By the same author:

Love in a Nutshell

THE REMARKABLE

Illustrated with Photographs

by Anita Leslie

Mr. Jerome

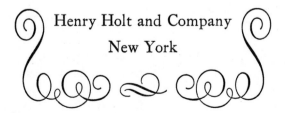

Henry Holt and Company
New York

Acknowledgments

My thanks are offered to the numerous relations of Leonard Jerome who assisted me in collecting material and allowed me to use letters and photographs. In particular I wish to express gratitude to my father Shane Leslie for handing over his snap albums and notebooks on family matters and for many remembered anecdotes; to Clare Sheridan for permission to use the letters written to her mother by King Milan of Serbia and for the accounts of life in the Tuileries and at Compiègne; and to Seymour Leslie for ransacking every box in his attic and for entertaining me with many charming reminiscences pertinent to this book.

Acknowledgments are also due Hugh Frewen of Sydney, Australia; Captain Oswald Frewen of Brede Place, Sussex; and my brothers John and Desmond Leslie, who all searched for fragments.

I am also indebted to W. de Witt Manning of Rochester; Dr. Blake McKelvey, City Historian of Rochester; The Board of Union College; The Board of Princeton College; Professor Wertenbaker, of Princeton; The New York Historical Society; The New York Public Library; and The Metropolitan Opera Guild.

My thanks are due to Sir Winston Churchill and Odhams Press, Ltd., for permission to quote from *My Early Life* and *Lord Randolph Churchill;* and to Lloyd R. Morris and Random House for permission to quote from *Incredible New York.*

To Bill, my husband,
who helped,
and to my children, Richard Tarka and little Leonie,
who did not

"I too lived, Brooklyn of ample hills was mine,
I too walk'd the streets of Manhattan island, and
bathed in the waters around it,
I too felt the curious, abrupt questionings stir within me."

WALT WHITMAN

PROLOGUE

Soft rain pattered on the attic roof. From the dormer window we looked out over hillsides of slate roofing and could hardly see the lake with its rush-lined shore where wild ducks had nested since days when the great Irish elk came from the forests to drink, or to slip and die, leaving their bones fossilized in the mud. An entire long corridor in one of the wings of our straggling house had been lined with glass cases containing prehistoric remnants dug from the bog. Bronze swords and petrified butter lightened a somewhat tedious collection of bones and massive antlers.

When it was wet, we used to be turned loose to play among these oddities, a diversion that kept us quiet in the sense that our screams could not be heard in the rest of the house. Tutors and governesses, groaning at their incarceration in the depths of Ireland could, for a time, ignore their charges who, they complained, had "too much American blood."

But today, we were, surprisingly as it always seemed in this house of our childhood, for good or for bad, grown up. The forbidden upstairs rooms had become ours by inheritance; we turned keys as we willed, opened monster cupboards built to contain the wired skirts of former ages, and rummaged through boxes of useless trinkets. Enameled lorgnettes with gold initials tumbled out of voluminous nightdresses of hand-embroidered lawn, and beneath layers of fine petticoats we found hats all decked with roses and ostrich plumes. One we knew well and carefully replaced. Grandmother had worn it "the day he proposed." Sentimentally she had carried it around for years in the brass-handled trunk, nearly four feet square, needing two men to lift it, which was known as a "hat box." In the end it rested here, in the rambling musty-smelling top story, where, as she often sighed, "there seems room for all the junk in the world." Camphor, lavender, and dust filled the air and made our eyes tingle, but we toiled on obsessed by this occupation, so perfectly in keeping with the drip of raindrops.

Trunk after trunk could be dragged out, and our fingers turned back layers of thick satin and rotting fragile lace. We found the eighteenth-century brocade suit worn by a great-great-grandfather Charles Leslie, one of the many Irish gentlemen who refused a peerage and voted against the union of Ireland to England. Evidently his best suit, he had worn it when being painted by Gilbert Stuart. The portrait hung in the dining room, but it did not reveal the quality of this brocade that sprang alive in our fingers. The years seemed to have been rolled up in tissue paper and locked here into cedar-wood chests.

From one vast Victorian trunk with a padded interior, we drew out the ball gown of heavy rose-colored satin embossed with flowers, which our grandmother had worn at Dublin's Vice Regal Lodge in the eighties. Then, gasping and laughing, we tried on the brilliant orange dress of thick corded silk made by Worth for Lady Randolph. Silken stitches inside the nineteen-inch waistband dated it 1876, and a ticket read: "Jennie's smartest day dress.

Keep." And in the dark recess of a high alcove, made presumably for the storage of countless riding boots, was an old-fashioned side-saddle, marked "Count Kinsky had this saddle made for Jennie after he won the Grand National on Zoedone in 1883. No one thought an Austrian could." (She meant, of course, win the race.)

In a tin box we found three parasols; small labels telling the story of each had been affixed to their handles. A delicate cane of carved ivory, bearing a white silk dome trimmed with a ruffle of black lace, bore the inscription: "Mrs. Jerome's parasol in the fifties. Her husband's first extravagance." I pressed down the catch and opened it carefully, half expecting the silk to crack, but the hundred-year-old material took the strain as if new.

The next parasol, drawn from its little linen bag, appeared to be made of ruched black lace, fancy and fluffy like a dark cobweb spread on its tiny stem of carved wood. This had belonged to Leonie, our grandmother, the youngest daughter of Mr. Leonard Jerome; and the third, a work of art, bore the legend: "Given to Jennie Jerome for her wedding to Randolph Churchill, April 14, 1874, and in her hand when she drove away." Her dark eyes must have flashed against the white Alençon lace, and the long exquisite handle of tortoise shell ringed with gold must have been clasped tight with excitement. For Jennie was a very inflammable person—we all knew that. And as we folded away these treasures in their black paper, the "best" dresses, the precious gifts that had been kept for a hundred years, we remembered little scenes, unwritten but recounted to us in our childhood, chiefly by that grandmother Leonie, who had been the youngest of the three astonishing Jerome sisters.

From the attic we wandered downstairs to the glass-fronted cabinet where, beside Queen Catherine Parr's needle case and old Bishop Leslie's 1640 "silver pen for writing on horseback," lay a tangle of family heirlooms. There was a bracelet woven of

3

hair from the heads of Christina Leslie's "nine lovely children," and a silver medal with a bullet attached reminded us of the role played in the 1854 Crimean War by one of these nine. Tom Leslie had been the A.D.C. Lord Raglan sent galloping off with that famous order that started the charge of the Light Brigade. Major Nolan, a superior officer, snatched it from Tom's hand and delivered the message with a wrong insinuation to Lord Lucan. As the "noble six hundred" charged, Nolan had his head blown off, which saved him a court martial. Meanwhile, Lord Raglan picked this Russian bullet from Tom's leg and posted it off with a line of praise to his mother. "Someone had blundered . . . but for once it was not a Leslie!"

A large glass box contained the Duke of Wellington's bridle and bit used at Waterloo; he had sent it to Charles Leslie with a note of thanks for paying for his education as a boy at Trim School, near Dargan Castle. (Mrs. Charles Leslie was a sister of the Duke's mother, Lady Mornington.)

Around these knickknacks a few later souvenirs had been stacked and forgotten. Leonard Jerome's consular sword, decorated with a medallion of Emperor Francis Joseph and purchased in Trieste in 1852, lay entangled with his horseshoe-shaped, gold racing badge, on which his name had been engraved. And folded around them was a thin shirt of white and blue stripes, the racing colors that gallant Kentucky had often carried past the winning post. Mr. Jerome's feelings for his greatest horse had been clearly epitomized in a colored print that hung in the hall. Kentucky, fine-necked and with rolling eye, occupied the entire foreground, while Leonard waved from a six-horsed coach in the back of the picture. A magnifying glass could reveal his friend James Gordon Bennett sitting beside him, while two ladies in bonnets, identifiable as Mrs. Jerome and the beautiful Mrs. Ronalds, peeped at the Jerome Park Clubhouse.

That was almost all we knew. Mr. Jerome had raced horses

and sailed yachts, and was an American, "rather a rare thing to be," a great-aunt had once told us, "nowadays quite usual, but then considered strange and original." The badge lured me on to the chest of letters where, delving among packets of envelopes, which my grandmother's unmistakable pencil had marked "family twaddle," I could decipher a medley of forgotten incidents, dimly illuminating a background for the brocade gowns and the three parasols.

I began to wonder what he had really been like, that Mr. Jerome of New York, who created a fine stir in the sixties and whose daughters had swept the board of London society for the next forty years. Faded sepia photographs filled several albums, but comments were scarce. One might start making a few inquiries, scribble down memories passed on by word of mouth, and perhaps tack the fragments into a pattern.

The first book mentioning old Jerome that I happened to pick up was *Clipperships,* by Frank Griswold. The author had never interested me before, although I had heard of him as a well-known sportsman. The bundles of letters revealed that he had tried to marry our grandmother. So had Freddie Gebhart, and after she refused him he "made a perfect fool of himself over Lily Langtry." Leonard wrote cryptically, "Tell Leonie it is well she escaped that match." One letter written to her years later fell from the package. It was from Griswold and commented in retrospect: "You are quite right about Freddie Gebbhart, he was a lovable boy that never grew up, and his weakness which was so attractive was his undoing. We often talk of him still. You were lucky not to marry him, or me either, for I was too much of a butterfly in those days to have made a good husband. It was the hunt after foxes and petticoats that occupied my mind."

Griswold admired the father as well as the daughter. "When I was a boy," reveals his book, "Mr. Jerome took me out in his sledge, built like a yacht to commemorate *Henrietta's* victory across the Atlantic. The thing that struck me most was that he drove the horses ten miles through the snow without putting on gloves." This at least gave a clue to great-grandfather Jerome's blood stream!

My father had done a good deal of family research. Every drawer and chest and cupboard of the old house contained notes in his neat script; and whereas it had been grandmother's habit to tantalize the future by tucking away some pincushion with an envelope saying, "Given to A——, by Z——, 1880, so in love, all letters burnt," her eldest son, the scholar of a sporting family, showed no such tact. When he added to the family documents, the dots were sure to be placed on the *i*'s. He had jotted down a few vivid impressions of that gaunt old American who died in a Brighton boardinghouse in 1891. No little family distress occurred when old Mr. Jerome refused to be comforted by religion. Carriages had drawn up at his London house daily, with flowers and jelly and Bibles. But after beginning with Genesis my great-grandpapa soon laid the Old Testament aside, remarking "What *horrible* people," and refused to read another word. He did not want condolence either. What he did desire was the sight of romping grandchildren, and this his doctor frowned at.

As the fogs descended cold and thick over the city, Mr. Jerome was ordered to Brighton for better air. His wife chose Lyon Mansions near the sea. She had stayed here with her girls when in flight from the Franco-Prussian war in 1870. Three rooms sufficed. Most of Leonard's fortunes were dispersed, and he had the simplest of tastes.

During the last days he lay quietly, watching the firelight flicker over his bedroom wall, flaring into sudden patterns before they faded into twilight. Soon, he knew, the coals must cease to glow. Soon it would be night and very quiet. But he liked the darkness as well as the day, for there had been enough of light and brilliance and violent pace. It made no difference to him where he died, an English boardinghouse with the sea rain beating

6

against the window pane would suffice for this brief backdrop. Having wrung much out of life, he was ready to go.

But firelight awakens the memory of old loves, and for him there had been many. He had cared with intensity, if not with single-mindedness. Music had been his quest, but not his goal. Women had learned they must share his heart with gallant horses and with great schooners straining under storm-canvas in Atlantic gales. . . .

A packet of newspaper cuttings fell at my feet, yellowed obituaries that called Leonard Jerome "millionaire and sportsman." Wall Street quoted him as a legend, citing fortunes lost as well as made; the racing clubs he founded named him "Father of the American Turf"; and crews he had sailed with spoke of a "staunch comrade." We knew more than this. Many a woman must have paused, wistfully thinking for a moment, "So he is gone. Dear Leonard, there was never another like him, and surely he loved me the best."

All of his acquaintances struggled to record his intense aliveness. Many of the notices used the word *gentleman,* throwing him into clear-cut perspective against a vital, ungentlemanly background. One New Yorker wrote: "I have known Leonard Jerome going on for thirty years now, and I've got just one thing to say about him. He was a white man and a gentleman if ever there was one"; and another: "One rode better, sailed better, banquetted better when Mr. Jerome was of the company."

There must have been more to his story. My father, a little boy of six, had been among the solemn grandchildren brought to wave from behind a screen when the old man lay dying, and Cousin Clare Frewen remembered her shoulder ribbons being tied into bows by grandmother Jerome for the occasion.

His three daughters, Clara, Jennie, and Leonie, had stood somberly by his bedside. In vain he tried to make them smile: "I've given you all I have," he said. "Pass it on."

He meant strength and joy of life, not the debris of his fortunes, and with gratitude he looked toward the screen beyond which his grandchildren were not allowed to venture. Yet there was not an American among them, and to one born and bred as he, and with no son of his own, this rankled.

Frequently he mentioned the eldest, Winston Leonard Spencer Churchill, his sixteen-year-old namesake. When this boy had been born to Jennie and her English husband, Lord Randolph Churchill, Mrs. Jerome had been shocked by a racing friend who wrote, "Interesting breeding. Stamina always goes through the dam, and pace through the sire." What might this first grandchild grow into? Would he unite Jennie's vital force and Randolph's nervous brilliance? Or continue his present determination to prove himself a dunce at Harrow? Might America hear of him? Old Jerome hoped so, but the boy belonged to that very aristocracy whose influence America repudiated in the War of Independence and again in the Civil War, when the Southern landowners had their way of life destroyed forever.

Leonard belonged to the hard core of new America. His grandson belonged to old England.

Could the double heritage enable any man to understand and serve both?

THE JEROMES WERE PROUD OF their Huguenot blood. Timothy Jerome, the first to become an American, had sailed from the Isle of Wight in 1710, and founded a home in Meriden, Connecticut. His son, Samuel, moved to Massachusetts and built a house about two miles from

Stockbridge (still standing and owned by Mr. Rodney Proctor). Samuel's son, Aaron, married Betsy Ball, a relative of George Washington, and settled as a farmer in the Berkshire hills. He experimented with new kinds of wheat, specialized in breeding cattle, and raised abundant crops to feed the local expanding villages. The eldest of his sons, born in 1786, was Leonard's father, Isaac Jerome.

In 1807 Isaac married a young Scots woman, Aurora Murray; and in 1812, when they had three sons, he bought land near his grandfather's Stockbridge home, which he intended to farm. But the War of 1812 kept him away for three years. When the snows of 1815 melted, Captain Jerome returned home with his troops, and asked his wife if she would move west. In the late summer of that year, Isaac and Aurora Jerome with several small sons moved by stagecoach to Syracuse, where Isaac purchased a large tract of land covered with beech, ash, and elm. He knew how to create a farm from virgin land, and the homestead flourished. Leonard was born on this farm in 1818, the fifth child among nine boys and a girl.

Leonard's earliest memories were of a large bustling kitchen where children were discouraged from falling under people's feet, and sent off on farm errands. The young Jeromes could all milk cows, feed cattle, and manage horses.

Aurora Jerome bustled around the house, sending everyone about his work. Servant girls were scarce and constantly being lured away to matrimony by the stream of young men moving westward. Aurora had to supervise the feeding of farm workers and family. She scented linen, indexed jars of preserves, and checked cider casks. When the potatoes, apples, crackers, and cheeses had been stored and the butter set in a cool place, when the smallest child had been plucked from her swirling skirts and laid in his cot at the end of the long day, she would sit down to make decorations for the house. Leonard remembered his mother

9

thus, stitching gilded fir cones around mirrors, working red berries into patterned mats, and making dolls from wool and straw. She even found time to redecorate the house annually.

The ten Jerome children were lucky to grow up in that rare countryside so lately carved from the wilds. As far as his recollection stretched, Leonard had known the glittering fantasia of ice in winter and spring carpets of flowers that slid from the departing snow. All through his boyhood he enjoyed the drama of harvesting and the smoking of hams before the weather grew cold. When snow fell, he tobogganed and romped with the other boys who were growing up in the pleasant white houses that were replacing log shacks throughout the countryside. In the village school he learned mathematics and Latin, while at home he was taught to be God- and parent-fearing. Like other boys, he yearned to escape parental discipline and dreamed of adventure in the undiscovered realms to the west.

The landowners of western New York tried to organize efficient schools for their offspring, but by the age of fourteen most boys started to work, and Leonard was no exception. He was expected to earn enough money to pay for the schooling necessary to enter college.

Each of the Jerome boys wanted a college education. Allen, Thomas, Addison, and Aaron, the four eldest, went to Princeton. Allen took a degree in theology. The others worked their way through two years but found the going hard, since their father could provide only very small allowances. Addison impatiently set off to New York City without a penny but confident he would soon be rich enough to help his younger brothers through their studies.

Meanwhile, Leonard obtained employment at the village store at a salary of one dollar a week. Bursting with pride, he accepted the responsibility of selling and debating the merits of scythes, axes, guns, fishing rods, plows, and barrels of whiskey and cider.

Almost all purchases had to be made through exchanges instead of using ready money, and it sharpened a boy's wits to deal with the shrewd farmers who came to "dicker."

One evening Leonard returned home to find a plan being made for him. Isaac's elder brother, Hiram Jerome, who was a judge in the town of Palmyra, sixty miles westward, had offered to take Leonard into his home, supervise his schooling, and see that he earned money during his spare time. Leonard had long considered himself a man, and he eagerly accepted the change.

J̲UDGE HIRAM JEROME BELIEVED in austerity and hard work. He disapproved when his nephew Aaron, while studying divinity at Princeton, wrote that he had staked his every penny in the famous Mulberry Tree Speculation, but when the rage for silkworms swept America and Aaron reaped forty thousand dollars' profit, the Judge could not but express a cautious admiration. A gambler by nature, and wildly generous, Aaron organized a hostel for destitute fellow students, and wrote jubilantly to his younger brothers that he would finance their way through college.

Leonard entered the College of New Jersey in the autumn of 1836. At the end of his first freshman term he stood well up in his class with an average grade of 83.6. After the spring vacation he made a daring venture by leap-frogging an entire year to join the sophomore class. In this advanced group his grades remained high until he became a junior, when he found himself in deep water. Mathematics were never Leonard Jerome's strong point, and the junior session was known at Princeton as the "mathematical year." He floundered with difficulty through the quagmires of analytical geometry, descriptive geometry, and differential calculus but ended the summer term with a grade of 69.

Soon after coming to college Leonard applied for membership in the American Whig Society. Escorted to the library building, he climbed to the top floor with a group of other excited entrants. They stood waiting on the landing until the door swung open to let them advance toward a red curtain hung across the east end of the room. To build up an atmosphere of drama, this was suddenly drawn aside and they found themselves in a large blue hall with bookcases in the corners. At the far end of the room sat the society officers. As the initiates walked forward, the members rose and the moderator solemnly accepted the new initiates.

The American Whig Society was pre-eminently a literary club. The members could develop their talents in debate or oratory without interference from the faculty, and books of their choice were discussed in public. They made and enforced their own discipline and fined those who "lay down on a bench or forgot themselves sufficiently to yell or tussle in public." During July and August, 1837, Leonard was appointed society treasurer and kept account of the fines, which ranged from twenty to forty cents. The book includes those listed against himself.

Among the great teachers of this time was the scientist Joseph Henry, who was contributing to the invention of telegraph. His lectures on electrodynamics and the decomposition of light were added to the basic formula for education, which rested almost entirely on Latin, Greek, and mathematics. In a popular demonstration he would lift a group of "sneezing coughing students weighing approximately 3,500 lbs. with an enormous magnet."

The outstanding figure at Princeton was "Johnny," Vice President MacLean, an old scholar with white hair in a long bob, who maintained college discipline and taught the Latin classes. A list of college pranks instigated by Leonard Jerome is also on record. Practical jokes age worse than witticisms. We read of raids on the village for signposts, gates, henhouses, and fences, mules led upstairs to the third floor of Nassau Hall, test tubes sabotaged before chemistry class so poor Professor Torrey's experiments exploded, and tar on the seats in the prayer hall. The humor of such escapades cannot survive a hundred years.

Leonard's frolics ended when Addison, now successfully established in New York, started his own firm and wrote he would be temporarily unable to provide funds. Princeton demanded a higher income than most colleges, and Leonard had been hard pressed to make ends meet. He had adopted the cheapest mode of existence possible, giving up his room in East College and moving to a small private lodging, but tuition fees were forty dollars a year while room rents stood at twelve dollars and board was seventy-seven dollars. Leonard could not make ends meet. Having jumped an entire year, he found extra cramming necessary, and the earnings to be made outside of study hours were, in any case, small. He wore his clothes until they were transparent and tried to eat "very little and very cheap," but to no avail. In August, 1838, he withdrew from Princeton and entered Union College, in Schenectady, where living expenses were lower.

After a holiday at home he traveled along the old Erie Canal to Schenectady, where he entered Union with advanced standing. Union College, which lay in a park on the town's outskirts, had taken its name in 1797 to signify "that the whole movement had welled up from the desire of a great number of people, of all social grades and racial stocks, and of all religious persuasions, with provision against control by any."

Within twenty miles of Schenectady lay the towns of Albany and Troy, both on the Mohawk River, but curiously different in atmosphere. On holidays Leonard ventured into a dreamy

Dutch civilization where the leisurely eighteenth century lingered on. This trim continental world was Leonard's first glimpse of a facet of Old Europe. He wandered the wide, tree-lined streets, watching the life in these wooden colonial houses and noting that, unlike New England only a mountain range away, Sundays here were enjoyed as frivolously as in far-off Holland.

On hot summer evenings the honest burghers, all with Dutch names and manners, would sit fanning themselves in rocking chairs on what they called *"stoeps"* and Leonard called "piazzas" and the English travelers called "verandas."

There were townsfolk still living in Schenectady who could remember seeing General Washington, and later La Fayette, riding down the old Post Road from Albany, and they liked to reminisce. Leonard was invited to a few meals in Dutch homes. The rooms were dark, yet gleaming. He carried away an impression of wide colonial fireplaces, wood stoves, copper luster, eagle mirrors, highboys, and mahogany davenports. Heavy old silver graced the sideboards and every object shone from constant polishing.

An arduous year rolled by. Leonard swam in the Mohawk and lay in the sun with other students, talking of vanished Indian tribes. In full summer there were flirtatious hay rides, with young people piled on the farm wagons, singing through the twilight. Occasionally he visited Troy and the other river towns, in each of which a different world had risen. Schenectady had shown him old Holland; Albany, shrill with early steamboats, opened up a river road with the swift-moving civilization of the Atlantic seaboard; and in Troy, only fifteen miles from Union, he found a city of musical taste that was becoming a usual stopping place for virtuosi on tour.

Here Leonard first heard musicians of standing. The concert hall with its padded red boxes and huge gas chandelier opened a kind of heaven to him. He could always scrape up enough for a cheap ticket and there, high among the worst seats, where plush gave way to plain wood, and gilt to black paint, Leonard sat with pricked ears and shining eyes, learning what wonders the world could hold.

His violin had long been abandoned, but he sang easily and for the delight of it. There were many musical evenings in the college, and then Leonard's clear tenor would ring out above the other voices, and fellow students laughed at his elation.

Leonard also learned to dance. His partners were young ladies, anxious to get up small parties in their own homes. From these amiable tutors he learned not only the cotillion and the waltz, but Spanish dances. "I will teach them all to you," he wrote his sister. And Isaac lifted an eyebrow—it might be fashionable, but was it *good?*

In July, 1839, Leonard graduated. He was twenty-one. All life lay ahead, and he felt not ill-equipped.

SHORTLY AFTER GRADUATION, LEONard moved to Albany. Having read law and been admitted to the bar, he obtained employment in the office of John C. Beach.

Competition was fierce. Youngsters had to "be go-getters, or get nowhere." Many fell by the wayside. As it had been in the wilderness when men pitted their strength against the elements so it was now in the tough, growing cities. To accept failure meant to die.

When, in 1840, Leonard ruefully discovered that Albany held far too many talented lawyers, he decided to return to western New York, where he reckoned the young expanding towns would offer more opportunity.

The journey home by way of "the longest canal on earth" was not devoid of pleasure. The packet boats, which were pulled along the waterway by two or three trotting horses, had become increasingly comfortable and elegant. A hundred passengers traveled on each boat, and canal travel was advertised as an excellent method of finding a spouse. "One comes into contact with new people and there is time to dally," explained a contemporary letter. Each boat now possessed "a decorated cabin for ladies, with real beds," and in the dining rooms, where the sexes sat at opposite ends of a long table, conversation blossomed with ease. The crews were guaranteed "sober and orderly," and one boat boasted that even the workmen who built her had done without "the stimulant of ardent spirits or liquid poison." The voyagers themselves, however, were not expected to abstain from wine; virtuous, well fed, and in amusing mixed company, they glided along the ribbon of water for hundreds of miles, and the cost of such travel including board and flirtations was only four cents a mile!

Disembarking at Palmyra, Leonard reported to his uncle who had just been appointed first judge of the Wayne County Court. Hiram Jerome had always wanted his nephews to become lawyers. He immediately employed Leonard, and suggested that Lawrence, the next brother, should follow on from Princeton.

Then came two years' hard grind in the Judge's office. Leonard, restive and burning with energy, fretted. He had begun to contemplate trekking westward toward the retreating frontier when Hiram decided to remove to Rochester. This at least was a change. When a small boy, Leonard had seen Rochester as a village of white houses sprawling across the Genesee River Falls. He found the town unrecognizable. The population had increased from a few hundred to twenty-three thousand. The original respectable milling families were busy legislating against billiard halls, bowling alleys, and disorderly newcomers. They welcomed judges and bright young lawyers.

The new Jerome office was established on the corner of Exchange and Main streets. Leonard was shortly made a partner and started to enjoy considerable independence.

At eight every morning he left his boardinghouse after a breakfast of hot cornbread, and walked briskly through the streets crowded with creaking farm wagons bringing in milk, wheat, apples, potatoes, and cheese. At twelve, work ceased throughout the town, and fashionable ladies would promenade while "idlers and dandies strutt as usual." The afternoon was filled with "noise and confusion, bustle and business." At five the farmers started to drive their wagons home, and by six "everyone was hastening home to supper."

Leonard would drag through the last of his legal work and then rush off with young friends. Pretty girls were plentiful all along the Genesee River, and in Rochester the "refined female academies" had become as numerous as the taverns. Leonard's singing voice and gift of quick repartee kept him in great demand at musical evenings and dancing parties, and many an eye lit up when young Mr. Jerome's footstep was heard on the garden path. "Rochester's social elite still functioned much as an enlarged family circle, with its hospitality checked only by the facilities of the larger mansions. The young folk kept a succession of gay parties running through each January and February in the numerous big houses, and no doubt the lists of guests, if combined, would supply a tentative social register. The old custom of gathering at four in the afternoon was giving way to the evening party, which sometimes continued until midnight, but the guests still attended as family delegations rather than in couples."

In the following year Lawrence joined the Jerome office as junior clerk. Whatever Uncle Hiram thought of his staff, the two brothers won a reputation of being "very popular with the young ladies, owing to the dashing manner in which they rode high-spirited horses."

An old lady writes in her early memories of Rochester: "My father (Samuel Wilder), when a bachelor, kept house with several of his like-minded brothers in pretty old Ravine Place, off Lake Avenue. There they were visited by all kinds of witty out-of-towners, as well as home friends. A simple life it must have been in those days, with lots of young fun and warm companionship. Among the visitors were the Jeromes from Pompey Hill and Palmyra. Lawrence and Leonard were constant visitors, and very inclined to borrow the Wilder brothers' smart waistcoats and cravates. But they were always screamingly funny boys, and could act a part as easily as breathing."

Two years passed during which the brothers, "screamingly funny" to contemporaries but perhaps less so to their elders, grew into well-known figures at Rochester supper parties and charades. Leonard won a reputation as an able lawyer, but Lawrence showed little desire to serve a full apprenticeship in the Judge's office, and he could often be observed searching with knitted brows for some more profitable, or at least more spectacular, pursuit. He was teased for wanting to put a finger in too many pies.

Suddenly, in August, 1844, Lawrence married Miss Catherine Hall, a dark-eyed girl of twenty-one who had been orphaned as a child and brought up by a band of old aunts in Palmyra. She and her two sisters were heiresses to a small fortune, and Lawrence fretted that he could not equal her income with his legal earnings. Soon he and Leonard decided they might earn more money in a publishing business just offered for sale. After many conferences they obtained a half-share, and arranged to take over entirely in the following year. It was a momentous decision for both young men, but it made no impression on Judge Jerome. Uncle

Hiram tried to dissuade them. He disapproved of youth looking for "easy money."

It was the very middle of a century in which the number of America's newspapers would leap from one hundred fifty in 1800, to thirty thousand in 1900. Leonard could not resist the lure of running his own paper. He invested all his savings and reckoned that an immediate profit could be made out of the printing office on the side. With this monetary security, a certain freedom might fall into his hands.

After much disagreement with the Judge, his nephews abandoned their legal careers and by 1846 they were joint owners of the *Daily American*. "Politics absorbed a fair portion, but by no means all of the energies of Rochester editors. New publications were frequently launched, occasionally with nonpolitical objectives, but it required more than the income from a few hundred subscribers to put a new paper on its feet, and many of these ventures proved ephemeral. The *American*, established in the mid-forties, enjoyed greater success and, under the energetic management of the Jerome brothers and the editor Alexander Mann, a staunch Clay supporter, soon challenged the Democratic leadership of local Whigs." * The financial side of the *American* was run entirely by Leonard. The circulation crept up to one thousand, then to two thousand, and eventually, they said, to nearly three thousand. These tiny figures were tremendous for that time. When the paper was running on a sound business basis, Leonard opened fire politically. "What we suffer from that Know-Nothing paper, the local *American!*" raged one of the town's prominent citizens. The *American* became known as a hard-hitting organ, expressly devised to oppose the Democrats (who upheld the rights of individual states, as opposed to strong centralized government). Leonard did not write the editorials

---

* Blake McKelvey, *Rochester, The Water Power City, 1812–1854* (Cambridge, Massachusetts, Harvard University Press, 1945).

himself, but he determined editorial policy and closely supervised his writers.

Through the impact of their paper, the brothers found themselves rich and famous, "big frogs, but in so small a pond." When a son was born to the Lawrence Jeromes they rented a spacious house in Fitzhugh Street, and asked Leonard and the seventh brother, Isaac, to move in with them.

Now that they had time and money, the Jeromes frequented the numerous balls given by the older families, who were intent on keeping out brash newcomers! A fine sense of snobbism was growing up. The tall, dark brothers with their Old World manners found themselves carried to the top of the tiny social tree. Now that Rochester's more violent period was over, many of the rough raggle-taggle who had made fortunes were turning respectable and trying to get into "Society." At all costs they must be kept out! The tiny core of early settlers resolved to resist the deluge of *nouveaux riches,* however pure or prim or cultured the second generation might be. As life became more comfortable, people had time to develop little snobbisms, and how they enjoyed them! In January, 1847, "the younger members of the leading families made one dramatic effort to re-establish their social ascendancy by a costume party at the home of Mrs. William Greenough, where the elite gathered to the number of seventy-six. The gala affair prompted two new young and dashing newcomers in Rochester, Leonard and Lawrence Jerome, to bring out an amusing account in prose and verse." Meanwhile, Miss Lillie Greenough, the young daughter of the house, who possessed a pretty singing voice, fell in love with Leonard.

Catherine Hall had a younger sister, Clara, a slightly unmanageable belle, who was a judicious flirt, but who often would "fall into moods." Leonard often took the twenty-four-hour canal-boat journey down to Palmyra to see her. At that time convention allowed a gentleman wishing to court to accompany his lady "to mid-week prayer service without offence, or they might join the family in an apple-paring match, or in a songfest around the piano in the sitting room." Leonard soon tired of the company of Clara's aunts. He suggested Clara seize on frequent pretexts to visit her married sister in Rochester.

The aunts became weary of the journey to and from Rochester, which took two days by stagecoach, or a day and night (of perpetual unwinking chaperonage) by canal boat. Clara thought that Leonard, unlike the impetuous Lawrence, would refuse to marry until his income equaled that of his bride, but she could not be sure. She could but take a feverish interest in the sales sheet of the *American*. With beating heart, Miss Hall watched the little paper's spectacular rise, and at last, one April day when the woods were whitening with blossom, Leonard Jerome came to Palmyra and led her up the aisle of the Presbyterian Church.

CLARA HALL POSSESSED A CURIous, dark, brooding beauty. Portraits show the melancholy, oval face fashionable in that period, hair parted in the center and looped low over the forehead, and black, mournful eyes. She possessed none of Leonard's surface fire, being secretive and rather shy. The aunts had found her detachment irksome. They "could not tell what the girl was thinking."

A strange, not very happy childhood may have left its mark. Clara could hardly remember her parents, both of whom had died when she was two years old. Only the stories of grownups gave her a shadowy picture of "a handsome father," who lay in

Palmyra churchyard beside the girl he had wooed in pioneer days. Relations assiduously compiled a family history. They traced coats of arms back to sixteenth-century England, and produced a detailed pedigree book for the delectation of future Halls. Ambrose, Clara's father, according to this research was "a tall man of striking personality." Clara listened with awe while his writings and speeches were read to her; the droning voices evoked a shadowy person forever watching from the habitations of the dead, ready to "strike." She thought of her mother differently, with longing and curiosity, for she had heard half-hushed rumors concerning her Indian blood. The old aunts could not resist whispering, and long before she understood the importance of a coat of arms, Clara knew herself to be a quarter Iroquois, a descendant of the tribe that for centuries had ruled the wooded hills around her home. They were gone now, the braves with their cruel courage and hard code, and the women who lived close to nature and were wise in the old lore of sun and moon and birth and death. Sometimes her mind grew confused at these tales she overheard, stories that always ended abruptly with, "Go away and play now, dear." And she would creep to a looking glass to peer at the reflection of a little sharp pointed face and wonder, "Will I grow up to escape into the woods?" And a quiver would run up her spine. She wanted to escape; she wanted a way out of this safe, comfortable house, which would be hers and her sisters'. "You are lucky girls," intoned the adult voices. "Why?" asked Clara innocently. But there was no answer because it was considered vulgar to speak of money, even when people thought of little else.

It was a relief to Clara's aunt when, at the age of twenty-four, she married the man of her choice, the only man she ever had looked at. None of her early letters survives and, apart from her portraits and the memories of her children, very little has been recorded. But through the veils of shame, virtue, and hypocrisy with which most anecdotes of the time were swathed, it is possible to perceive the outline of a person who caused consternation by not accepting the usual. Clara loved what she could not understand. Perhaps that is why she loved Leonard Jerome. She certainly loved him all her life.

After bringing his bride back to Rochester, Leonard acquired the red brick house next to Lawrence's, and built a connecting passage so that the two brothers and two sisters and their offspring need not cross the lawn to visit. Clara, delighted at having an independent home of her own, created a framework of red plush, tasseled curtains, and dark mahogany furniture in which to entertain her husband's varied and "oh, so interesting friends." Chief of these was the brilliant young attorney-ethnologist, Lewis H. Morgan, who had been at Union College with Leonard. Morgan had just started writing up the customs of the Iroquois and defending the red man with an outraged sense of justice. He was also an expert on the beaver, and would sit in the Jerome parlor discussing with passion the unbelievable engineering feats of this little animal.

Leonard was inundated with work. Apart from the Whig cause, the chief issues of importance in the forties were slavery, temperance, and women's rights. The Female Charitable Society, the Ladies Temperance Society, and the American Female Moral Reform Society deluged Rochester with conventions during these years. Although they used men speakers and were without a vote, zealous, public-spirited women were fiercely beginning to prove their power.

For over ten years the Rochester Antislavery Society had been hammering its views into the press, and in 1849 the city's newly elected Whig representative declared his sympathy for the Negro cause at an antislavery bazaar in the new Concert Hall. Funds were collected to build a city library, to give aid during the Irish famine, and to form a Rochester company to send young men out to California as "diggers" in the gold rush of 1849. There was agitation for a ten-hour day for working men, for new bridges and sewers, for gas to replace the sixty oil lamps that illuminated the city, for a larger jail, for the abolition of bawdy houses, and for the curbing of "wayward women" (who were arrested for wearing men's clothing, or even for having "a red face"!). Most important was the long-drawn-out battle regarding free education. The principle of taxing one citizen to pay for the education of another citizen's children was considered "undemocratic."

Among Leonard's more enjoyable outings were the Saturday afternoon trotting races, where he could train his already keen and practiced eye for a horse while Clara, attired in the latest fashion, chatted with her friends. Satin gowns, high-buttoned boots, and ostrich-feathered bonnets were fine correct attire for respectable matrons. Unconventional as her character may have been, Clara always assumed the exterior trappings of respectability, and both the Hall sisters were considered perfect matches to curb and mould their exuberant spouses.

During the weekdays when Leonard and his brother disappeared to their offices, the Jerome ladies enjoyed themselves re-decorating rooms and changing the settees from corner to corner. Soon Clara begged to replace the mahogany furniture by more fashionable rosewood and walnut, and the Turkish carpets by those of Brussels. New figured papers started to cover the walls, and around the windows heavy damask curtains were held back by gold lilies to reveal muslin curtains, which were presently superseded by sets of real lace. The parlor blushed crimson and purple around its white marble fireplace, and those shell bouquets in glass domes, which had seemed so ornamental to the old aunts in Palmyra, were cast aside for expensive ormolu mirrors.

With scorn she recalled the plain Georgian style in which her father had built his houses. Not for her were bare rooms and pale colors. The fungus of fancy Gothic was spreading through the land, darkening windows, laying stripes on wallpaper, and presently insisting that Mrs. Leonard Jerome, as a lady of high fashion, should dress in the same shades of deep red with which she draped her dining room. But the Jeromes blossomed happily among magenta hues, and a year later into their nest of silken plush, gilt, and ebony a daughter was born. She amazed them with beauty all the more enthralling because it was so unlike their own. Little Clara threw back to some fair ancestor, and her parents could rave over her blue eyes and golden hair. Never had a baby more frilled gowns in her wardrobe or gaudier bonnets. Leonard walked about as if bewitched, the arrival of his first child seeming to be an event unique in human history.

In 1849 the Jerome brothers had participated in Silver Gray rallies of the Whig party. When the two wings of the party resolved their differences, Leonard and Lawrence, already dreaming of wider horizons than Rochester could unfold, decided to sell the *American*. They made known in Washington their availability for political appointments. Then, as now, America employed two types of diplomats—professionals whose lifelong careers corresponded to those of their European counterparts, and semipolitical appointees who were given posts in acknowledgment for their work on behalf of the party.

Leonard was rewarded for his services to the Whig cause when, in March, 1850, the United States Senate confirmed his appointment as Consul to Ravenna (then in the papal states). Clara was delighted. She realized a promising diplomatic career might open up for her husband. But Leonard seemed to have kept several other irons in the fire. He never traveled to this consular appointment, and two months later the *American* announced his election as Secretary-Treasurer of the Merchants State Telegraphic Company. Rochester had already been the scene of conflicting telegraph ventures. Several important business men had invested in the Morse line across the state of New York and, when local control had been lost, several of them undertook the construction of a private line across the state. A firebrand Irishman, Henry O'Reilly, formerly of Rochester, who had been frozen out of the previous telegraph ventures had decided to launch a line in competition. There was general surprise when Jerome, a Presbyterian and a Whig, became linked with an Irish Democrat. Leonard, however, had no intention of losing his individuality.

In the early summer of 1850 Leonard left Rochester for New York City, where he opened his own office from which he helped O'Reilly press forward the construction of the Merchants State telegraph. Such energy was poured into this effort that the Morse faction eventually found itself forced to buy up the new telegraph line for $65,379.

Ravenna went without a consul while Leonard fought O'Reilly's battle. In December, 1850, somewhat belatedly, he resigned the appointment. During the following winter the Leonard Jeromes lived at 292 Henry Street, Brooklyn, a red brick house just large enough to house Clara and the baby, and brother Addison and his wife, who moved in with them. Addison was well ensconced as a broker in Wall Street, and Leonard found him congenial company. The two men were out every evening together while Clara kept house as best she could amid the half-unpacked crates, trunks, and boxes that she had packed so diligently in Rochester with all those belongings "suitable for Italy."

WHILE CLARA FOLLOWED a sedate, maternal existence in Brooklyn village, the Jerome men ventured into the fast-paced and extravagant world that surrounded Wall Street. Every morning the brothers left the house together "in great hurry and spirits," and took the South Ferry to Manhattan, where they debarked in the heart of the turbulent city. Clara spent the day supervising the Negro servants (who wore bright bandannas), scribbling notes to friends, and walking along the quiet leafy streets where it amused her to look into little gardens. The glue-pot and fret-work saw whiled away many hours for her contemporaries but never amused her. She liked to see things "really happen." Occasionally a fire might be signaled in the neighborhood. Then she hurried into bonnet and street dress to enjoy the sight of the old volunteer fire brigades racing their equipment to the scene. Occasionally competing teams arrived in such a state of exhaustion they were unable to man the pumps. It was customary for spectators to shout encouragement to the red-faced gentlemen volunteers, who sometimes were clad in ruffled shirts, long-tailed coats, and high beaver hats.

On fine afternoons she took the baby Clara down to the riverside, where she could feed pigeons and watch the paddle boats and tugs and sailing skiffs on the East River. A kind gentleman sometimes let them peer through his telescope and they could see right over the low roofs of Manhattan Island, which lay fringed by a narrow forest of masts.

Now and then Mrs. Jerome crossed by ferry for a shopping expedition to Broadway, and once or twice Leonard walked with her to Wall Street to show her his office in a pleasant three-storied house with tall windows and green shutters and to point out the office buildings of their acquaintances. One or two banks recently had put up new buildings for themselves, replacing eighteenth-century houses by heavy stone façades with thick columns designed some two thousand years previously for Roman temples; but the majority of brokers' offices remained in simple, spacious Georgian houses. Leonard always insisted his office should face south and have a large window easily opened "to let the sun in."

All day long, carts and barrows rattled over the cobbles and gentlemen in top hats strolled along the pavement shouting financial secrets into each other's ears. When the offices closed, there would be a flood of famous personages walking toward the omnibuses of Broadway and many diversions were laid open to them on the way.

The Jerome brothers soon became an integral part of the lively New York scene, for they developed several interests apart from those concentrated in the Merchants State Telegraphic Company. After office hours ended, professional friends sought their company for the evening to talk over new projects and enjoy themselves at the same time. Leaving the Street, they immersed themselves in an atmosphere of excitement. Sometimes they dined in one of the splendid new hotels that were being built to catch the stream of business men who poured forth from Wall Street each evening.

Famous restaurateurs provided cushioned seclusion for those who wished to continue their business discussions; and no little thought was given to the many "overworked" gentlemen who would be eager for relaxation and pleasure. The pious owner of a famous licentious establishment declared: "American men are driven to bouts of dissipation by the relentless pressure of money-making."

The potentialities of a new continent were well reflected in the brain-storm pace of mid-century New York. It was noisy and exhausting, but Leonard loved it: the clatter of huge horse-drawn omnibuses, the crowded sidewalks, and the hundred gas-lit bars and restaurants of Broadway, where pretty teen-agers from every state were recruited as waitresses. As the new rich grew more boisterous and self-assured, the older families deplored their ostentation. But they were powerless to stop the tide. Caught by his business associates for dinner and supper parties, Leonard came home to Brooklyn later and later. Clara began to wonder if she liked being the wife of a financier. Leonard's wife had been brought up to admire subdued manners and quiet tastes. Yet she could not but notice with interest those large brownstone houses elaborately carved and colonnaded, which new millionaire families were building above Madison Square and along Fifth Avenue. There was a steady movement northward toward the open country where Central Park was being planned. Old Astor had died worth twenty million dollars, an unprecedented sum at the time, and he had set the pace for the next generation.

With robust strength and high spirits Leonard plunged into the vulgar, exciting whirlpool of financial New York. He took up its zest and flourish in Wall Street and at stag dinners; "the new Mr. Jerome" became famous for wit and quick repartee. However, a contemporary recorded that in this tough and corrupt metropolis Leonard kept to his own set of rules. "I never knew him to take a drink in a bar or public place," wrote this person, "yet he belonged to the city with all its garish brilliance. No man ever became more completely a New Yorker."

While Clara developed a small circle of friends and entertained at home, Leonard ventured into the musical world. He attended concerts and operas, often alone, for Clara's lack of ear caused her much shame. "Oh dear," she once wrote, "it's such a pity I can't *appreciate* more." When Leonard did persuade her to leave the housekeeping and attend a concert with him, she would find herself lost in a mist of sense impressions. Next day she had to stay out of the voluble family criticisms. Leonard's ability to concentrate enabled him to talk glibly with professionals and Clara's heart sank when the subjects of counterpoint and leitmotiv arose. No Jerome could understand that, to her, music meant only a flood of sound that swept through her mind, arousing strange emotions. She could remember not one bar.

New York had a capacity for enthusiasm that exceeded that of any city in the world. When Jenny Lind, the greatest concert singer of the century, arrived in New York, cheering crowds lined the streets to watch P. T. Barnum drive the "Swedish Nightingale" to her hotel. Twenty thousand fans spent the evening shouting for her, and the New York Musical Fund Society, accompanied by red-shirted firemen carrying flaming torches, serenaded her Broadway hotel until after midnight. Tickets for her first concert were sold at auction for unprecedented prices. "Twenty or thirty dollars to hear Jenny are paid by those who live hand-to-mouth."

Leonard went, of course, battling his way through an adoring mob to reach Castle Garden. The thirty-year-old singer with her plain features and serene, shining eyes appeared in a white ball gown. She responded to the wild reception, which the audience accorded her, with deep curtseys and donated the twelve thousand dollars received for her appearance, to charities. Leonard missed few of her performances, and when she was criticized for "lack of passion," he retorted, "Her voice is indescribable in quality, like the dawn. Who wants more?"

When he met her, he apparently wanted considerably more, but Jenny Lind was famous for virtue as well as for generosity. Leonard had always liked pretty women. Miss Lind changed his taste. He was fascinated by the simplicity of a great artist unconcerned with her appearance. And amid her triumphs, and despite her "purity" (which unkind critics called a publicity stunt) Jenny Lind could not help remarking that, of all her admirers, Mr. Jerome was "the best looking."

Meanwhile Clara produced a second daughter. She showed some disappointment the child did not prove to be a boy, for she had set her heart on a son to be called Leonard.

"Why not name her Jenny?" suggested her husband.

Elegant preparations for the new baby had kept Clara too busy to read the papers, which resounded with the wonder of Miss Lind.

"Why?" she remonstrated, "Just plain Jenny? No Jerome has been called that before."

Leonard did not press the issue but he firmly ruled out Aurora. "Let her have one short, pretty name," he said.

"Jenny Jerome," exclaimed Clara. "It sounds outlandish!"

But Leonard smiled winningly, and, as always, he obtained his way in the end.

"Very well then," agreed Clara. "It shall be as you wish, but I think it is hard on a girl to have to go through life as just plain Jenny."

"She'll manage," said Leonard softly. He walked to the frilled cot, stared down at the small object which lay there with its tiny face encased in a frilled bonnet and marveled at the bright little eyes that were so like his own.

ALTHOUGH HE HAD RESIGNED HIS appointment to Ravenna, Leonard, hoping for more political favor later, assured Clara that he would enable her to travel to Europe at the first opportunity. She waited in Brooklyn for two years while Leonard and Addison, always on the brink of making fortunes, hustled their way around Wall Street and spent their evenings in the garish brilliance of the new gas-lit restaurants and theaters. When they made for home in the early hours of morning, Brooklyn lay dark and quiet with shutters drawn and curtains pulled. Clara and the baby daughter would be fast asleep when the brothers tiptoed in. And in the morning there was hardly time for greeting before they had flashed away, leaving the chubby hands waving in one window and Clara's wistful smile in another.

Always observant of her surroundings and eager to improve her home, Clara implicitly accepted the standards of her age. In the west she had seen classical houses of the colonial period superseded by fancy brick and darkened rooms. Now she regarded with interest a city blossoming into sham Gothic. Not unnaturally, she shared the general enthusiasm for reproductions of Italian masters hung in ornate frames. New York copied everything it heard of—Greek, Turkish, Egyptian, or Chinese. Harriet Beecher Stowe scolded the rich citizens for their pretentious taste: "Of what use are brick houses, whose fronts are plated with brown sandstone with expensive entrance doors trimmed with carving, lacking bathrooms and a good kitchen?"

Clara, with hours to spare, immersed in books and magazines, studied every new fashion trend. Occasionally she and her sister-in-law, Julia, crossed on the ferry to take a horse omnibus and observe the large Broadway shops. Although conservative by nature, Clara knew what the fashionable world expected, and her expert eye enabled her to differentiate between overdressing in "incorrect" bright colors and any hint of dinginess. Dresses must be sober, but *obviously* costly, and etiquette decried "any material, however expensive, which might give the look of calico to even the most decided lady." Worse than the stigma of cotton was that of wearing "reddish lilac," a color considered sufficiently ungenteel to endanger social status. As a gentleman grew wealthier, the hoopskirts of the female members of his family grew wider, and trimmings and ornamentation more elaborate. The invention of the sewing machine, far from helping the housewife to run up quick garments, led to a surfeit of braiding and embroidery. Clara used materials as heavily embossed as the rest, but she looked lovely in some of the new gowns, particularly those with fragile transparent undersleeves and wide collars. As

Leonard obtained successes in the city he urged her to spend more lavishly, and she tried in all ways to please him. But the pace of New York did not suit her. With a trace of wistfulness, she saved from her personal income to buy him a bejeweled card case, and with her own inexpert hands she embroidered a velvet smoking cap, hung with a tassel. But her husband had become too busy to notice trifles.

In January, 1852, this life, so arduous and gay for Leonard and so conventional for Clara, abruptly terminated. The Senate confirmed Mr. Jerome's second political appointment, and with joy Clara started to prepare for residence in Trieste. What little time could be spared from shopping and packing she devoted to solemn efforts to absorb the history of the Austro-Hungarian Empire "so that I should know *something* about the place to which we were going, but what a complicated and involved story it did seem." Leonard, kept occupied day and night by business arrangements and conferences concerning his future duties as consul, had to leave preparations for departure entirely to Clara. She stored furniture, obtained new places for the Negro domestics, supervised crates of "necessaries for the Italian clime!" and ordered a suitable trousseau for the journey. It was the age of special costumes. No lady traveled without a traveling dress, or stepped on a boat except in a sailing bonnet, or dreamed of appearing in a new city without trunks of specially devised ensembles.

Although steam passenger ships were running a regular service between New York and Liverpool, Leonard, who always loved to see the great clippers tacking in from Sandy Hook, insisted that they cross the ocean by sail. They traversed the North Atlantic in the westerlies, and then turned south, entering the Mediterranean through the Straits of Gibraltar.

The harmony of this Atlantic crossing was not enhanced by the addition of a young songstress to the family party. Miss Lillie Greenough, deeply in love with Leonard ever since her mother's fancy-dress party in Rochester, had spent a year persuading Mama to allow her to accompany the Jeromes to Italy. She was romantically minded, and the possessor of a moderately good voice. Thoughtlessly, Leonard had offered to pay for her training; now the poor girl must not be disappointed. The propriety of the arrangement did not in any measure alleviate Clara's irritation. She was busy with her own family, and not in the slightest interested in Italian singing technique or the possible renown of Lillie in grand opera. Yet she found herself forced to chaperone and supervise "a feather-wit" who hero-worshiped Leonard in an embarrassing fashion.

In April the party disembarked at Marseilles and traveled along the flowering Riviera to northern Italy, the whole of which lay within the confines of the rambling Austro-Hungarian Empire. Passports were unknown in those days, except for a barbaric land such as Russia and the troubled Italian states. Lillie promptly lost her special papers. Clara exploded with wrath, "She cannot even look after her own pass. *I* have to look after everything."

Venice, Padua, Milan, and Turin were governed from Vienna, and Trieste itself had been under Hapsburg rule since 1382. During several centuries Trieste had remained the Empire's sole outlet to the sea; in 1852 it counted as the most important Mediterranean port, and three years before the Jeromes' arrival Emperor Francis Joseph had granted it the status of *Reichsunmitt-Albarkeit,* making it subject only to the imperial government. Trieste, in fact, was a tiny city-state within the vast Empire.

Perched on the blue Adriatic with all the exports and imports of Austro-Hungary flowing through its great harbor, the city was packed with rich merchants who, like the Venetians of earlier times, traded with the entire world. America was just beginning to open up interests in the Adriatic, and Leonard found it easy to stimulate trade between his country and the eastern Mediterranean lands.

Having settled into a pleasant villa, and familiarized himself with the un-onerous duties of the consulate, Leonard organized a pleasant life for his household. Singing teachers were found for Miss Greenough, who trilled away at her exercises, and Clara, venturing forth in an open carriage, enjoyed the views of bay and mountain, the soft temperate climate, and the lively people. It was a different world for her, a throbbing little world full of ancient history, and her letters home were studded with romantic stories of Venice.

Since many ports in the Adriatic had been founded by emissaries of the Doge, most villages near the sea were Italian-speaking, and despite Austria's sovereignty, this remained the chief tongue of Trieste. Clara tried valiantly to master her Italian and German grammars, but she had as little ear for languages as for music. During drives in the country she was forced to notice that not only the townsfolk but many unlettered peasants seemed able to pick up a foreign language more easily than she. Within the Austrian ruling class it was granted that three or four languages should be perfected in the schoolroom, and Clara determined that her daughters must learn French and Italian while young.

The Governor of Trieste, to whom Leonard presented his credentials, was a Viennese aristocrat who enchanted both Jeromes "by his manners, the art of his conversation, and his supremely unpractical outlook on the world." Later, when they were invited to the castles and manor houses of those Italian counts and dukes who held whatever posts they could procure befitting their rank (this last was of immense importance to all of them), Leonard sometimes experienced tedium in their company. "They spoke more languages than I, but none paid for their own education, and surely it is more important to think clearly in one idiom than to chatter in five."

It was not so to his wife, for whom the charm of all foreigners proved irresistible. A few evenings at the Governor's palace, where she met not only the nobility but rich Viennese merchants whose villas lay scattered around the bay, completely bewitched her. Her eyes were opened to a way of living she never had glimpsed among the successful men of America, and from now on everything Austrian must be deemed perfect.

Concerning the merits of the Italian aristocracy she remained more guarded. They amazed as much as they beguiled, for the men, apart from those who procured posts in the Austrian government services, obviously had no intention of ever doing a stroke of work if they could help it. As for the *contessas,* they appeared to be more interested in lovers' compliments than husbands' careers. Molded by her strict Puritan upbringing, Clara was slightly shocked.

Entertaining in Trieste with well-mannered servants and perfectly trained cooks proved far easier than it ever had in Rochester or New York. The blue bay surrounded by pastel-colored mountains made a backdrop of theatrical splendor for the Jerome villa, which possessed a large garden with "exotic blooms and English lawns" where the babies could romp all day, and their parents could give open-air parties at night. During the summer no Triestians ever seemed to go to bed and the formality usually attendant on diplomatic entertaining faded away in the warm enchantment of the Adriatic. There were even bathing parties at dawn, when the men and women separated as modestly prescribed, splashed out into different bays, and then returned to a vast outdoor breakfast. Clara wrote, "The gorgeous picnic seems as correct as a formal reception for ambassadors and princes as well as our merchant friends."

Once Leonard had become the proud owner of a small white yacht, the consulate saw little of "that energetic American gentleman." He never had owned a boat before, and was forever "missing lunch while taking sailing lessons from a dreadful old fisherman in a red cap." There were also hunting parties with Austrian friends to blue Lake Zirkintza and Monte Nevoso, the Snow Mountain of legend.

In winter most of the Viennese departed to their capital, and as the bitter bora blew down the stark, treeless mountains, the Jeromes, creeping cautiously out to dinner in their closed coach, saw ropes fastened along the streets for people to cling to, lest they be blown into the sea. Entertaining on the grand scale started again in early spring, and Clara, growing more vivacious and talkative every day, forced Leonard to take her to all the balls given in the castles and mansions built along the coast. The flickering candelabras and masses of southern flowers, the old tapestries, and mixture of Latin, Slav, and Germanic tastes enchanted her. And so did the dancing partners. These were provided largely by the battleships of the Austrian Navy, which could disgorge large numbers of well-polished officers for all parties.

Clara, "an elegant brunette with American vitality and Paris gowns," found herself inundated with compliments "so daring one blushes, and yet too graceful to offend."

She met Archduke Maximilian, a naval officer of twenty-one, and danced frequently with his friend, Baron William Teggethoff, who, she admitted years later, "seemed to be, though one should not say it, rather taken."

Trieste was a tiny world, glittering and light-hearted. Night after night, Clara found herself dancing into daylight, and as Leonard drove home beside her he would be whistling a haunting new Strauss waltz. Never before had life permitted them to be so carefree. She would lean back, close her eyes and, as the stars died out of the pale pink sky, completely forget about Miss Greenough practicing scales in the attic.

HE LIFE OF TRIESTE WAS SO DIF-
ferent from that in Rochester and New York that Leonard did
not at first notice the brutality with which the pieces of the old
Empire were kept glued together. Behind the pageantry ticked
a slow time bomb that would explode in the pressure of the next
century. A foreign consul, however, was prone to see the light-
hearted side, and Trieste was a city of many enterprises, packed
with people from different nations. Ambitious men flocked there
for a few years to make quick fortunes before retiring to Paris,
where the art of living had reached supreme heights.

Leonard liked the Austrian Governor of Trieste. At the palace
receptions cosmopolitan merchants of the port mingled with
local counts and dukes and presented an entertaining assortment
of men, all intent on weaving their various destinies in the structure of the swaying Empire. Among them Leonard Jerome, the
North American, Puritan by training, Latin by temperament,
stamped a vivid impression. He was a character, this *"ricco
Americano."* The "gay dogs" of Trieste tried to draw him to the
gambling clubs, but hours at the tables bored him. Seeing him
grow restless at faro, friends urged him to the theater, but he
never mastered Italian sufficiently to enjoy the witty, if licentious,
topical plays for men only. Only the Stadt Theater with its opera
company, to which the stars of Milan and Vienna were frequent
guest artists, held him riveted night after night. Verdi, Doni-
zetti, and Bellini were his favorite composers, and he often
traveled to Venice for star performances. Those of his compan-

ions who had grown up knowing the score of operas by heart laughed at the zeal with which *"ce cher Jerome, ce businessman Américain"* became a connoisseur.

He showed almost as much interest in the Imperial Stud at Lipizza, a few miles from Trieste, where the famous Lipizzaner stallions were bred and kept on show for foreign visitors. Polite comment (from Englishmen in particular) was expected, but Monsieur Jerome became *"passioné."* After he bought a pair of Lipizzaners, Clara decided that as a topic of conversation she would rather bear with musical scores than equine pedigrees. Her poetical feminine mind veered away from technicality. And even Lillie began to look pained when the subject of Lipizzaner sires arose. So Leonard, finding a poor audience in his home, would cry out, "Send for the children!" And the Misses Jerome toddled in, accompanied by their Italian nurse. The little girls loved Papa, whose long mustaches could be pulled with impunity. Mama proved quite a different matter, for fragments of a valuable lace inclined to tear off her gowns, and when beads, braid, and ribbon littered the floor, maids had to be rung for and gaieties ended.

Eager to please Leonard, Clara ordered all her dresses from Paris. "Do look well, Clara," he would urge, and he faced with equanimity those bills that arrived in the wake of enormous boxes containing hoop skirts of satin or brocade or muslin. A lady had plenty of time to devote to her toilette, time to change into two or three dresses each day, and to "attire herself for the evening," a complicated process necessitating several hours and the help of several maids. Here in the romance of this southern setting such efforts were well repaid. When Mrs. Jerome swept forth in a cloud of tulle, she had a sparkle in her eye that had never been seen by the aunts of Palmyra. Clara soon ceased to strive to attain "intellectual heights which just wear one out." She laid by her French and Italian grammars, because they "spoiled too many precious hours," and took to sight-seeing instead. With some trepidation, wearing an enormous sun hat and swathed in veils to protect her complexion, she even accompanied her husband on yachting trips down the lovely coast of the Adriatic.

They tried the Brioni Islands, anchoring near wide beaches and rustling woods of oleander and myrtle. "Paradise," sighed Clara. But Leonard fidgeted and longed for a brisk wind. One autumn they reached Venice, glided across the glass-green lagoons in a gondola, and then traveled overland to Florence, buying pictures and gazing at cathedrals along the way. They ventured with some trepidation into the states of Naples and Sicily. Here Mr. Gladstone, splendidly British and meddlesome, had just paid a visit of inquiry and written an outraged letter to the world concerning the thousands of political prisoners working in chains.

A week after their return to Trieste, Leonard took Clara to Vienna where the winter season of 1852 proved particularly gay with "a great passion for court balls." These were "informal but exclusive. Only the diplomatic corps, and families with the required number of quarterings were invited." The melodies of Johann Strauss were inundating the city, and Francis Joseph and his brother, the Archduke Maximilian, created much flutter by attending many informal dances. On Shrove Tuesday their mother, the sour old Archduchess Sophia, ended the winter season with a ball that crowned all the others, and lasted from 8:00 P.M. until midnight. Then the court retired into seclusion for Lent.

As visitors to the glittering capital, the Jeromes fancied they could feel the pulse of the Empire. But they counted a different beat. Leonard observed Vienna with coolness. Clara, completely captivated by Viennese society, could only find everything "quite quite delightful."

THE PRESIDENTIAL ELECTION OF 1853 replaced President Fillmore, a Republican, by President Pierce, a Democrat. Jerome and other American diplomats, who held political, as opposed to professional, appointments, tendered their resignations. Clara was deeply disappointed. She could not help feeling that she would have made a perfect ambassadress to Vienna or Paris, posts that might have been offered had her husband's diplomatic career continued longer. With the end in sight, she spent the spring in an orgy of sight-seeing, exploring the caverns of Postinina by candlelight and peering from the shelter of a beribboned parasol at the old churches of Trieste. Brow puckered beneath poke-bonnet, she labored through verbose guidebooks on the amalgamation of Byzantine and Gothic. But "one has to be a very diligent student to understand the muddles of Mediterranean architecture, and the afternoons are so hot."

Leonard regarded the date of departure gladly enough. He had enjoyed Italy for a time but the tempo was not his. In the mornings he had driven from villa to office, admiring his prancing horses all the way. After attending to business, he strolled to a club for an *apéritif* before a late lunch. The usual Italian siesta terminated with a sail or a swim. Then, drying whiskers and mustache, Leonard drifted to various entertainments along the coast. He and Clara both had been amused by the long-drawn-out Italian dinner parties. Back in New York they would miss the torrents of conversation, which were elegant and subtle if not quite proper, and the light wines and heady laughter, the old silver gleaming by candlelight, and the eyes languid and blazing in turn, invariably full of admiration for the tall American consul and the *bella bella signora* his wife.

Before leaving Trieste, Leonard and Clara commissioned an Italian named Schiavoni to paint their portraits. In July these were shipped off with a collection of what they hoped were old masters and a huge crate of antique furniture, which fell to pieces in transit. Leonard did not have much to pack. His consular uniform was laid in moth balls and his court sword, with its fine steel blade and engraved motto *Vive le roi* (hardly appropriate for an American Whig), sent home for a future son.* He was eager to introduce the Lipizzaner strain to America and visualized the day when his own carriage would be drawn down Fifth Avenue by the high-stepping beauties of blood royal. There was much to attend to. Babies and maids must travel one way; two horses and a groom, another.

In late summer Leonard and Clara with the children and their Italian nurse started a leisurely journey across Europe, by horse-drawn coach. They crossed the Alps and tarried on on the lower slopes of Mount Cenis. Jennie wrote, "I remember how, as we crossed the Mont Cenis in a *vettura,* the deep snow filled my childish mind with awe and astonishment." In the autumn, accompanied by maids, grooms, and nurses, they reached Paris, where Clara started to purchase gowns at the *grandes maisons.*

After the tension of North Italy, where feelings ran high against imperial Austria, Louis Napoleon's city of gaslight and crinolines appeared remarkably content. The new Emperor distracted attention from governmental difficulties by rebuilding the capital Roman fashion for his amazed citizens. Gigantic buildings, new boulevards, monuments, and columns sprang up daily, and a glittering court was being created "in great haste," its tone grow-

---

* The son never materialized, but the sword hangs today in Castle Leslie, the home of an Irish grandson.

ing not *nouveau riche* but *nouveau royale*. Clara decided that here, not in Vienna, lay the center of the world she loved, and Leonard promised to bring her back. If she could not return as ambassadress then she must come for love of the fair city.

The fact that France, England, and Turkey were at war with Russia seems to have affected the lives of ordinary people scarcely at all. The incidents of the Crimea were hardly mentioned in the Jerome ladies' letters. Far more pertinent to the general interest was the rumor, sent across the Atlantic by Clara herself, that straw hats would shortly replace bonnets.

Then news arrived from Addison saying his firm of brokers, Fitch, McNeal, and Jerome, had failed. It was imperative for Leonard to return hastily to America. When, to Clara's sorrow, the family embarked, one glance at her husband's keen face showed that he felt no grief at leaving. He had been yearning for that financial jungle of New York. Amid the potentialities of the high-strung city he had always been sure he could battle his way to victory.

On a sailing ship plunging across the South Atlantic, two faces looked westward. The Jeromes came home with different aspirations. Leonard remained an American to the core. Clara left her heart in Europe.

THE CITY TO WHICH LEONARD JEROME returned in November, 1853, was the center of a blunt, brilliant world. He was glad to return to its limitless horizons and to the companionship of men who rose from nothing to fantastic financial power—men who thought in terms without boundary. Vanderbilt, Jay Gould, Jim Fiske, and Daniel Drew were among Leonard's friends and adversaries in the toughest financial arena in the world. Courage belonged to them all; kindness, to very few. "These boys did not like to be clamped down on." They were fussy to see that "sufficient freedom was granted to the individual" and inclined to take the law into their own hands if they could not buy out a legislature! Walt Whitman, who once lived near the Jerome house in Brooklyn, wrote, "New York is more than a city; it is a way of life." It was to this life that the Jerome brothers belonged, by inclination and by understanding.

After a brief visit in Rochester, Leonard brought his family back to Brooklyn, where he and Addison purchased a house lying two blocks nearer South Ferry than their previous joint home. This residence, 8 Amity Street, became the base from which the Jeromes conducted their Wall Street forays during the ensuing years. Addison's firm had recently failed, but what of it? "Leonard did not wait to unpack before he plunged. Every dollar he had not settled on me was in constant use on the market," said Clara. Having provided for their wives, the brothers considered themselves free to gamble away the rest, or to make fortunes if luck held. Clara sighed at her enforced return to America, but Leonard swore he would be a rich man within a year, and once again every morning he and Addison vanished toward the ferry that carried them to work. It was very late when they recrossed the river and walked home through the dark streets and quiet gardens of Brooklyn.

Leonard devoted all his free time to his one pair of horses, which he drove jubilantly among the swarms of fast pacers exercising on Third Avenue. Elegant carriages and sleighs abounded, but Leonard's turnout proved the cynosure of all eyes. He had always been a natural horseman, and years of practice now made him an artist with the reins. Many a girl whisked by

44

amid the jingling bells of her fur-covered family sledge sighed on hearing that Mr. Jerome was already married.

Despite the failure of his firm, Addison swiftly recovered his prestige and among the grand ventures that were sweeping America, the brothers grew steadily richer. Many contemporary projects were financial tidal waves that grew completely out of control. While vast rivers were being harnessed, new cities sprang up on the edges of the ever-receding wilderness. Many an incandescent fortune flared and died speedily like a rocket soaring against the night sky. Leonard called Wall Street "a jungle where men tear and claw." But jungle air suited him. The all-powerful operators were fair game.

During this period the development of railroad lines throughout the nation caused financial pandemonium. Most lines were sketched out on paper and built too quickly for their ultimate effects or worth to be assessed by the company founders.

Leonard recognized the potential dangers of many of these projects, which were out-of-hand financially before the first engine ran. At that time, overissue of stock could be considered normal procedure, but when the New York and New Haven railway companies sold forged stock and were involved in enormous scandals, the public grew resentful. Mr. Jerome stepped forward as a kind of railroad reformer. While buying heavily in companies whose stocks he had ascertained were in actual existence, he simultaneously exhorted political friends to "clear up the chaos." He saw that if railway investments grew safer they would immensely increase in value, and he persuaded the congressman from Rochester, Freeman Clark, to secure the passage of a railroad reform bill restricting several forms of over-issue. Leonard Jerome's name began to resound through the street as "a man who could get things done." In the midst of the incredible corruption and gigantic swindles one man of integrity and nerve could stand up boldly and gain the confidence of an outraged public. A sour rival said, "That damn fellow has cashed in on honesty."

While the big shots battled a way to fortune, their women-folk conspired to enter the tiny nucleus that called itself the old aristocracy. It seems that when sudden wealth lays the world at women's feet, they only wish to scale some pinnacle where they aren't wanted! The portals of the New York nobility proved exceptionally strong. Unable to storm the citadel, the "rich no-bodies" built a new social ring that gave fascinating original entertainments, and the grandee stock became uncomfortably squeezed. Apparently Clara knew the way through the bar-ricades. She would soon be able to add to the mansions that were creeping up Fifth Avenue, and her breeding through Ambrose Hall would allow her to drop cards on the elite (no mention was made of her beautiful mother's antecedents, one may be sure!). Yet entrancing as it was to step into the select circle of old New York society, Clara still yearned for Paris.

While Leonard, who refused to belong to any one circle, persisted in inviting a mixture of people to the house, Clara drove diligently around in her new carriage, dropping cards on the "right" people. She gave small, formal dinner parties for guests carefully selected to match each other's tastes. Even Leon-ard noted with pleasure her Paris gowns, modeled on those de-signed for the Empress Eugenie. The Italian pictures were hung, and Clara's discourses on Italian art caused much admiration. The rage for antiques had just begun to spread through America. Starting in Boston, this cult was destined to obsess the upper classes for generations. The new rich speedily learned they simply had to have old furniture. Not being able to drag it from attics, they were only too grateful to learn from Mrs. Jerome that such things as junk shops existed and that it was "genteel" to snoop around the shops of art dealers.

On the fringes of society it was becoming the habit for wives (as well as mistresses) of successful men to load themselves with jewelry for dinner parties. Clara, issuing from the fastnesses of well-bred drawing rooms, dropped quiet snubs to those of Leonard's friends who were newly emerged from the welter. With disappointment they learned that only pearls could be worn by a lady on informal occasions.

When Leonard spent his first sensational gains on a magnificent diamond necklace for his wife, she counted the operas and entertainments at which she would be able to wear it and then looked at him with shining eyes: "And if we ever went to a court how splendidly I could show it off!"

"Don't worry, Clara," he laughed. "You shall have your court too." In the fifties ladies dressed in velvet to show their affluence; they also hung rooms with velvet and sat on velvet, but they cultivated the most unvelvety thoughts and were forever watching steely-eyed for an opportunity to "cut" some unfortunate of whom they disapproved. The maneuver for cutting had been developed into a minor art. The deliverer of the thrust would step forward as if to speak to the intended victim, then as that person moved or smiled in anticipation, would deliberately stare through her. Clara with a gentle nature had no wish to assert such powers, and she quite liked some of the new upthrusting families, but the strident note of New York jarred her. She did not sense the drive which made it the most exciting machine on earth. The flamboyant new set whom Leonard met through his business connections often sighed at the number of restrictions that followed the lofty pursuit of social climbing, but nevertheless they learned what they could from Mrs. Jerome's hints, and even her censure was kindly.

During the summer of 1854, Leonard, whose taste for sailing had been whetted in the Adriatic, bought a yacht, the *Undine*, in which he made several trips to Newport. Leonard thought that Newport, an Old World fishing village, would be a satisfactory summer base for Clara and the babies. He could visit his family by sea whenever the fray in Wall Street eased. Clara delighted in this new move. She never visualized the marble palaces that later would overwhelm the picturesque town.

By 1855 Addison had made a complete financial recovery. Having re-established himself as a broker-banker, he proceeded to build a mansion at 33 West 20th Street, then a fashionable part of the city, and to settle two million dollars on his wife, "so the poor thing shall not be worried again."

Leonard, himself a magnate of no mean repute, spent most of the summer shark fishing. He left Clara and the children in the country and wrote complaining of the exorbitant cost of a professional crew (not an unusual shock for gentlemen of fortune who take to the sea):

> . . . I wish we could always keep a yacht. I had rather have one than all the other luxuries that are indulged in by people of wealth. My dear little pickininies and you, my ever faithful and true wife . . . how happy I shall be to see you again. The boys are pulling me by the coattail, so good night. *Dite a Talla che Papa vena* [*sic*] *a casa subito . . . tre o quatro jorni* [*sic*] *. . . addio.*
>
> *Leonard.*

Talla, who was little Clara, received the news joyously, but her mother was silent. She did not approve of "the boys."

In November a third daughter arrived and was christened Camille.

LAWRENCE QUICKLY JOINED LEON-
ard and Addison in New York. The brothers shared a quick wit,
which kept them in constant demand for dinner parties. By day,
they strolled on Wall Street, playing the roles of broker-merchant-
bankers; by night they became Manhattan's gayest gentlemen.
They earned and spent in unison. Addison's mansion on West
Twentieth Street became the scene of many entertainments, and
here in 1856 the famous firm of Travers, Jerome, which lasted so
long in Wall Street, came into being.

Addison, without social aspirations but liking to astound his
men friends, had given a dinner with particularly good wines.
The guests sat talking and drinking, until in the early hours
Leonard rose to his feet and amidst roars of laughter, announced
the founding of a new firm by himself, Addison, and William
Travers, the celebrated lawyer-wit, owner of a stable of fast
trotters. The Three Musketeers, as the directors called themselves, toasted their partnership in rare port, and toward dawn
those who could stand gave a smart salute to each inauguration
speech.

This was the evening when William Travers, creeping home
on tiptoe, originated the reply which has become a famous vaude-
ville joke.

"Is that you, Bill?" his wife called as the floor boards creaked.

Travers always stuttered. "Y—yes," he said, "wh—who did
you expect?"

Within a month, the Musketeers proceeded to work. Their

49

attacks in Wall Street produced spectacular results until Leonard, over-confident from success, took a tip from a friend. This man, who was treasurer of the Cleveland and Toledo Company, knew his stock to be false, but just before it crashed he off-loaded it on the firm of Travers, Jerome.

Leonard's entire personal fortune disappeared. He had settled a considerable amount on Clara, and she accepted with complacency the news that the move to a Fifth Avenue mansion must be postponed. "Leonard Jerome never flickered an eyelid in public, but he was sore displeased that one he trusted had let him down."

To everyone's surprise he announced a year's retreat for himself. This period was to be devoted to the study of Wall Street psychology. While he took no part in active speculation, Clara ran her reduced household with tact. She did not care if he made money or not; in fact, she seems to have been slightly ashamed of her husband's financial flair. And for the first time, Leonard was grateful. "How dear seem Clara's airy notions in comparison to the shoddy values I meet elsewhere."

She believed in her husband. He had made money before and probably would do it again. Did it matter so long as their life together remained smooth and the correct moral tone was upheld? "I will not find it in me to worry," she told her sister. They were not tempted to sell their pictures, for none of the new millionaires, intent on furnishing private art galleries, would have thought of purchasing unobtrusive early Italians.

Leonard minded deeply. His lost fortune represented years of effort, and the sneers of enemies in Wall Street galled. Jerome was mocked as "one of the brightest meteors that has flashed by." But the children saw more of their adored papa, and Clara seemed content. "Only dear Leonard's *real* friends now enter our parlour. I know them and like them."

Among those who stood by him, in the parlor and elsewhere,

were Henry Clews, the banker, and August Belmont, famous financial adviser to the Rothschilds and to the Democratic Party. Neither of these men had started life in America. Henry Clews, educated in England to take Holy Orders and accept a country curacy under his brother, had made a trip to New York before going to the university, and this brief kaleidoscopic vision "turned the dear boy's head," to an extent that resolved him to combat his parent's wishes, to break away from quiet country security, and plunge into the maelstrom of Wall Street. He became one of the city's greatest financiers, teased by few save William Travers, whose inimitable voice was heard in the Jeromes' drawing room: "I s—s—say, Clews, s—s—since you are a self-made man, why the devil didn't you put m—m—more hair on y—y—your head?"

The other friend, stocky, stanch August Belmont, said that no man in America delighted him more than Leonard. Belmont and Jerome shared a very special passion for horses (and rather more complicated, for ladies of high mettle). Some of their upbringing corresponded; they had been born in the same year and started work young, but August Belmont was the son of a well-to-do yeoman farmer in the Rhenish Palatinate. Apprenticed at the age of thirteen to the Rothschilds in Frankfort, he had been sent in 1837 to America as their first agent. During the next forty years Belmont's advice regarding United States securities enabled the Rothschilds to build a new financial organization of immense power, and he became New York's outstanding magnate.

Clews from the English gentry, Belmont from the Rhine, and Jerome bred of the New World: the friendship of these three became consolidated by inordinate school-boyish enthusiasm for sport and horses. The German and the American in particular shared exuberant tastes; their country breeding on soil that had not been corrupted by artificial processes may, to some extent, have given them the strength to enjoy all they won. They lived

51

like tornadoes; apparently nothing ever went wrong with their livers or nerves, and Leonard accepted occasional ruin as a good steeplechaser does a fall—just a passing event to learn from.

The lean year passed. Clara bore patiently the impossibility of going to Mrs. Schermerhorn's famous costume ball, to which only the "six hundred indisputable members of New York's elite" were invited. Leonard had no great urge to shave his whiskers and gambol in Louis XV period attire, but Clara was disappointed when she heard that the two-hour German cotillion would be danced for the first time in America. Having learned endless cotillion steps in Vienna, Clara would have been completely at home. "Never mind, Clara dear," said Leonard, when he realized what she had missed, "you will have more parties than you want some day. Wait and see."

New York society, at which Astor's grandson was now jeering for its "tyrannical exclusiveness," refused to open its portals to the hulking figure of Commodore Vanderbilt. His language kept him beyond the pale, and though the handsome old man made occasional efforts to get invited, he simply could not "quit cursing," and his uncontrollable admiration for the weaker sex caused even the housemaids to fly from his proximity. During the fifties, when Cornelius Vanderbilt had reached only the ten million mark, the upper crust of New York society ostracized him heartlessly. Finally, the Commodore built the *North Star,* an enormous steam yacht, and sailed away to Europe. In France and Russia he was accepted as a rough-mannered grand duke might have been accepted, yet he never lost the urge to return. During the next twenty years, despite his social frustrations, he would turn his eleven million dollars into a hundred million.

When Leonard's year of contemplation terminated, he hazarded a new gamble. Scraping together every available dollar, he threw for high stakes. Within a month, he had multiplied his firm's capital ten times. Once again Manhattan swallowed him soon after dawn and returned him past midnight. Clara wondered, "All this for a brownstone house in Fifth Avenue?" But Leonard dreamed more of stables than of houses. With his first winnings he started a racing stud to equal August Belmont's. "After all, I'm fond of the fellow, but one can't let him have the pick of everything—he's got the best pictures, the best porcelain, and the best chef in New York as it is."

The Three Musketeers exasperated Wall Street by mingling ruthlessness with frivolity. Their failures could be jeered at, but the steel-hard tycoons found their successes hard to stomach. In Wall Street it was lese majesty to laugh about money.

Meanwhile, in a luxurious room high above the junction of Pine and Nassau Streets, the firm of Travers, Jerome inaugurated what it airily called its "Observatory." Here, in a splendid setting of red plush and polished woods, Leonard, entertaining his business acquaintances, thoughtfully "observed." The luncheons and dinners served in this room were unhurried and the conversation, stimulating. Wines showed the choice of a connoisseur, and guests seldom realized their views were being dissected as under a microscope.

Among the most frequent visitors to the Observatory were the financial editors of two New York papers, the *Herald* and the *Tribune*. Since his own venture in Rochester, Leonard had fully comprehended the powers of the press. If these men wished, they could break a company, and in the instance of the Cleveland and Toledo, Leonard decided that such action would be beneficial. After careful research he knew the whole company to be rotten, but only an unprecedented press campaign could reveal its true state. Both the *Herald* and the *Tribune* started to publish the facts dug up by Leonard, and not only this company, but also the corrupt Michigan Southern (which Leonard swore to break even if it carried down the whole market) were exposed and smashed. His threats had been laughed at, but during the panic that followed the press exposure of these companies Leonard made a far greater fortune than the one he had lost.

A story is told that one day Leonard was standing on the pavement near the old Stock Exchange, predicting the failure of certain securities of which he disapproved, when a broker stepped up. He pointed to the edifice of the Ohio Life and Trust Company, saying, "Say what you please, that company is good stock at all events." Leonard scowled and said he would not give fifty for its stocks, then standing at 103. The word traveled around. No one believed him, but two months later the Ohio Life and Trust Company failed for several millions and dragged not only Wall Street but the entire commerce of the country with it.

Leonard Jerome's frankness became famous.

"Those Jeromes are doing well," wrote a contemporary, adding not without a touch of irritation: "Sometimes it pays to behave like a gentleman."

WHEN LEONARD CONSIDERED IT safe to leave his business, he acquiesced to Clara's pleadings to return to Europe for two years. He strolled down to South Street and wandered past the trading schooners and ocean clippers whose high bowsprits stretched almost across the street, while the busy dockyard traffic passed underneath. Had it not been for his family, Leonard would have dearly loved to choose a ship and sail off around the world. But domestic ties held him to civilization. Clara did not enjoy an ocean crossing, so he chose the most seaworthy bark he could find and booked passage for her and himself, the three children, a maid, and a nurse. In the early spring they reached France.

On their arrival, they found Paris in a ferment of excitement, wondering if Emperor Francis Joseph would blunder into war with Piedmont-Sardinia. Leonard took an apartment at 63 Avenue de Champs Élysées and strolled off to investigate the studs of France. On September 13, 1858, he wrote lengthily to Lawrence:

"Paris is not yet as agreeable to me as New York except on Sunday. The pleasure carriages that passed my window yesterday, 12 A.M. to 8 P.M., averaged about 50 *a minute*. I amuse myself with music in the morning, walking or riding in the afternoon, and theatre visiting and billiards in the evening. . . . I think I shall spend next summer at the Isle of Wight, a great place for yachting and horses. . . . I advise you to teach languages to your sons young. Boys run to things they shine in. Whatever they *succeed* in, that they are inclined to do well.

"I wrote Travers by the last mail to send me a wagon and harness. If not already dispatched, cancel. I find horses here abominably dear. 2,000 francs is nothing for a pair that you would not drive a second time. They do not admire speed. Showy, high-stepping, short switch-tail and arching neck is the description that generally answers. I have been looking about only to find French horses so little to my fancy that I have ended by buying nothing. So if you happen to see a pair of horses you think would suit my driving, good size, good travellers, you may send them over."

Clara bloomed at Leonard's side in this new element. They drove, they visited, they saw theaters and operas, and went to private concerts and salons and gave "delightful, intimate little dinners." The dukes of this and that paid calls, and Leonard sent flowers to more than one prima donna. Voices remained long in his memory, far longer than the faces of lovely women. According to family research, Clara was the only woman he ever looked at twice who couldn't sing.

While Leonard visited race courses with the dandies of Paris, Clara ventured gingerly into the imperial court. Apparently the Empress simply heard of an interesting American lady and asked her to the palace. Clara, fluttering with pleasure, assured the Empress she liked dancing. When she came home, she tried on her diamond necklace before the mirror, saying, "I have found the court I want!"

In January, 1859, Leonard wrote again to his brother. "We have been to the grand ball at the Tuileries and were presented to the Emperor and Empress. It was universally conceded that Clara was the handsomest woman there. I never saw her look so well."

And then, suddenly, war came. Louis Napoleon, leading a new *grande armée,* hurried to the rescue of the Italian states. His enemy Francis Joseph, obsessed with the importance of nipping in the bud revolutionary movements within the Austrian Empire, could not conduct any army with efficiency. For the second time within sixty years, Europe saw the noble house of Hapsburg trounced by an upstart Bonaparte.

The French victory of Magenta was followed by Solferino and, by June, Napoleon had entered Milan at the head of his troops and the French fleet was blockading Venice (where Clara's dear Archduke Maximilian held an inefficient nominal command allowing him to take no proper action).

Napoleon won the war within a few weeks, but he was too ill to think clearly or take advantage of victory. When the obvious moment came to reduce Venice, push into Austria, and form a cohesive Italy, the oppressive summer heat seemed to sap all his powers of decision. After one hideous day looking over the battlefield strewn with wounded, Napoleon III, who loved humanity, felt his nerve falter. Weakly, at just the wrong moment, he let armistice proposals begin. Francis Joseph's elaborate system of centralization, Germanization, and police repression had completely broken down, and the dawn of Italian unity lay in sight; but Napoleon's fatal conclusion of a half-won war merely humiliated Austria and left the Italian peninsula as unsettled as before. The foolish loser and the well-meaning victor returned to their respective capitals in equal unpopularity. "What have you done with *our* triumphs?" raged the Parisians. "Did you go to war just to stop *en pleine gloire?*"

To allay the discontent of his capital, Napoleon ordered a grand parade of returned troops to take place on August 14. Tiers of seats were built around the Place Vendome, and for hours on end the Emperor and his little son took the salute, while Eugenie sat enthroned beneath a canopy of green velvet and golden bees. The setting was very impressive. As the Second Army of Italy marched past with tattered banners and trophies of war, regiment after regiment showed gaps in their ranks. These were the places of the dead.

It was impossible not to be moved. The Parisian mob cheered and wept, but it was the showmanship they applauded, not this new Napoleon who led soldiers to war and threw away the prizes.

Mr. Jerome witnessed the parade, but with all her zeal for "history in the making," Clara dared not move from St. Germain-en-Laye. The next day on August 15, Napoleon's birthday, she gave birth. Again the hoped-for Leonard turned out to be a girl, a funny, little, brown-eyed creature. Rather sadly they christened her Leonie (French feminine of Leonard). She was their last child.

WHEN LEONARD NO LONGER
dared to remain away from New York, he returned by steam
packet with his wife and four small daughters. He found his
friends Vanderbilt, Belmont, and Clews obsessed by the possibility of civil war. President Lincoln had stated: "I shall swear
that I will, to the best of my ability, preserve, protect, and defend
the Constitution of the United States. It is not the Constitution
as I would like to have it, but as it *is,* that is to be defended."
The clash of interest between the industrial North and the agricultural South might have been resolved, but the Southerners remained prone to high-handed action, and Lincoln was unflinching
in regard to secession. "Can a squabble over high tariffs and free
trade lead to civil war? Surely not?" wrote Addison. But slowly
events were moving toward that moment when, against the will
of all thinking men, blood instead of words decides an issue.

Meanwhile Clara was to be given her mansion. "I'll build you
a palace yet!" Leonard had often called, as he hurried to South
Ferry. "Wait and see!" She had waited and now she saw.

The fashionable were edging northward. By 1859 Madison
Square had been incorporated in the domain of elegance and the
large houses there contained the city's first indoor water closets,
which had been attacked for being "not only unsanitary but im-
moral." Leonard bought a large site on the corner of Twenty-
sixth Street overlooking the square and adjacent to the mansion
of Mrs. Schermerhorn, redoubtable leader of New York society,
who was decreeing like Empress Eugenie that the vulgar polka

must not be danced at *her* balls. Unfortunately, even Mrs. Schermerhorn could not effect the removal of an immense marble palace called the Louvre, which also overlooked Madison Square two streets down. Despite the installation of several social leaders in the vicinity, this establishment defiantly continued to flourish as a rendezvous for the city's most expensive demimondaines. Boasting sparkling chandeliers, marble columns, gold paneled walls, and plashing fountains, it naively advertised itself as the "most refined of its sort in the world."

It was not sufficiently refined, however, for Mrs. Schermerhorn and Clara, who launched a drive to have the Louvre banished from their neighborhood. Their efforts always remained handicapped by the fact that they were not supposed to know about "such things."

Professional architects had only just begun to exist, and Leonard freely redesigned the plans he was offered. Unlike the usual ornate brownstone, his mansion was to be of red brick and white marble, a strawberry pie amidst rows of chocolate blancmanges.

Long before the central portion could be ready for occupation, Leonard enticed the builder to deviate from the original design and add a rambling fancy stable and a private theater as wings to the main structure.

According to the New York *Tribune:* "Jerome was the friend as well as the patron of artists and actors. His passion for the theatre and opera was only surpassed by his love of horses. He built his stable before he built his house. It was of brick, faced with marble, three stories high, with a mansard roof. He filled it with horses and carriages of the finest makes. Except for the Emperor's Mews in Paris, it is doubtful if any stable in the world at that time surpassed Jerome's. Black walnut, plate glass, carpeted floors and other costly decorations ornamented the place. Above the stable he built a private theatre, handsomely adorned. . . . In front of his stable Mr. Jerome built his house and for years it was the centre of fashion. From its doors one Sunday afternoon he drove the first four-in-hand ever seen in this city. . . ."

Clara looked askance at these additions to her home. Did she really wish to live in a house "built in front of a stable," a house that might be described as an annex to an opera? It was all "very very trying," and despite her bathroom with French fittings, which really did shock the older generation, Clara hankered increasingly for Europe. The court of the Second Empire, where distinguished Americans were feted, offered a setting more to her taste than the restricted *beau monde* of New York. Foreign climes seemed even more attractive when neighs and arpeggios began to resound through her windows. Parisian friends wrote her that interesting events were taking place in Europe. The Archduke Maximilian had once complained of the Napoleonic court, "the Emperor is lacking in nobility . . . Eugenie quite a thoroughbred but lacking in the august quality of an Empress . . . parvenu etiquette keeps coming through . . . whole impression is of a make-believe court occupied by amateurs who are not very sure of their parts." But the American Mrs. Jerome, quite sure of *her* part, disagreed with all the Archduke's criticisms save one concerning St. Cloud, where "a very improper piece was performed which, according to our ideas, ought not to have been played before ladies."

Now she heard the Archduke had again visited Paris to seek French backing for Francis Joseph's Mexican project. On these occasions parvenu rifles are as good as any others.

Madame Jerome naturally had attracted admirers in French society, and this partly compensated for Leonard's inability to keep at bay that circle of vulnerable feminine hearts that sprang up around him in every land. In contrast he (almost unique among husbands in Paris) had no cause for jealousy. Clara brought up in the Puritan code was "too good to occasion aught but fair comment." This, however, did not help her countenance

Leonard's lapses. Her pleasure when dear Miss Lillie Greenough was finally married off had been made known to all the family. No more musical evenings to arrange for the doting songstress, no more chaperoning, no more eulogies necessary for Lillie's mama! Leonard also seems to have shown a slight relief. His protégée had a few charming notes, but her emotions exceeded her art.

Lillie's first letter to Leonard after her marriage survives undated:

TROUVILLE.

My dear friend,

I have not heard from you for such a long time. I believe I entirely lost your good opinion because I am no longer a young lady? Oh, don't forget to love me just the same. I am the same to you. I love you more than ever because I feel you are never getting as strong love from anyone else. Have you really not written a word of kindness or congratulation? Is it possible you can give me less in this way? What am I to do with my temper is a question I ask of myself every day. It is an unpleasant thing to live with, is my temper. It worries me and I cannot help getting angry. You know it is my nature and it kills me. Ah, well enough. You will say a pleasant beginning.

My husband (the first time I have written that hateful word) is kind and I am living just as I have always wished to, at Trouville (you know that is the fashionable watering place in France) in a house to ourselves. We have hired the house for the season, have plenty of room, and are going to have the two boys and Mama (who will come to spend a little time with us), a yacht of our own, carriage and horses, two men servants, plenty of nice neighbours, and so you would think I would be happy. Well, I am in one way, very, but you know. Then we have a nice piano and I sing and Charlie composes for me and accompanies me.

We first thought of travelling in England and when we got to Dieppe in true bridegroom fashion (we were four days getting there) we went to the same hotel where we went, Mama you and I in our first travels, and I was so continually reminded of you and kept so constantly talking about you that my worthy husband was frightened at the contrast I would probably draw and after staying in Dieppe for five days we decided—I say *we* because I was afraid myself—if we went there, I should probably bring on a fit of the blues for my own benefit and one of jealousy for his, so we decided to come to Trouville.

I have not heard once from Paris owing to our moving about so and having no settled plans about anything, but I expect letters today. Just think how lonely poor Mama must feel all alone. I have written to her to beg her to come here and spend a little time with us. . . .

Do write to me and congratulate me won't you? Say something kind at least. If my life is going to be as long as these first two weeks, I shall not want many birthdays. Poor America, I have almost forgotten about her as you forget me. What are your plans? Don't for heaven's sake forsake me. If you can't love me as you used to, don't let me know it.

YOURS AS EVER,

Lillie.

THE JEROMES MOVED INTO THEIR new home along with the carriage horses, the champion hacks, and two fast trotters. No sooner had the clang of workmen's hammers died away than the voices of practicing singers arose from the miniature opera house. Leonard was never at a loss to know what to do with money. He became a music patron in the grand manner.

Meanwhile Clara labored to decorate her own apartments appropriately. The ballroom shimmered white and gold beneath its immense chandeliers and the drawing room flamed in dark red. She tried to enjoy it all while secretly dreaming of a small salon in Paris where ambassadors whispered state secrets and a poet or two strolled in to show his work. The poets of New York were Bohemians who caroused in a smoky cellar and had to be dubbed unsuitable for a lady's drawing room.

As Lillie Greenough's sighs faded into the distance, Mrs. Jerome had dared to hope that certain aspects of life would become easier. But the private theater had risen on her doorstep, and worse trials lay ahead.

Adelina Patti was now famous in New York, and before long Leonard met the seventeen-year-old phenomenon. She told him of her surprise when, on being pushed suddenly into the role of *Lucia* by her brother-in-law, the impressario Strokosh, on an unfashionable evening, she found the half-empty house rising in uproar at the end of each act.

"They say my voice equals Jennie Lind's. Does it remind *you?*" she asked Leonard. He answered truthfully, "It's the only one that ever has."

Now she was the darling of New Yorkers, their first artist to reach supreme heights. Four times a week she sang through an opera to exulting crowds. She was so young and her gift, so perfect. What could any man have to offer? Flowers, jewels? No! No! That, to use the favorite adjective of the age, would be vulgar. Only kind Mr. Jerome could produce a toy out of the ordinary for a little prima donna. His private theater was placed entirely at her disposal for the trying of new roles. And who gave her the most stimulating criticism? Who spoke of a woman's soul as well as of her technique? And who was always ready to drive her home in his superb sledge? New Yorkers saw them often together and gossip began.

Leonard Jerome "dazzled society with the glitter and novelty of his carriages, the costliness of his blooded horses. He excited its dubious admiration by his extravagance and assurance. Both were obvious in all his activities: his fantastic speculations, his scandalous love affairs, his incredible parties. . . . He made, lost, and again made fortunes; he was reputed to be worth more than ten million dollars." * But this was only half the story. He had a strength that never flagged, a capacity for attending to detail, and a violent interest in everything he touched.

When the Jeromes gave their first tremendous ball, the new house had to be transformed into a fairy palace with walls of sweet-smelling roses and gardenias and plashing brooks. Piping difficulties arose concerning the access of the water main to the dining room, where two fountains were supposed to cascade among hillocks of flowers. Leonard swept aside the decorators. "I'll fix it up," he said. "Send the plumbers to me." Fountains that spouted champagne and eau de cologne were then devised. Guests inebriated in the vicinity of one could recover beside the other.

A person present at the Jerome's first big ball recorded: "Invitations were eagerly sought by the 400 of that day, and all the wealth and fashion and beauty of the metropolis took part in the dance. Two fountains were placed in the centre of the auditorium, playing cologne and champagne, and the floral decorations were marvellous. The front of the theatre was illuminated and the sidewalls covered with crimson tapestry. The Supper must have cost thousands."

Clara's diamonds and satin ball gowns now required an inventory to keep in order, but she knew the rules. She never appeared in the latest fashion; that would have been considered showy and ill-bred. She simply kept the Paris importations in her wardrobe and wore them a year later when the Empress's approval had stamped them as good taste! Gowns and gossip and

---

* Lloyd R. Morris, *Incredible New York* (New York, Random House, 1951).

calling on the right set took a certain amount of time but, as Leonard slipped from her clutches, Clara turned more and more to the consolations of the nursery, where her eldest daughter was now a dreamy ash blonde ten years old.

In 1860 Leonard became financially interested in the New York *Times*. He purchased one quarter of that paper's shares and directed the financial editor. "The Observatory set the moral atmosphere for Wall Street. Mr. Jerome did well through his climb to virtue . . . his name became known throughout the country as one of the boldest, coolest, and most successful manipulators in the Street."

The sixties certainly presented an amusing epoch in which to be suddenly rich. So much *could* be done to a house. Furniture arrived in crates from the leading cabinetmakers of New York. Pieces of walnut, ebony, tulip wood, and rosewood ornately carved or inlaid with pearl crowded the large darkened rooms. Chandeliers threw rainbows of crystal from the center of her ceilings; glass decanters and goblets were bought from the new Brooklyn industries, and electroplated and pearl-handled knives made yet more opulent the large dinner table. Bronze statues supported gas jets, while cast-iron mirrors, fountains, and balconies were inserted into unused corners; light had to be kept out by foliage as well as by sets of curtains. Sèvres, Dresden, and Worcester porcelain stood in niches until the only rooms in which it was possible to move freely were the nurseries, hidden behind a final filigree of carved woodwork, where the four lively daughters lived in the charge of a beloved colored mammy and a governess.

Delmonico, the famous restaurateur, found his talents stretched to the utmost when Leonard, August Belmont, and William Travers arranged a competition among themselves in sumptuous dinner parties. "Here three gentlemen come to me and order three dinners, and each one charges me to make his dinner the best. I am given an unlimited order."

The chef, a true genius, threw hysterics but succeeded in improvising novelties for each one. Leonard added to the originality by placing a gold bracelet with a jeweled pendant in every lady's napkin, but Belmont capped this by platinum trinkets. Travers could only add the diamonds of his wit.

Fifth Avenue watched Mr. Jerome's social audacities with amazement. That any man could have so much *energy*. Was it really very well bred? Clara wilted and turned pleadingly for friendships to the old families, who were retreating behind increasingly high social barriers.

Yet in the stiff, dark drawing rooms where life continued to be conducted with iron decorum, Mrs. Jerome maintained a brave front. No complaint concerning her husband's activities ever slipped from her lips. The sufferings of a lady in such circumstances must be accepted without a sigh. The code was rigid. But she received indirect sympathy.

The most unsuccessful of Leonard's extravagances was the *Clara Clarita,* the family steam yacht (named for his wife and daughter), on which he spent one hundred twenty-five thousand dollars. The interior was left to an unsupervised contractor and the daughter wrote years later: "Mamma's face fell a fathom when she first stepped aboard and saw the luxurious, impractical furnishings in pale-blue silk and hammered silver. 'What *has* all this cost?' she asked."

Leonard, who had given no thought to the project, became soon irritated by constant mechanical troubles.* He replaced the

---

* According to press clippings, *Clara Clarita* knew one brief moment of fame late in 1865 when the Atlantic cable was reported broken. "Mr. Jerome having been informed of the difficulties under which the company labored, and that Mr. Everett, the able and skillful engineer, was willing to undertake the repairing of the cable if a proper steam yacht could be had, gracefully offered the use of his beautiful steam yacht, the *Clara Clarita,* and we are informed that she will proceed at once with Mr. Everett to the Gulf of St. Lawrence. This liberality on the part of Mr. Jerome will not only prevent any delay in the transmission of cable messages but will enable the Telegraph Company to meet the expedition

engines, but when he realized his family did not want to live aboard, he relegated the yacht to the "limbo of expensive failures." His heart belonged to sailing ships henceforth.

A̶DDISON JEROME DIED SHORTLY before the outbreak of the Civil War. He left his wife two million dollars. The Jerome brothers, who gathered for his funeral, discussed at length the political situation. They resolved to work actively in support of President Lincoln's policies.

As part owner of the New York *Times,* Leonard exerted considerable influence. The war enormously increased the circulation of newspapers, and fresh power fell into the hands of the owners. The New York *Herald,* which had been launched twenty-five years before in a rented cellar by old James Gordon Bennett, had the largest circulation. Its impropriety could be guaranteed to fascinate the masses. Every edition contained amorous scandals, few of which were mentioned a second time, and even the personal column made salacious reading. Bennett desired not to mold public opinion, but to become a millionaire. Having achieved this ambition, and having been snubbed by society, he retreated into sulky isolation in his country place and only saw a few business acquaintances, among whom was Leonard. The New York *Times,* in which Jerome held a quarter of the shares, aspired to "correct grammar and unbiassed reporting." In fact, it attempted to emulate that unique organ, the London *Times,* regarding poli-

with a vessel of which not only American yachtsmen but every man in the country may be proud."—Every man except her owner!

67

tics and foreign affairs. Henry Raymond, its founder and editor-in-chief, shared Leonard's enthusiasm for the theater and drove a smart span of bays. The two were often seen whispering together.

"Reckon I'd like to know what Raymond and Jerome are talking about," said a man in Central Park.

"I'll tell you," responded his friend. "Just hosses."

What *could* a millionaire do in New York if he didn't like fast horses? Stay outside the pale presumably, a sinister spider like Jay Gould; or live in seclusion in a marble mausoleum like A. E. Stewart, the "richest merchant in the world," while the other boys showed off their teams.

Leonard made society revolve around him until it grew giddy. "He outdid all who were bent on cutting a figure." The shocked, the cross, and the weary scolded in vain. He drove his own turnouts with horses that were "trained to rear and prance as they turned the street corners." Old ladies, as well as young, lost their emotional balance as he careered by. His team of trotters, competing in Harlem Lane, evoked a popularity with the masses similar to that which in England is accorded to those who enter a horse for the Derby. And now, with boyish enthusiasm he took up the organization of racing and steeplechasing, which in North America had existed only in an unorganized, disreputable fashion.

It is difficult to conceive of the calm prevalent in civilian life during conflicts prior to the twentieth century. Those who were not in the actual firing line considered it natural to carry on with normal pursuits and amusements. Letters of the period redound with chit-chat concerning fashion, sport, and "delightful soirees." In this hour of national crisis Clara busied herself defending, not the Constitution, but a fashion launched by the Empress Eugenie of "coyly looping up the skirt at one side to show one foot and ankle." In this atmosphere no one thought it curious that owners of Southern studs should hurry them into enemy territory to ensure the animals' safety and comfort. Leonard took a keen interest in these horses (the only refugees of the period), and devised plans for building race tracks and instituting an American jockey club similar to the English one. "Impossible," snorted contemporaries. "The gambling laws will never allow it."

"I'll raise it above all that," retorted Leonard. "Wait until war ends; you'll see."

Throughout the bitter years of fighting, the New York *Times* ardently supported President Lincoln and the Republican administration. Wall Street speculation continued as before, and the intelligent analysis of economic and political issues, which only the *Times* offered, made it indispensable to the serious reader. While political activities held him in New York City, Leonard continued to run his brokerage and to work with Commodore Vanderbilt in various railway ventures. Each time he made a fortune he threw it after the disappearing tails of several which had gone before. Over ten million dollars ran through his fingers.

An example of plans gone wrong was Leonard's venture into a government emigration scheme. In the second year of the war, President Lincoln offered freedom to all slaves (a military, rather than political, expedient). Various amateur attempts were then made by Union supporters to solve the race problem by deporting freed Negroes to Brazil or Africa. These projects were not successful, but Lincoln was so anxious to get any colonization schemes started that, without being able to go into the matter thoroughly, he permitted a contract with a Mr. Kock, who offered to lease a suitable island in the Caribbean, and Leonard became involved in what appeared to be a benevolent government scheme. The Jerome firm raised the money to pay for the voyage and five thousand Negroes were shipped off to a dot of land, known as the Ile des Vaches. Having landed the bewildered Negroes on what seems to have been a desert island composed of sand and cactus, the authorities in charge realized that all food and water would have to be shipped from Haiti. Mr. Kock disappeared with the lease money and was never seen again. When official investigators reported the likelihood that the island could never support human beings, tempers flared up both in the Department of the Interior and in the Jerome office. Mutual accusations of irresponsibility flew faster than the enemy's bullets. Barrels of food and water had to be sent at large expense until the island could be evacuated. This hardly seemed what was meant by "colonization," and the ex-slaves must have puzzled at such uncomfortable freedom. Despite losses in this fiasco, Leonard was still able to contribute large sums to the war wounded and he wrote a check for thirty-five thousand dollars to help in the construction of the *Meteor,* a ship designed to catch the blockade-running *Alabama.* His gifts, however, could not approach those of Commodore Vanderbilt, who presented the Navy with a steamer costing eight hundred thousand dollars.

Meanwhile, Clara worked away at "sanitary commissions" for the soldiers. Bandages were rolled and lint scraped by the "highest-bred hands of the city," which may have given some solace to the wounded in an age before anesthetics.

In the autumn of 1863, seven-year-old Camille, the loveliest of the four Jerome daughters, died at Newport of a sudden fever. Her desolate parents brought the child back for burial in Greenwood Cemetery.

During the remaining months of the war, Clara hid away in her villa, and Leonard attended only to urgent political business. When General Lee's army was finally brought to a halt at Appomattox and the South surrendered, New York City speedily forgot it had once given acclaim to Mayor Wood's proposal for secession and rejoiced wildly in Yankee victory. The Jeromes were all in New York at the time of President Lincoln's assassination, and Jennie has described what she saw of the funeral: ". . . our house in Madison Square draped from top to bottom in white and black, and the whole of New York looking like one gigantic mausoleum."

Leonard, who, throughout the war, had earned thousands for charity by the performances in his theater, now opened a campaign for a Southern relief fund. "We must ease the bitterness," he wrote. When Henry Clews (who with Leonard had subscribed to every government loan and organized many Union meetings during the war) built up plans to help the South recover its lost wealth and prestige by diverting foreign capital to regenerate Southern agricultural and commercial interests, Leonard placed a large amount of his own money in Georgia bonds.

The expansion of industry during the Civil War had created many fortunes of unprecedented size. Cornelius Vanderbilt, who had been the government's wartime shipping agent, was now a unique citizen. He possessed twenty-five million, and this figure was to be quadrupled. Leonard found his own modest three million doubling itself in the gigantic new railway schemes that occurred during and after the four years' conflict, but he could not say, like the Commodore's rival, Daniel Drew, that: "I got to be a millionaire afore I knowed it, hardly." Old Daniel Drew, tattered, semiliterate ex-cattle dealer, and his young henchman, Jim Fisk, were the outstanding entrepreneurs who made overwhelming wealth out of dealings with the Army during the Civil War.

Through cooperating with Vanderbilt in the Harlem-Hudson railway battle, Leonard cleared several millions for himself. No matter what the project, Leonard did most of his thinking in a small sailboat. Then, when "the salt spray had tightened up his ideas," he would blow into his Wall Street office like a hurricane, give orders and sweep out again. Mr. Jerome's nickname of "The Comet" began to stick.

THE DYNAMIC RHYTHM OF GROW-
ing New York never struck a responding chord in Clara. She
seemed impervious to its verve, its raw splendor. Even Leonard's
most cultivated friends, witty William Travers and clever, English Henry Clews and weird, brilliant August Belmont slightly
jarred her. She preferred Europeans in their own settings.

Travers' humor, which exactly fitted the America of the time,
left her unmoved. He and Larry Jerome took a schoolboy delight
in boarding a horse-drawn Broadway bus, treading on each other's
toes, and pretending to fight violently, shouting "How dare you,
sir!" and demanding to be set down so they could take their coats
off. When the frightened passengers stopped the bus and looked
for a policeman, they would walk off arm-in-arm, roaring with
laughter.

At dinners Travers could silence bores with jokes they did not
grasp. A deadly talker running out of subject matter once asked
if oysters had brains.

"Well, y—y—yes," purred Travers, "just enough to keep
their mouths shut."

A famous shaft was launched when a crowd of Wall Street
businessmen were watching the end of a yacht race at Newport.
As the boats passed the winning post, the name of one rich broker
after another was called out. Then came the inimitable voice of
Mr. William Travers echoing from the club steps: "And where
are the customers' yachts?"

August Belmont contrived to dominate New York City "at

almost every level." Enigmatic, dapper, short, strong, limping from an old German duel, hard as nails and uncannily astute in finance, he became Leonard's rival in more matters than one, for Belmont boasted the best chef, the best paintings, the best porcelain, and the best trotters. In addition, according to Frank Griswold, ". . . his connoisseurship of horseflesh and women were considered authoritative." Whatever that may mean. Belmont had a very dashing wife. "People like Belmont and Jerome do not enter society; they create it as they go along," said Griswold's mother.

Despite her shyness, Clara was very sure of her own judgment concerning things artistic. Few New Yorkers, however, saw any virtue in the panels of angels she had brought from Florence, asserting they "had been done before artists learned how to paint properly." And in time she grew slightly ashamed of liking them. Perhaps they did look rather odd among the carved mahogany and striped wallpapers. Happily, Leonard had purchased a Raphael as well, and her friends had at least heard of him.

Clara could never hope to shine in the horsey world. She admired, but could not seek to emulate, Mrs. August Belmont, who with elegant French manners and amazing jewels won renown as "Queen of High Life." The niece of the famous Commodore Perry, hero of Lake Erie, had been born into the highest stratum and after marrying August she soared naturally to elegant leadership. Not only could Mrs. Belmont converse, enchant, and put people at their ease, but she electrified the common herd by allowing a nude by Bouguereau to hang in her drawing room and by driving herself at high speed around Central Park. Clara did not envy Mrs. Belmont's daring taste in art, but her light fingers and quick nerve, and her all-around ability to show off with horses, would have served her purpose of catching Leonard's eye. "So silly to admire courage and have none," she said. Unable to handle any reins adroitly, she determined her daughters should be of harder fiber, and she supervised their upbringing in detail.

Already they rode and danced and skated with expert precision, and in an age when the vapors were still fashionable Clara Jerome insisted on cold baths, fresh air, and strenuous exercise. "Strong women make beautiful women," she admonished. They showed every sign of having inherited Leonard's immense physical vitality, and people turned to smile at the rosy-cheeked girls driving their donkey cart along the new wide avenues of Newport.

Despite her antipathy to certain professional singers, Clara entered wholeheartedly into her husband's charitable schemes. It must have been extremely convenient for Leonard to be able to entertain himself while raking in large sums for charity at the same time. "I believe you *can* serve God and mammon if you try hard enough," said a prominent New Yorker. "Look at Jerome."

"We have a new girl rehearsing the part of Lucia tomorrow," Clara scribbled. "She *can* sing, but O dear what temperamental scenes occur!" The most memorable artists to grace the Jerome stage after Patti left for Europe were Minnie Hauk, for whom Clara evinced a particular tenderness, and Mrs. Ronalds, whose singing voice and beauty, as well as her gentle birth, elevated her to a unique niche in New York society.

To the chagrin of many less-talented ladies, the exquisite Fanny Ronalds could not only hit high C but drive her own drag in masterly fashion to Newport picnics. It was impossible to compete with such feats. Clara wisely did not try, for Leonard's horses, trained to rear and caper, caused her to close her eyes.

For years Leonard had worked to perfect himself in the art of showy driving. From boyhood he felt an instinctive understanding of the high-mettled horse; riding around Rochester, trying Lipizzaners in Trieste, gallivanting down Harlem Lane with his first trotters, he had never ceased to study and improve his hands. Now he heard that the Duke of Beaufort had taken to driving a four-in-hand around England seeking to revive the romance of old coaching days. Leonard's eye lit up. Such a pastime exactly appealed to him.

Soon from the stables in Madison Square emerged a spectacular vehicle "built to Mr. Jerome's special requirement," and New York saw amateur coaching for the first time.

The social-snob chronicler of the time, Ward McAllister, recorded Jerome's inauguration of what was later to become the smartest sport of the city. "He turned out daily with his drag or coach loaded with beautiful women, and drove to every desirable little country inn and about the city, where one could dine at all well, crossing ferries, and driving up Broadway with the ease and skill of a veteran whip, which he was."

August Belmont followed suit. Being a multimillionaire, he devised a still more costly coach, and with German thoroughness mastered the art of four-in-hand driving. The two friends astounded New York with the spectacle of their rival coaches, but Belmont did not achieve the effect of Jerome. Leonard devoted Sunday mornings to this new amusement. A shocked newspaper criticized him for driving up Fifth Avenue waving to friends who had turned out for the smart church parades: "Gay and laughing ladies in gorgeous costume filled the carriage. Lackeys, carefully gotten up, occupied the coupe behind; Jerome sat on the box and handled the reins. With a huge bouquet of flowers attached to his buttonhole, with white gloves, cracking his whip, and with the shouts of the party, the four horses would rush up Fifth Avenue, on toward the Park, while the populace said, one to the other, 'That is Jerome.' "

IN 1865 LEONARD BOUGHT A RACE
horse for forty thousand dollars. This was great-hearted Kentucky, who was to prove ten pounds better than any horse of his day. In August, soon after entering the Jerome stable, he won the Inauguration Stakes, the first race ever run at Saratoga Springs, and Leonard in impeccable spencer and morning coat knew the pride of leading in a winner to the cheers of the crowd. He and William Travers had vowed they could raise horse racing from disrepute to the high standard it obtained in England. They would maintain a royal sport, not rowdies' outings.

Saratoga Springs enchanted Leonard. He had studied the course with William Travers (who presented the Travers Stakes, the first stakes ever given for a flat race in North America), and they decided that a race track for New York City ought to be laid out on the same lines. They named it Jerome Park and founded a jockey club, which they hoped to keep as strict and incorruptible as the one in England.

New York in the sixties sizzled beneath its elaborate social ramifications and diverse methods of showing off. Behind the accumulating fortunes, behind the façade of brownstone mansions that crept ever farther from the vulgarities of Broadway, lay a strange tangle of crude, tough, corrupt circles of power. Where respectability began and ended did not always distinctly show.

"Boss" Tweed, who was Street Commissioner, head of Tammany and ruler of the city's polling boxes, used as his right-hand-man one John Morrisey, a gangster-pugilist who ran luxurious gaming houses both in New York and at Saratoga Springs. The whole of New York feared Tweed. It knew the machinery of the city was controlled by his hands, and that millions were extracted by him in bribes. But he was efficient and, by making the law conform to his wishes, he remained legal. New Yorkers were hardly surprised when "the Boss" took up with Morrisey, the notorious leader of the dreaded Dead Rabbits Gang, which commanded the immigrant Irish vote in the Bowery; but they suffered a real shock when Commodore Vanderbilt made friends with the ex-prize fighter in his gambling house at Saratoga. When they saw Morrisey matching his fast horses against the Commodore's in jovial competition in Central Park they wondered where the underworld ended and respectable society began.

If anyone knew the answer to that question, it was Leonard Jerome. If a man trod on the fringes of high finance where gangsters met bankers, he needed to know his way around. And Leonard did. Clara would have fainted had she understood the caliber of the men whom her husband was often up against. Leonard, however, stuck to straight methods that even the gangs respected. They knew where they were with him, and some curious trait in his character—his deliberate frankness, perhaps, or his flamboyance—appealed to the riffraff. At any rate, John Morrisey, having instituted a system of repetitive voting in city elections * and bribed the City Council in order to secure the appointment of Tweed's nominee as City Chamberlain and made a fortune from his sumptuous casino on Twenty-fourth Street, had the grace to announce that he "sure liked Mr. Jerome's driving."

Now that Leonard was sponsoring a new sport calculated to enthrall the multitudes he had to beware of tough twisters only too eager to enjoy a rake-off. The moral responsibility lay on his

---

* According to Tweed's evidence in court later.

shoulders from start to finish. He had battled in New York City for sufficient years to understand where and how rackets started. But the gangs appeared to be hypnotized by the novelty of this new venture and the verve of its inaugurator. They wanted to go horse racing too. If Mr. Jerome would provide a track where they could gamble and flaunt their mistresses, they wished him luck.

Leonard started by purchasing the old Bathgate estate of 230 acres at Fordham where, for half a century, the Bathgate family had privately bred and tried out their horses. The property possessed a unique formation, with a large hill, called the Bluff, standing in the center of a natural race track. On this eminence, the stands and clubhouse were to be erected, while the track curled in full view around it. With William Travers and Lawrence enthusiastically sketching and making notes and suggestions, Leonard walked every hillock. Already they could visualize the horses, hear the thunder of hoofs. To August Belmont, who joined in the project with zest, Leonard wrote, "It will pass Saratoga in charm. We have the most picturesque scenery, hills, a hollow and a really good view, and I am insisting on a competent engineer." This turned out to be Charles Wheatley, designer of the Saratoga course.

In the following April, the American Jockey Club held its first conference in Leonard's office, at 46 Exchange Place. The committee laid down its aims thus: "To promote the improvement of horses, to elevate the public taste in sports of the turf, and to become an authority on racing matters in the country."

The moment it was finished, Leonard leased Jerome Park to the jockey club, and volunteered to stand an annual loss of twenty-five thousand dollars if the expenses could not be paid. He possessed a childish enthusiasm and drive that brought flat racing into repute throughout the country in one day. Thousands of people who had never previously heard of "the turf" now found it their favorite subject.

In September, 1866, with unsurpassed fanfares the American Jockey Club held its first race meeting. According to the press, this opening of Jerome Park "proved the social event of all time and started a new era in the horse-racing world." General Ulysses Grant, victor of Appomattox presided as guest of honor in the "royal box" of a grandstand holding eight thousand. New York's smart set turned out in magnificent clothes, and the pleasure-hungry fans followed joyously. Every woman present from richest to poorest had a new bonnet for the occasion, and the shimmer of silk and satin covered Leonard's green hill. Newspapers could hardly find space to print the race results, such were their exclamations over the fashions, well-known faces, beauteous ladies, and gorgeous gowns. And in the center of it all, serene in their clubhouse, the Jerome brothers and August Belmont and William Travers surveyed the perfectly laid course and scintillating crowds. Mrs. Belmont, all beaded and befringed, and Clara, rustling in puce silk, could fan themselves and sigh with satisfaction while nearby in white, beneath a ribboned parasol, the exquisite Mrs. Ronalds distributed her soulful, enigmatic smile to a band of top-hatted admirers.

Needless to add, the leaders of the great New York "rings" were there, John Morrisey "in sober black," and Boss Tweed (with nine years yet to run the city as his own, before imprisonment), and diamond-covered Jim Fisk, whose plan to effect a corner in gold would be broken by Ulysses Grant, who sat laughing with Clara Jerome on the grandstand.

Every lady present did not necessarily possess a diploma of respectability; those without one atoned for lack of virtue by stylish turnouts. Josie Woods, the young and lovely owner of New York's most expensive "establishment," arrived in her luxurious victoria, escorted by liveried footmen. "I wonder what is engraved on their buttons?" whispered William Travers. The virtuous declaimed it "impossible to follow such a profession and look so good, and dress with such taste." For doe-eyed Josie wore only costly silks in subdued colors as a real lady should, and her manners were affectingly genteel. To the relief of many, the millionairess-abortionist Madame Restall did not appear. She had built herself a colossal brownstone palace at the corner of Fifth Avenue and Fifty-second Street and outraged society by whirling around Central Park at fashion-parade hour in a magnificent barouche with her nose in the air like a duchess, but she did not care for a day in the open and the respectable were spared the sight of her.

Rich and poor trekked from every part of the city, and a babel of different tongues arose, Italian, German, and the Irish brogue. The green grass blazed with human beings, and a roar of voices echoed long after the last race when the white dust driven from a hundred departing carriages rose high in the evening sunlight. "Never was there such a day for pomp and glitter and excitement."

Clara drove home "faint from so many people, but all a success," she wrote, "only very bad for Clara and Jennie. He would take them to the Club House."

New York retained an inordinate enthusiasm for its race track, and the "social glories" continued to occupy press headlines. The American Jockey Club obtained a membership of thousands, held in firm control by the committees. Leonard never had to donate his twenty-five thousand, but stipulated that the club must not be allowed to degenerate into a mere money-making concern. Jerome Park was to be run as a cherished creation, a kind of untarnished sportsman's dream. Money must be earned elsewhere.

Leonard evidently spoiled his daughters, who pressed him into combating their mother's strictness. Jennie has described these years with "lessons, and matinees at the opera 'to improve our minds,' sleighing and skating for pleasure, and on red-letter days a drive to Jerome Park on my father's coach, where I always occupied the seat of honour next him. Sometimes, from afar, I could see the blue and white of his racing colours come in first, which was a great excitement. On one occasion I was hoisted upon the back of his most famous race-horse, the celebrated Kentucky, whose sire Lexington, and dam Magnolia, by Glencoe, were of the best blood in England."

There were "several delightful summers at Newport, where my father had built a charming villa, more in accordance with one's idea of a seaside residence than the gorgeous white marble palaces which are the fashion nowadays. There we were allowed to run wild and be as grubby and happy as children ought to be."

Jennie made her worldly debut at the age of ten, when August Belmont gave a fancy-dress party. Leonard had ordered a pretty little costume to be made for her, copied from a print of a French vivandière. She did not sleep for a week with excitement, but on the evening of the party her father found her in floods of tears, "because I don't look as I thought I was going to." Years later she added, "a situation which, alas! was often to repeat itself."

MINNIE HAUK WAS RUMORED to be Leonard's daughter through an early romance. She had been born in New York at about the time of Jennie Lind's visit, and, curiously, the gift Leonard admired most seemed to have been wished into this small dark-eyed creature. Song came as naturally to her as to the nightingale. After a childhood spent in the wilds of Kansas, where she had rambled with Indians and gathered prairie flowers while "singing at the top of a baby voice," Minnie traveled back to New York during the Civil War. A man-of-war brought the Hauks up from New Orleans, and Minnie's mother, whose whole life centered on this precious and precocious only child, launched her as best she could into a musical set. Leonard first heard Minnie sing after a dinner party when she was still a schoolgirl with hair in long plaits. He could hardly believe his ears. With August Belmont he promised to finance her musical education and as foremost patrons of the old Academy of Music they arranged for her to be given an audition there. Minnie hoped to please with the "Casta Diva" from *Norma*. The manager listened with surprise to this small person's rendering of the opening recitative ending with pianissimo *La* in *Alt* developing into a forte and then dying into a pianissimo. "Enough," he cried. "Study and you will be great."

Leonard and August Belmont now vied with each other in encouraging their discovery. They took her out to be petted and spoiled, treating her to cakes and ices along with their criticism. After a year she had mastered ten or twelve Italian operas, and her poetic renderings of the more emotional airs gave promise of real art. An untrammeled outdoor childhood had given her strength, and perhaps the very lack of any early forced education had kept her mind receptive. She certainly showed an unusual capacity for learning long passages of music by heart. At fifteen she was ready to make a small debut; ". . . with the aid of Mr. Jerome and other kind friends who had taken great interest in my progress, I succeeded in doing so."

From the first Clara found something touching in the fiery little brunette. Never had she taken such an interest in any singer, and her nervousness exceeded Minnie's before a performance. The girl seemed sufficiently unself-conscious to leap on to any stage and sing with the same abandon as when she had tried to entertain the Indians in Kansas.

On the night of her public debut at the Academy of Music * an old singer saw the young star jumping for joy in her blue silk costume. He warned her, "In later years you will not dance before your looking glass before appearing on the stage." And she was to learn from Patti herself the increasing nervousness that besets mature artists, but now at fifteen, fresh from the prairies, with the high true notes ready to burst from her childish heart, Minnie made so guileless a picture that Mrs. Jerome could hardly refrain from kissing her. That exuberance, that disregard of all save the moment's excitement—where had she seen it before? On the back of a photograph of Minnie, Clara penciled one indiscreet clue: "so like Jennie, but less good-looking."

Her own girls, galloping wildly on their ponies, had indeed become her very life, but here she found another version, a high-strung incarnation of Leonard in song. She could not but be fascinated.

Minnie's career launched in the Jerome Theater to that picked "Four Hundred" swept forward without a hitch. Destined to become the first great American prima donna, she toured the States and then, well-chaperoned by a forbidding and stately mama, left for Europe. She conquered Paris and Moscow before accepting contracts with the Imperial Opera House in Vienna and the Berlin Court Theater, neither of which had engaged an American singer before.

Adelina Patti became, through Leonard Jerome, her inspiration and her friend. It was Minnie Hauk who first sang *Carmen* in London, and although this opera aroused consternation on account of its novelty she "made people like it."

* Forerunner of the Metropolitan Opera.

83

Toward the end of her life Minnie found herself sitting amid the faded costumes in which she had won fame in so many cities and she wrote nostalgically in her memoirs: "At my feet I noticed a piece of stuff which had fallen out of my very oldest trunk of all. I picked it up. It was a remnant of the *rose moire antique* dress which I had worn when I made my first appearance in opera at Mr. Jerome's theatre in *Linda di Chamonix*. A world of memories of the past came rushing and flooding through my mind. I sat with this lovely piece of rose moire clasped in my hand. . . ."

Seymour Leslie, a grandson of Leonard, has written this account:

"The end of Minnie Hauk was romantic as her beginning, for she bought and restored Wagner's famous villa of Triebschen, on the Lake of Lucerne . . . the house where most of the *Ring* was written. I went through it in 1928, just before she died. Royal photographs, silver-framed, cluttered the piano, every table, every *vitrine*. She willed Triebschen to the city of Lucerne as a Wagner museum; and here in 1937, took place one of the most moving and historical of musical events. Toscannini conducted a picked orchestra of the finest musicians in Switzerland in a program that included the exquisite 'Siegfried Idyll' . . . played for the first time since that far-off morning when Frau Cosima Wagner awoke to receive the most immortal of child-birth gifts. There, we sat, with Wagner's grandchildren and Minnie's old admirers. It was a glorious day and even the lake steamboats had been muted for the occasion. Few of us knew that we owed it indirectly to the inspired Testament of Minnie Hauk . . . or perhaps to her far-away and forgotten patron."

HE YEAR OF 1866 WAS AN eventful one. Financial panics rocked Wall Street; the Atlantic cable was laid; Clara's youthful beau, Tegetthoff, created naval history at Lissa; the Empress Eugenie started to wear humming birds in her hat; Mrs. Ronalds gave her famous fancy-dress ball, and the Jerome brothers participated in the first transatlantic race.

Meanwhile, a skating craze developed, which kept the smart set with their rude health and strong ankles whirling and gliding on every pond in Central Park. The Jerome girls, of course, became star performers. Leonard flooded a large area near his race track, and a special train ran guests out to waltz and pirouette while a band played encouragingly in the crisp air. Two cottages were furnished by the skating rink, and Clara supervised hot luncheons. "It would take Leonard to devise the details," wrote a visitor. "We were comforted by waltz tunes and sausage rolls. I can't tell you how lovely a scene it made, with the band playing, and everything glinting in the sun." And, the center of attention, her whole little body given to the rhythm of the waltz, legs twinkling, and cheeks scarlet with excitement, skimmed Miss Jennie Jerome. Clarita, less daring, and baby Leonie, unable to equal their sister's fancy steps, circled precariously around the edge.

Mrs. Jerome sat by the sparkling lake wrapt in furs and worry. She worried about Jennie: Obviously that child ought to have been a boy; such zest and energy might then have been in keeping.

And she worried about Leonard's friends, the gay ladies and strange men whom Commodore Vanderbilt took around in his sporting set. The old man's bluff ways and untempered tongue amused Leonard, and the Vanderbilt trotters, yachts, shipping lines, and railroads, all backed by a maelstrom of millions, gave them plenty to joke about. Leonard could not stand glum tycoons; Vanderbilt had charm—for men, if not for refined ladies —and if high-society drawing rooms did not always receive him, there were wider worlds that did. Clara had to admit she liked the Commodore, "not despite, but because of, his lack of airs and graces."

But now Vanderbilt had taken a fancy to John Morrisey, a person who definitely could not be asked to *her* home. Dressed soberly in black, Morrisey allowed only a few large diamonds to sparkle in his cravat and on his fingers. He did not drink, and after watching the brother of New York's Mayor Wood lose ten thousand dollars in a night at one of his faro tables, Morrisey would remark piously, "I never gamble myself." "A character," Vanderbilt called him, and established Morrisey as his "political agent." Since Jerome had entered as Vanderbilt's partner in the Harlem Railroad, the three men were often seen together.

Respectable citizens frowned. Unable to stomach such intruders socially, they yet feared the power of Tweed's ring. No one wanted to fall afoul of John Morrisey, or to delve too deeply into his affairs; they merely wished he would stay put in his sumptuous underworld casino and not be seen about. Well-bred folk disapproved but could not resist watching as the suave intruder with the broken nose matched his horses in Harlem Lane against those of Vanderbilt, Jerome, and Belmont. And the snobs, not daring to speak out, shook their heads and cast angled glances to see how Mrs. Jerome was taking it.

Clara did not think Morrisey a nice person at all, but she feared to say a word of reproach lest it result in Leonard's going away

86

from home more. Her husband never mentioned the real powers in that strange background from which he emerged with an occasional diamond necklace for her. How could she understand those hard hitters and corrupt politicians against which he had to pit himself? Less and less did he discuss mutual plans. Perhaps it was her fault. She could not understand music or horses or finance, and yachting made her sick. How could a quiet, motherly person amuse such a husband when all glamorous ladies of New York went out of their way to catch his eye?

It was very different for Mrs. Ronalds. It was only too easy for her to obtain attention. A superb ice skater, she came to Leonard's flooded field and she practiced figure eights in a shortened hoop skirt while Jennie swooped after her.

Only Fanny Ronalds could show so much leg and not be criticized. Fanny could sing and manage horses. Fanny could skate in circles. When Fanny went out in boats, her cheeks turned pink instead of green. Everyone marveled at Fanny. Had she so wished, in her enchanting, authoritative manner, Fanny could have got away with murder very prettily.

Clara's thoughts took refuge in those years in Europe where she had been at her ease among people, where Leonard's eyes had lighted up each evening when she appeared in a lovely new gown. She would never forget the night when they went together to their first Tuileries ball, and he had said as they came home in their carriage, "Clara, you were the handsomest woman there." She cherished that evening's approval; could she ever win it back? How could she shine before him? Certainly not on skates!

When summer came, they all went as usual to Newport where the quaint little eighteenth-century town with cobbled streets and vistas, which came to an end "like the quick steps of old ladies," was beginning to disappear. Here Mrs. Ronalds took daily driving lessons with Leonard. She showed exceptional talent with the reins. Everyone gaped, and everyone talked. The comments were not always kind.

Meanwhile Clara busied herself with the children, who, hardly surprisingly, had a tendency to show off. She found it extraordinary, and very hard to curb.

THE WANDERING EYE NEVER ceases to wander, a fact that presents consolation to certain wives. No one had held Leonard's attention for long, not even Patti with her unbelievable octaves and dramatic fire. But Mrs. Fanny Ronalds, siren of New York society, became a lasting friend.

Born in Boston, she had overwhelmed family opposition and persuaded reluctant Puritan parents to send her to Florence to train a natural singing voice under the best masters. She might have stormed every musical citadel in Europe, but Pierre Ronalds, a young American of fortune, persuaded her into early matrimony. They returned to New York where the alliance disintegrated. Fanny bore three children, and then, according to a firsthand account, "The husband neglected his wife. In fact, he would disappear for months at a time. She had to look to her brave men friends for sympathy, and these she found in abundance."

Then Mr. Pierre Ronalds disappeared from the picture; contemporary memoirs hardly allow him another peep around the frame. Most of those who were lucky enough to meet Fanny gushed about her beauty, her voice, her expressions. One habitually reticent Englishman, Mr. Greville Moore, in his *Memories of an Old Etonian,* otherwise written in the traditional British style of understatement, bursts forth, "Her face was perfectly divine in its loveliness, her features small and exquisitely regular. Her hair was of a dark shade of brown and very abundant."

Leonard met her when she had just shed her husband and become the sensation of New York, but a very well-bred sensation. She dressed perfectly, entertained on a grand scale, and showed herself a gracious patron of music; in fact, she represented what any respectable mother might have wished for had her daughter proved irrevocably and through no fault of her own to be *une femme fatale.*

The story of the first meeting of Clara Jerome and Fanny Ronalds became famous. Leonard had not known Mrs. Ronalds for long, but gossip flared easily in that small slippery social world, and when Mrs. Jerome, on entering a ball room, was unexpectedly introduced to the lady whose name she must have heard linked to her husband's, an embarrassed hush fell on the immediate spectators. Would she use the deadly weapon of the public cut?

Clara took the proffered white-kid hand. "I don't blame you," she said softly. "I know how irresistible he is."

After opening her house in New York, Fanny continued to study singing, but an amateur prima donna finds it hard to find fulfillment and she could not demean herself by "going on the stage." The problem was neatly solved by Leonard Jerome's private bandbox opera, where she began to sing in aid of wounded soldiers.

Lovely Mrs. Ronalds—the best of every world was hers for the asking—walked carefully among proffered bouquets. If she seemed to over-sparkle at Leonard's fabulous parties, the malicious were forced to admit she seemed to have become a dear friend of Clara's as well.

In the summer mornings she drove with Leonard at Newport,

89

learning how to conduct her own plunging horses, his hands on hers, gently showing how to send the messages along the reins until she could skilfully manage her own four-in-hand on crowded Belleville Avenue. Each evening she sang at the piano. But afternoons were spent with the Jerome children, who "allowed her to become a favourite." She gave them "a species of small dog cart and two donkeys, which rejoiced in the names of Willie and Wooshey." This most winning of gifts could be seen tearing up and down Belleville Avenue, "a terror to the smart folk in their silks and feathers who drove majestically by."

Naturally Leonard was not alone among Mrs. Ronalds' admirers. August Belmont, usually able to mask his feelings, was becoming visibly affected. The two men had been friendly rivals so often, but now neither could fathom what tactics the other would try to employ. Only Fanny knew, and she kept silent.

Frank Griswold, whose mother was an intimate of Mrs. Ronalds, wrote in his privately printed memoirs: "There were two outstanding men at that time who were most prominent in all social and sporting matters. They both drove coaches and four, and had large racing stables; both were married and in the prime of life. These two men fell desperately in love with Mrs. R——. L—— and A—— were rivals who kept the house of their lady filled with flowers and attempted to satisfy her every desire. She proved to be an accomplished general, for she managed these two great men, as well as other aspirants, with much skill."

One day Fanny thought it would be delightful to give a fancy-dress ball but complained that she could hardly afford it. "Too bad," Leonard agreed. Then, after some thought, he suggested that she deposit a few hundred dollars with his firm to see if he could improve matters. A week later the investment was returned to her, multiplied into thousands.

Mrs. Ronalds set to work with ardor. She would give the most glamorous fancy-dress ball ever seen in New York. A guest wrote: "It was the talk of the town. Invitations were sent out three months ahead, so there should be time to get special costumes from Paris. Such hot-house fruit and flowers, such music, canvas-back ducks, terrapin, and old wines had never before been seen on Manhattan Island. The ball was a grand and glorious function which produced some little sympathy for the absent husband, owing to the extravagance of his young wife. Thousands of dollars had been spent on flowers alone, and the ball lasted until six in the morning."

The hostess excelled herself. She impersonated Music, and wore a wonderful white satin gown embroidered with bars from Verdi's *Ballo in Maschero*. Her harp-shaped crown, especially designed and constructed in Paris, consisted of sparkling quavers and crotchets lit up by the tiniest gas jets, which were supplied from a holder hidden in her hair. A guest wrote: "This made a great impression; the harp glowed and sparkled all the time that Mrs. Ronalds received her guests. . . ." Everyone quivered with excitement. How daring and how explosive!

Exquisite as ever beneath her ingenious headdress, Fanny caused the sensation she had intended. But many guests were shocked, for peeping from her satin skirts were red boots hung with tinkling bells. Not quite good form for a lady, even when representing Music.

Happily this stupendous outfit did not have to be relegated to oblivion. It reappeared some years later when Mrs. Ronalds attended a yet more famous fancy-dress ball, that of the Duchess of Devonshire in London. But times had changed; now the crown could be ignited by an electric battery!

Frank Griswold, well-known American sportsman, recounts a nice ending to Fanny's party. He happened to be present on a day twenty years later when Leonard Jerome and August Belmont were lunching together at Jerome Park. Mrs. Ronalds' name was mentioned, and Leonard looking across the table asked, "August, do you remember Fanny's celebrated ball?"

"Indeed I ought to," replied Belmont. "I paid for it."

There was a sad, faraway look in Jerome's dark eyes as he said, "Why, how very strange. So did I."

YACHTING, LIKE HORSE RACING, revived with a flourish after the Civil War, but transocean racing had not yet been thought of. All through the summers of 1865 and 1866 Leonard spent what time he could spare from coaching and Jerome Park and the Observatory, out at sea. Since the evenings in Trieste, when he had learned to sail his own little boat with an Illyrian fisherman for master, Leonard had developed a passion for taut canvas and high wind. He raced *Undine* and *Restless* along the coast of Maine, and as long-shore racing grew in popularity, he became a prominent member of the New York Yacht Club, a discriminating group quick with the blackball. To this club he brought an unhappy, uncontrollable boy of twenty-five who did not know what to do with himself or where to turn for headstrong adventure. This youth was James Gordon Bennett, Jr., the only child of the greatest publisher of his day, whose press had dared assail Astor at his death as a "self-invented, money-making machine," and who himself now merited that epithet.

Mrs. Bennett, finding it hard to make headway in New York society, had whisked her darling son off to Paris for a sophisticated education. Now he was brought back to be loosed on the elite with a French accent and a large income. Young James found himself much in demand socially—and was bored stiff. He did not want to be "classy"; he wanted to "feel able to breathe." This was a rude thing to say when the best people were inviting him to their houses. Soon his parents scolded him and, as often happens when this treatment is meted out, the scoldee took pains to avoid future contact. This proved easy as far as his father was concerned, since James Gordon Bennett, Sr., indulged in picturesque seclusion in a vast house in Washington Heights; but Mrs. Bennett, after spending so much time and money on polishing her one jewel, despaired to see her fair-haired boy scorning society, scorning newspaper management, and groaning for "something worth doing in life." Like many frustrated human beings, the boy turned to the sea for escape, but his sailing master tried to win a race by cutting through Plum Gut instead of sailing over the prescribed course. The opposition papers seized on the charge and used it as a handle to belabor the *Herald*. James's father, bitterly resentful of his son's inability to keep out of trouble even in sport, banished the youth from New York much as a medieval king might dismiss an erring son from court. Stamped as a ne'er-do-well, haunted by reiterated reminders of "that wonderful education" he had so ill-deserved, James finally found consolation in the company of two older men whose early lives had been entirely different from his own. Leonard and Lawrence Jerome did not treat him as a wealthy fop. With them he found "the companionship of real men at last!" They forced him to summon courage to live down the ignominy caused by his cheating skipper. With their moral support James ventured once more into the yacht-racing world.

In October, 1866, after a yachtsmen's dinner at the Union Club, Pierre Lorillard and the Osgood brothers, all sporting millionaires with no uncertain notions concerning their own prowess with boats, fell into excited discussion concerning the seaworthiness of the centerboard yacht. Lorillard owned *Vesta,* a centerboard schooner 105 feet long, and the Osgoods sailed *Fleetwing,* a keel schooner built the year before, with a length of 106 feet.

Lawrence and Leonard, who were also sitting at the same table, threw forth their opinions, but no one listened in the fray of flying words.

"Don't shout so—try it!" cried Lawrence.

"Try the Atlantic, and give each ship her chance!"

Within a flash the owners were hurling bets of thirty thousand dollars on the table.

And then young Bennett joined the group, heard of the match, and begged with such vehemence to be allowed to enter his *Henrietta* on the same terms that, despite the fact she had been beaten both by *Vesta* and *Fleetwing,* they allowed him in. Ninety thousand dollars lay on the table; the winner was to take all, Leonard holding the stakes.

By dawn they had fixed the date and set the course. The race would be sailed from Sandy Hook to the Needles Rocks off England's south coast in the stormy month of December, "when there's wind enough for all." Each owner was to sail his own boat, and the match was to be a test of endurance as well as of speed.

As the starting day drew near, dramatic efforts were made to obtain first-class crews. The original contestants, Lorillard and the Osgoods, thinking better of their hasty challenges, decided not to sail themselves. Their boats would venture out in charge of the finest professional skippers obtainable. Only young Bennett insisted on the privilege of sailing in his ship through the mid-winter storms, and the Jerome brothers thought it would be "good sport" to join in.

Bennett's *Henrietta,* a keel schooner like *Fleetwing,* was 107 feet over all and carried a crew of twenty-four.

In *All the Year Round,* a weekly journal conducted by Charles

Dickens, the following descriptions occur: "Some difficulty was experienced in securing seamen to cross the Atlantic in such vessels, and in such weather. The men were willing enough to engage but their mothers, wives, and sweethearts, interfered and persuaded them not to sign articles. Moved by such feminine solicitations, the picked crew of the *Henrietta* deserted her a few days before the start, and their places had to be supplied by a lot of land lubbers. . . . Invitations to prominent yachtsmen were declined for various reasons, and the gentlemen who served finally in this capacity were almost all volunteers. . . . From seven A.M. on Dec. 11, the day of the start, no communication was permitted between the yachts and the shore, partly to prevent any further difficulties in regard to the crews, and partly because several kind but frightened friends had conceived the idea of subpoenaing some of the yachtsmen as witnesses in trials of which they knew nothing, in order to preserve them from the perils of the sea." *Fleetwing* had the same crew difficulties but, at the last moment, nine whaling sea captains volunteered to man her.

At the start Bennett was loudly cheered as "the only man who goes in his own boat." Spectators noted that *Vesta* and *Henrietta* had both decked over their spacious cockpits, making for icy hardship but greater safety. "A pity the *Fleetwing* hadn't taken the same precaution, for the seas would be big out there, and cruel and hungry." The three ships scudded away into a fresh wind, and *Vesta,* with her centerboard up, clearly set the pace. Then they disappeared into the green sea and snow-filled breezes.

Meanwhile old Mr. Bennett, fuming in his monumental palace, was anything but pleased, for opposition papers declared that everyone who sailed in the race would be drowned.

The ships' logs survive. During the first week *Henrietta* chalked up 250 to 280 miles a day. Then she ran into a full gale, and when Captain Bully Samuels, famous master of clipper ships, decided that she could be driven no longer, preparations were made to heave to under close canvas. "The storm trisails happened to be stored in the cabin, and as the sailors came silently down, coiled the tackle, and carried up the sail on deck, the scene reminded one of the bringing forth of a pall for a funeral. A pause in a race like this seemed the burial of all our hopes. Nevertheless, it was some consolation to be informed by Captain Samuels that, in his thirty years experience, he had never seen a vessel that could face a gale for so long."

During this gale *Vesta*, who might have sunk had she attempted to heave to, scudded on, running dead before the wind, and gained a fair lead.

At 6:55 P.M. on Christmas Eve, *Vesta* made the lights of the Scilly Isles. Fifty minutes later *Henrietta* picked them up. But in the two hundred miles up the channel to the Needles, *Vesta* threw away in poor pilotage the ascendancy she had gained in mid-Atlantic driving.

At 10:00 P.M. *Henrietta* brought land abeam and raced up the channel at thirteen knots, compensating for the lost hours. Soon after noon on Christmas Day, she picked up the Cowes pilot, who set free loud cheers with the news, "*Henrietta* is first boat in, and a good 'un." At 3:45 P.M. she passed the Needles with everything set, and so won the race in thirteen days, twenty-one hours, and forty-five minutes. Eight hours and fifteen minutes later, at midnight of that same Christmas Day, *Fleetwing*, who had taken a more southerly course, roared past the Needles reefed down in a fierce gale, and *Vesta*, again losing her way through poor pilotage, took last place forty minutes later.

But *Fleetwing*, who had not decked over her cockpit, bore sad tidings. Six of her stalwart crew had been swept overboard and drowned. The ship's log reads: "Wed. Dec. 19th. This day commences with a light breeze from S.S.W. 2 P.M., in all light sails, gale increasing with heavy sea. 7 P.M., blowing a gale; running under two-reef foresail and forestay sail (storm canvas). 9 P.M., shipped a sea which washed six of the crew out of the cockpit; hove to for five hours under two-reef foresail. 2 P.M., kept off; latter part moderate, wind hauling to west; set square sail. Lat. 47—20. Long. 37—27. Distance run, 199 miles.

The five-hour search in the dark, with icy seas breaking against the ship's sides, had been almost hopeless from the start. Men cannot live for long in the North Atlantic in mid-winter; oilskins and sea boots shorten their struggles.

One hopes that the millionaire owners of *Fleetwing* looked after the families of these gallant seamen who died trying to win them laurels. Surely they did. Generosity was ever the hallmark of American sportsmen. International interest had been aroused by the great race, and the sportsmen of two continents had kept their attention riveted on the Atlantic all that December. The yacht clubs of Europe were waiting for the three brave yachts slashing their way before the westerlies.

Members of the Royal Yacht Squadron hurried to welcome each ship as she anchored in the sheltered harbor of Cowes. The crews were bathed, feasted, and sent to receive acclaim in London and Paris. At some of these entertainments we learn that "Lawrence Jerome was the life and soul of the party and told stories that greatly amused the Britishers. He was a very large man, full of humour and wit and a practical joker. . . ."

The tables were turned when a member of *Henrietta's* crew managed to abstract a sheet of royal notepaper from Osborne House, and on it write a command to Mr. Jerome to dine with Queen Victoria on a certain evening.

Jerome was both pleased and distressed when he discovered that he was the only member of the party so honored. His shipmates sat about and jollied him along as he dressed for the banquet, but did not reveal the truth until the gig had actually put off from the yacht bound for the Royal Landing.

97

When Jerome was recalled and climbed back on board *Henrietta* his relief was so great that he danced a hornpipe on deck.

A public banquet was given in Paris and "the eulogistic articles in the English and French papers were cabled to the New York *Herald*." Papa Bennett's annoyance faded when he saw his son blossoming into the hero of the hour. According to a writer of the eighties: "This ocean race was the turning point in James Gordon Bennett's career. When he returned to New York, he began to devote himself to business. . . . The foreign staff (of the *Herald*) was reorganized and ordered to use the cable instead of the mails. Editorials were telegraphed from London. Stanley (the renowned explorer) was engaged to report the Abyssinian war and repeatedly beat the British dispatches with his news. The *Herald* supplied the London journals with its telegrams and became a power in the English metropolis. The acquaintances which Bennett made as a yachtsman became of the greatest service to him as an editor." *

Such a transformation in the Bennett heir caused general comment; in the storm-swept sea he had grown up and even his socially ambitious mama smiled. Did not J. P. Morgan state, "You can do business with anyone, but you can go sailing only with a gentleman"?

"Right—although it depends what you mean by a gentleman," said Leonard Jerome. He was thinking of hard-driving Captain Samuels, and of the stout crews of flush-decked *Henrietta* and *Vesta,* crouching half-frozen in the lee of weather cloths during long hours of watch, and putting all their heart into the handling of canvas in shifting freezing winds, and of *Fleetwing's* six sailors lost in the roaring ocean.

The world excitement died away, but lasting tribute has been

* Stephen Fiske, *Off-hand Portraits of Prominent New Yorkers* (New York, G. R. Lockwood and Son, 1884).

paid to this first great race in Alfred Loomis' modern history of ocean racing. He writes: "Ever since, in a score of ocean races, have seamanship and dogged determination and inscrutable luck mirrored the greatness of the historic match between *Henrietta, Fleetwing,* and *Vesta.*"

WHILE LAWRENCE REMAINED roistering in the yacht clubs of England, playing his impossible pranks, amusing guests at dinner parties, his wife Catherine remained in New York. According to her in-laws, Sister Carrie was becoming rather grim in middle age. Once a grave, modest girl with downcast eyes, years of mingled adoration and disapproval of a flamboyant husband had turned her silent and solemn. While Lawrence had grown famous on two continents as a humorist, her only wish was to be taken more seriously. Everything the Jeromes did worried her, and they, in turn, referred to her as "a plague." While Clara shrank from all forms of publicity, Catherine brooded because the family name received the wrong sort of recognition.

Both Jerome brothers had contributed financially to the building of a wide avenue leading to Jerome Park, and for some reason Catherine took a personal interest in it. "I admire that avenue," she announced. Her indignation was intense when local authorities named it after Alderman Murphy. This was "really too much!" After some pondering Mrs. Lawrence Jerome set out in her carriage to visit a large metal foundry, where she placed a considerable order and hired a band of craftsmen. Overnight the

Murphy nameplates were removed, and impressive bronze ones bearing the words JEROME AVENUE were irrevocably riveted and welded in their stead. Evidently the local council felt too tired to carry them away. Bronze lasts, and the subway goes to Jerome Avenue to this day.

Meanwhile Leonard inadvertently received more limelight than he desired on two showy white horses from his stable, which appeared drawing the carriage of a certain lady. All New York recognized his gift.

Clara had been brought up in the belief that a wife who speaks a cross word loses power over her husband forever. She merely announced that she was in poor health and thought it would be better if she sailed for Europe to consult a French physician. The three girls and Dobbie, their Negro mammy, were to accompany her. She visualized taking an apartment in Paris while Clarita and Jennie, in their teens, and little nine-year-old Leonie, could receive a French education. Leonard would then be freer.

He let her go. Within a month, she had mustered her personnel, packed belongings, and said good-by to the house in Madison Square, turning without regret from the rooms she had so carefully furnished with ebony and scarlet plush. Henceforth the address of the Jerome ladies would be 70 Boulevard Malesherbes.

Paris was about to hold a World's Fair. Thousands of foreigners flocked to France, eager to see the latest marvels, which included "locomotives, 50-ton guns from Krupp in Germany, aluminium, fuel oil, and American rocking chairs." Among the visitors there were of course, many crowned heads—Alexander II of Russia, Victoria and Albert, and the King and Queen of Prussia. Clara, for whom royalty held much appeal, immediately recovered her health and prepared for a diverting time. But first she had to organize the girls' education. Because of their special talent, music took highest place, but they must also become "polished conversationalists in French and German." The "Jerome Program" left very little time to spare.

No sooner had they moved into "an apartment containing many gilt mirrors and padded chairs" than a series of news bulletins arrived, which must have made padded furniture less a luxury than a necessity. Ladies swooned all over Europe, and quills were scratching little notes dotted with exclamation marks at every aristocratic writing desk. Shortly after a Polish patriot attempted to assassinate the Tsar as he drove in the Bois de Boulogne with Louis Napoleon, the Emperor Maximilian was shot by a firing squad in Mexico. Contemporary letters stress the "inconvenient moment," at which the telegram announcing this news arrived. Eugenie was dressing in the Tuileries to present prizes at the Fair and all festivities had to be canceled. The court went into mourning, and so did Mrs. Jerome. Meanwhile the populace of Paris raged because their Mexican loan seemed beyond redemption. If the Emperor got shot it must have been his own fault. Why should their small savings disappear in the dust along with that tiresome Hapsburg? Ominous clouds rested on the city; the atmosphere thickened as before a thunderstorm, and when Maximilian's Empress Carlotta capped the drama by going mad in the Vatican, the pens of a thousand social scribblers squeaked with horror. Queen Victoria wrote in her inimitable style, "too horrid, poor dear unhappy Carlotta bereft of her reason, and her husband killed . . . What a shocking end to their luckless undertaking which I did all I could to prevent, and which dearest Albert was *so* much against."

Clara sympathized with them all but could not resist a twitter of excitement when her gallant Admiral Tegetthoff departed for Mexico to retrieve the Emperor's body. It was all so dramatic.

Leonard, alone in his large somber house in Madison Square, received the news with coolness. He was himself approaching a fall. During the past seven years his profits had been immense.

"He led the street now to the exclusion of everyone. Tobin even, with all Vanderbilt's influence, had not the power of Jerome over men's opinions. The latter was the pet as well as the king . . . almost worshipped as well as watched and imitated." * How long could it last?

By now a contemporary could write, "Jerome had weathered more cyclones, and triumphed over more conspiracies against his fortune, than would have sufficed to ruin a hundred ordinary men." His biggest defeat lay ahead.

In 1861 Leonard had cornered the Pacific Mail Steamship Company. He took the stock when its selling rate was sixty-two and carried it up in the next few years to 329. His realizations even at the earlier stages of the rise were enormous. A stream of dollars ran through his fingers and burned holes in his pockets. Ever since 1848, when California joined the United States, there had been a great demand for ships that would ply the Pacific coast at ever cheapening rates. Jerome regarded the issue as vital, and his ships made the most intensive effort to compete and head the list. At the close of the Civil War the Pacific Mail Steamship Company, almost entirely owned by Leonard Jerome, was considered the soundest investment in the country. It was his favorite venture, his financial hobby.

When Vanderbilt shrewdly switched from ships to railways, Jerome held on to this line. An 1872 article in Harper's weekly, describes the situation: "In 1868 the leading part in Pacific Mail was played by Leonard Jerome. He had made a fortune of several millions out of the stock. He understood Wall Street and the public temper thoroughly. Born a *Preaux chevalier,* in another age he would have led charges of dragoons (complicated chronologically even for a Jerome). It contented him today to lead Wall Street. To this man it now occurred that if the public were willing

---

* Stephen Fiske, *Off-hand Portraits of Prominent New Yorkers* (New York, G. R. Lockwood and Son, 1884).

to give $240 a share for 6 million of new stock in the Pacific Mail, it would be well to feed them with more of it while the appetite lasted. He accordingly proposed and the directors sanctioned a further issue of 10 million of stock. But like many other operators, Mr. Jerome was infatuated with his own property. When the new stock was issued he offered to take the whole issue off the company's hands at $200 a share. The offer was accepted. This was the turning point in his own fortune, and those of the Company." The stock did not find support elsewhere and remained on his hands, ruining him.

The failure of this vast expansion of Pacific Mail came at a moment when Leonard Jerome was already tiring of the role of millionaire. He was too many-gifted to cling to money; he began to wonder if the chase was worthwhile. Money had become boring, a bore to make and a bore to lose. The tranquillity of retirement with Clara might hold charms he had not hitherto appreciated. She had demanded little; and other women, so much. Patti had long disappeared to capture London and Paris with her trills, and besides, as a jealous rival put it, ". . . her charm only just exceeded her tantrums." Autumn was in the air.

Despite his enormous Pacific Mail losses, there would always be the remnants of other fortunes to live on, pleasantly and quietly. Leonard visualized himself as a family man at last.

In April, 1868, he leased his house to the Union League Club and in October, after attending the debut of Ethel Agnes in what the newspapers still called "Jerome's Private Theater," he left for Paris. It was rumored that, at fifty, Leonard Jerome was retiring to Europe. He would be known as a sportsman, as the promoter of turf clubs and winner of yacht races. Wall Street would see him no more.

In the apartment which Clara had taken in the Boulevard Malesherbes he found her calm and gentle as always. She was getting plump, but the new flounced gowns suited her and the drawing room was decorated in her favorite way, with hanging baskets of flowers and garden vases of terra cotta from which green plants struggled in search of light and air. She had stepped in on the last brilliant whirl of the Empire, and she was pouring forth the gossip of the French court. Leonard wrote to Lawrence of gaiety and gaslight and Offenbach and of "the extraordinary architectural changes made by Napoleon and Haussmann."

"It is curious, Clara dear," he remarked, "to find 'home' in a Paris apartment." Clara smiled at the unintentional compliment. Home would always be where *she* was.

Only the girls were not quite as he had expected. Leonard puzzled at their lack of docility. Clarita at nearly eighteen was, his wife told him, interested in quite the wrong type of men. It was distressing—one might almost say alarming—to have a daughter so blonde and innocent with sweet upturned blue eyes who did not agree with her mother. For Mrs. Jerome had decided exactly the type of match her daughters were to make: They must all marry into old Huguenot families. Their husbands were to be aristocratic, but definitely Protestant. This limited suitors to a very small circle, one in which Clarita took no interest at all. For a time she had foolishly smiled on the Emperor's companion in exile, the Duc de Persigny, twenty years older than herself and married to a jealous lady who opened and read the notes he sent Miss Jerome (which were then censored by that lady's angry mama). And no sooner had that been stopped (if indeed it *had* been stopped, for the Duke's carriage seemed to be always at the door with a message), than Clarita fell in love with the young Marquis de Tamisier, who was out of the question as a husband.

"Why?" Leonard asked Clara.

"His grandfather, Carrier de Nantes, was responsible for those terrible drownings during the Revolution! Think of it, *les noyades de Nantes*. Happily, he came to a dreadful end himself."

"But the grandson hasn't done anything?"

"He keeps proposing to her. Wants to marry into our family. I couldn't stand it," snapped Mrs. Jerome.

Leonard found his eldest daughter blossoming into a frivolous blonde with a misleading gentleness of manner that made it difficult to speak to her on serious subjects. She herself ventured few opinions to the family save that M. Worth was "mad on azure and pale green." Her eyes were mild but her chin determined.

Poor Jennie suffered from her elder sister's habit of smiling on older men, for at a children's party where she had difficulty in dancing the mazurka the Duchesse de Persigny came up and suddenly boxed her ears.*

The younger daughters, marshaled by a troop of French and German governesses, were studying music with the best teachers in Paris. All three of Leonard's daughters had inherited his musical inclinations, and they played the piano unusually well. Jennie, whose flamboyant beauty was already beginning to show, might have become a virtuoso. Her master, impressed at such competence, had assured her she could earn her living as a concert pianist if she wished, an idea that fired her imagination. "I'm *never* going to marry. I am going to be a musician," she announced with assurance.

Her mother winced. *Ladies* did not become pianists. They played pieces.

Leonie enchanted her father. The quaint little girl had no looks at all, but a vitality and intense independence. Her short, grubby fingers plucked melody from the piano with a plaintive charm that her father found most fetching. He praised and encouraged her renderings of Chopin and insisted that Jennie, who with

---

* The Duchess was a daughter of the Prince de la Moskowa and a great-granddaughter of Maréchal Ney. As ambassadress in London, she won a reputation for eccentricity, often appearing late at official dinners and apparently soaking wet from her bath.

flashing eyes and no small talent was pounding out the *Sonata Amorosa,* should not reap *all* the attention. Leonie was obviously going to be a real problem. Her hasty temper, coupled with a habit of naughty repartee, caused complaints from all the servants save Dobbie, who had managed her since childhood. Leonard could laugh at quick wit, but even he was put out by her violent temper. On the first day the girls had tea in the drawing room, Leonie was teased for walking in the Champs Élysées with her toes turned in (at that time correctly reared young ladies turned toes *out*). In a flash she had seized the tablecloth, dashed china and cakes to the floor, and was led to bed in hysterics. Home life was not exactly as peaceful as Leonard had anticipated.

"Why are the girls so wild?" he exclaimed.

A trace of a smile flickered over his wife's lips. "Well dear," she answered. "They are *your* daughters."

PRINCESS METTERNICH, THE AUStrian Ambassadress, and the Duchesse de Mouchy (Eugenie's most intimate friend) and many famous court beauties habitually drove out with four horses in great state "helped by the magnificence of their appearance to give to Paris that air of elegance and distinction which could neither be surpassed nor emulated by any other capital in Europe."

Among the strollers who most enjoyed the sight of splendid equipages were the two Jerome girls who, "still plagued by governesses," walked sedately along the wide avenues envying their elder sister who met these celebrated ladies in society.

Napoleon's court had become a rendezvous for international beauty and fashion. "Wandering stars, English, American, or Spanish, were always welcome there and the permanent circle counted many foreigners besides the Empress." The young Jerome sisters greatly admired Eugenie and her dazzling entourage, which had thrown the other courts of Europe in the shade. They could hardly wait to grow up and be presented in their turn.

Louis Napoleon was teaching other monarchs that it could prove an advantage to be a parvenu. Most hereditary princes were apt to wet-blanket their own entertainments. The present royal couple might often be sneered at as "cosmopolitan adventurers brought up in the world and not to the purple," but they had a wide range of friends of various nationalities, and with the prestige of a throne and unlimited resources and a sense of the picturesque they were able to turn imperial functions into unique entertainment. Eugenie's flair for the dramatic helped the gayest capital in Europe to dance a swifter, more lighthearted rhythm than had ever been seen before.

Naturally the Tuileries provided the court at which Americans were most likely to enjoy themselves. Here no one seemed shy or stiff. What if the monarchs did enjoy wild games of catch and paper chases through the woods around Biarritz! What if the somber palace with its inadequate lighting and lethal drainage had been garnished with what the *ancien régime* sniffingly referred to as *couleur de théâtre?* Mrs. Jerome found more charm in Eugenie's famous blush than in all the long-lineaged royalties with their blue blood and shiny noses. The Empress possessed an indefinable, translucent beauty, a variability of expression that no portrait could reproduce. We know that she soared above other women, not from the painters' brush which records only a pretty oval face and large blue eyes, but by her effect on those she met.

The American Ambassador in Madrid (who particularly disliked Eugenie, owing to the encouragement she had given to the Mexican venture) wrote: "But when I met her yesterday, simply dressed, wearing her hat, and speaking Spanish, her features lighted up, and fingers, fan, and little feet all in animated movement as she talked, I laid down my arms on the spot; I lost the battle at first onslaught. Yes, she is beautiful, more lovely than words can express. . . . And how sparkling she was at the Banquet that evening!"

Could mere coquetting have reversed this sturdy Yankee's opinions? Her famous good-night bow, "like a swan curving its neck," caused him to forgive all her unwise political efforts.

Eugenie considered herself well fitted to be an empress, and the Jeromes were not alone in considering such charm more interesting than pedigree. As for the Emperor, he was the most genuinely sympathetic man in the world; his thoughtfulness of others' feelings gave him the stature of a gentleman even if he did occasionally shock the Hapsburgs. His son's doctor wrote: "It is really curious to see how strongly he has the instinct of practical benevolence, and the satisfaction he feels in doing good incessantly, wherever he goes."

Clara Jerome, of course, knew more intimate details concerning the imperial couple than her daughters did. She said, "You could not know the Emperor without loving that kind heart. His servants idolized him." What if he *were* unfaithful to his autocratic wife? Many another woman had suffered that affront without receiving a throne in compensation.

Leonard, who had been horrified by the political cruelties of Emperor Francis Joseph, found in Napoleon III a human being he could respect "if only he were not so ill; it rots any man's judgment."

While Clara preened herself in new diamonds and court gowns and the girls received a high degree of "French polish," Leonard followed his own pursuits. He bought a few pictures to add to his New York collection, he went to the opera, and he investigated the possibilities of running a racing stable in France.

Almost every morning he rode in the Bois de Boulogne with the Prince de Sagon (later Duc de Tallyrand) a famous Empire buck who had originated the Auteuil racecourse and Circle de la rue Royale. The most eccentric of Paris beaux, he liked to astound society by his fetes and extravagances. Though born of different worlds, he and Leonard had much in common, and the Prince showed his pity for the two older Jerome girls, who were not yet "out," by organizing juvenile picnics for them. Jennie mounted on a "seemingly fiery chestnut" often accompanied her father and the Prince on the morning rides. Little Leonie had less luck; the governesses hung around her like crows at a corn bushel. One day the Prince organized a picnic at St. Germain for the whole family and Leonard brought along some of his American friends. Jennie writes, "As Mr. James Gordon Bennett was driving us back on his coach, we came to grief near the Arc de Triomphe and were nearly killed." A likely end to any picnic with Bennett junior. More sober he may have been after that wild Atlantic racing, but not sufficiently so to be put in charge of children!

Once again Leonard saw Adelina Patti, who was singing Italian opera in London and Paris until at the height of her fame she accepted an offer of marriage from one of the Emperor's equerries and temporarily retired from the stage. For a time her place remained vacant. Patti's manager tried new artists in vain. Then Leonard pulled a string and soon after he had the satisfaction of seeing the seventeen-year-old Minnie Hauk selected to take the leading roles in the Italian opera season of 1869. "Miauk," as the hotel concierges called her, was the youngest prima donna to have appeared in the renowned *Salle Ventadour*. She became the first American singer to succeed in the great opera houses of Europe.

Her Paris debut as Amina in *Somnabula* is described by Maurice Strakosch in his *Memoires:*

"I had done everything I possibly could, for the theater was completely filled with the elite of Paris. The Imperial couple, whom I had specially invited, were present, and the little American girl really sang herself into the hearts of the French. In the last act an unforeseen incident amused the audience hugely and contributed more to her popularity than the beauty of her voice and her art in using it. When crossing the bridge, she, in her childish way, hesitated and finally stopped, frightened. Suddenly the words, 'Go on, Minnie,' were heard by the whole audience, coming from behind the scenes. At the tittering that followed, Minnie continued her walk faint-heartedly, and when the curtain went down she had won the game. Auber, the octogenarian, who sat in his accustomed corner stall, wrote to her with lead pencil on his card: *'Bravo, ma chère enfant!* May "Go on, Minnie" become the motto of your life.' "

Leonard, who only three years before had teased this unsophisticated child into singing after a dinner party, was strangely moved when he heard her acclaimed a worthy successor to the great Patti. His advice to her to study Patti's technique reaped results, for Minnie wrote: "It was my good fortune to hear Adelina Patti in all her brilliant roles, giving me a chance to make an intensive study of her art of vocalization and breathing, something which I may have imbibed, for both in Vienna and Berlin the critics declared they noticed a resemblance."

One particular evening remained in Clara's memory, when Minnie was asked to sing at a reception in the house of Theophile Gautier, where many Paris intellectuals were gathered including Auber, Flotow, the Duc de Broglie, Ferdinand de Lesseps, the younger Dumas, Alphonse Daudet, and Ernest Renan. Minnie had chosen two arias from *Rigoletto,* Leonard's favorite opera. A young musician named Bizet accompanied her on the piano.

Flushed by success, Minnie did not pay much attention to his shy compliments. Neither artist could have foreseen the interweaving of their names in the future. Bizet died unappreciated and unknown. It was ten years after this casual meeting that his opera *Carmen* was produced for the first time and Minnie Hauk sang the lead to an astounded London.

It is hardly surprising that Mrs. Ronalds arrived in Paris at about this time and, when winter froze up ponds and lakes, the spectacle of *la belle Américaine* skating in a hoop skirt became the sensation of Paris. Her exploits on the ice attracted the attention of the Empress, who liked to surround herself with beauties, and she was invited to the French court. Fanny Ronalds, with her elegance, her charm, and her musical talent, found no difficulty in skating into the royal entourage. She soon took a place as one of the many lovely ornaments of the Second Empire. She and Mrs. Jerome drove around together, paying calls, and young Clara was "brought out" ceremoniously in their wake.

Clara made her debut at one of the Tuileries balls and, despite her confusion at having to walk up the grand staircase between the *cent gardes* in her first low dress, she was able afterwards to give a coherent description of the scene to those two pairs of greedy ears in the schoolroom. "When the company was assembled, the doors were flung open and *Sa Majesté l'Empereur* was announced." Then after a pause *Sa Majesté l'Impératrice* appeared, "a resplendent figure in green velvet, with a crown of emeralds and diamonds, spiked with pearls, on her small and beautifully shaped head. The Emperor and Empress walked around the circle of curtseying and bowing guests, addressing a few words here and there, and then proceeded to the ball room."

An old photograph shows Miss Jerome attired for this ball in a white crinoline. The tulle skirt billows around her in the style of a Winterhalter portrait, and her golden hair hangs in ringlets on her neck.

Leonard did not share his womenfolks' enthusiasm for royalty. When Minnie Hauk had departed for the Imperial Opera of Moscow (well-chaperoned by her mama), and Mrs. Ronalds toward Algeria where she thought it would be amusing to subjugate the Bey, and Patti had shown her preference for the role of Marquise in a salon rather than that of a prima donna before the footlights, Mr. Jerome returned to New York. He wrote, "The two Claras are having a wonderful time. I leave them to it."

In New York he found his unwatched finances deteriorating. On Black Friday in 1868 Jay Gould and Fisk brought ruin to Wall Street and, despite the fact that President Grant stopped their plan to corner the gold market, they paralyzed the business of all America while reaping fresh millions for themselves. Gould secretly had tried to bring the President into their scheme, and oversure Fisk boasted to a congressional committee that the President was going to "play ball." In his last-minute decision to stop their gold plan, President Grant made bitter and powerful enemies within the "rings," but he could not prevent a national disaster.

Jerome, when the power lay in his hands as after Vanderbilt's Harlem battle, always worked to avert the ruining of smaller folk. "I prefer the role of financier to that of highway man," he wrote laughingly. Now he suffered, as everyone outside the rings did, from the shaken confidence and panic of the entire country. He revolted against the jungle that once had excited him. He longed to pull out but he could not. For the first time in her life Clara would be distressed by curtailment of income, for whether at Compiègne or the Tuileries, their eldest daughter needed an immense repertory of expensive gowns. Taking a tip from the Austrian Ambassadress Princess Metternich, who said, "I *made* M. Worth, you know—or was it he made *me?*" the ladies had decided to purchase all their dresses from that expensive gentleman.

Clarita went to a succession of *grands bals* at the palace, as well as to *les petits lundis,* those informal weekly dances which the young Prince Imperial was allowed to attend. *Mademoiselle Jerome, la voilà!* She could be seen gliding through the drawing rooms of both old and new nobility (they were just beginning to tolerate each other), and her after-dinner piano playing caused many hearts to miss a beat. The oldest man she ever danced with was the Comte de Flahaut. "Just think of it," she blurted, "He was Napoleon's aide-de-camp at Waterloo and Queen Hortense's lover."

"Hush!" snapped Mama. What a word for a girl to have learned! Perhaps there were drawbacks to bringing girls out in France after all.

"Mademoiselle Jerome" was written on numerous imperial invitations. On heavy cream paper, headed *Maison de l'Empereur,* they were issued from the chamberlain's office in the *Palais des Tuileries:*

> MADEMOISELLE,
> *Par ordre de l'Empereur, j'ai l'honneur de vous prevenir que vous êtes invitée a passer six jours au palais de Compiègne du dixième au quinzième novembre.*
> *Des voitures de la cour vous attrendront le dixième à l'arrivée a Compiègne du train spécial partant de Paris à deux heures pour vous conduire au château.*

This, dated November, 1869, seems to be the first time Clara traveled without Mama. One can see the picture: a young girl on a special train (heavily chaperoned we may be sure) with a frantic lady's maid in charge of her trunk. The fuss of packing and preparation surely had brought a flush to her cheeks; and her blue eyes, which remained bright and expectant to the end of her days, must have been shining.

A letter written to her mother by Clarita at Compiègne, briskly depicted palace life:

> . . . This morning I went down to breakfast. The Princess Mathilde shook hands with us, and the Emperor asked me if I would like a ride. . . . We "suivred" very well—and got in at the death of the *cerf*. It was five o'clock before we got home. The rendezvous was beautiful, the whole city of Compiègne and its environments turned out to it.
>
> In the evening I put on my white with marguerites, for the Prince Imperial was to have a Cotillion. We played *chat et souris,* so he ran after me and in and out, and I finally caught my foot in the Duchesse de Mouchy's dress and fell. . . . We have been asked to lengthen our stay until Tuesday—so I shall need another dress—something white, trimmed with anything you think pretty. I think I must have it—in fact two, if possible—for these ladies dress so much and never appear in the same.
>
> Dear Mamma, I love you and you are so sweet.
>
> Addio,
>
> *Clarita*
>
> P.S. I need a new light opera-cloak badly—merely something to throw around me to go to the dinner table.

It was obviously essential that dear Papa should also remain sweet. If every evening demanded a new white dress, he could not consider it the moment to relax. While his daughter tripped in and out of the imperial palaces, Mr. Jerome struggled alone in the city his family had scorned and deserted. Now was the time he longed for a son, a lad who would be an American, strong and confident as he had been, ready to learn from experience and fight his own battle, ready to take over responsibility.

When it was rumored that Jerome had passed his heyday, criticisms of him appeared in the press. Had he not driven down Fifth Avenue on Sundays? Was not betting allowed at Jerome Park? Certain persons attributed the failure of Pacific Mail and shaking of Wall Street to direct divine intervention. The New York *Times* argued in his favor: "Nothing goes on at Jerome Park which the purest minded person could object to. There is no bribing of jockeys, no 'dosing' of horses with laudanum. Never did the history of racing in any country begin with so fair a page."

The dressmakers of New York rose up to defend the races that gave them much trade: "Has not Monsieur Worth presented handsome stakes to the Ascot meeting? We will do the same!" And a band of well-meaning Puritans asked for a croquet to be added to the race track as a harmless divertisement.

By his own tremendous endeavor, Jerome had created this course; he had raised horse racing from the disrepute into which it had fallen and placed it upon the level of the English turf. Now picnics, croquet, and dress parades were the defense of his efforts! With a groan of boredom, Leonard wrote to his family, "Everyone getting tiresome here. I'll make you a little something and come across. Paris sounds delightful and a change."

He was in his fifties, physically on the crest of the wave, for his vitality had lasted. The whole wide world lay open to him to explore. He longed to travel, to sail the oceans, to see strange sights while there was time; but just as he had begun to tire of finance, it became incumbent on him to fight once more in the tottering frenzy of the Street. His daughters' tastes left no alternative. Sustained by that unflagging health of the frontier-bred, he tried to earn afresh.

One evening after working long hours he thought it would be "good fun to take a party to the Circus." At an age when he might have known better (but the very strong never do), he leaped into a contest with a professional weight lifter. Friends cheered him on while he wielded a hammer that sent a weight soaring up a pole. The pretty ladies who inevitably formed his background applauded, but the effort strained one whole side of his body and he collapsed soon after.

"Will you never learn?" pleaded Clara when she heard. He wrote back wistfully. "Can it be that one gets too old for circuses? I know I *ought* to feel too old, but the truth is I enjoy such nonsense as much as before."

THE COURT CIRCLES INTO WHICH Mrs. Jerome and Mrs. Ronalds drew Clara for a worldly debut were quicksands of dissension. Legitimists, Orleanists, and Republicans criticized every Bonaparte move, while the Mexican campaign had shaken the Empire's popularity to a degree which the daily procession of beauties in splendid carriages could not counterbalance. Eugenie's great charm seemed to be accompanied by an equal lack of wisdom. The Emperor struggled against her authoritative attitude and no longer permitted her to attend the council, but it was hardly possible for a man so tolerant of the faults of others to construct a new liberal Europe from scratch. Eugenie, surrounded by *soupirants*—men who sighed for her unassailable virtue from a distance—continued to exasperate all parties. Reared to make a great match for herself, she had aimed just too high. Never did she manifest the natural practical statesmanship which in history has so frequently and surprisingly shown itself in common-born women whom destiny has lifted to a throne. The feminine world might strive to copy her hats and her grace; a bewitched American ambassador might write, "Perhaps for an Empress she was too much of a coquette, but as an Andalusian and a woman she was the most perfect creature I have ever seen anywhere," but none yearned to be governed by the former Melle de Montijo. In the autumn of 1869 the Emperor packed her off to open the Suez Canal, a task for which her dramatic beauty and sense of theater seemed particularly suitable, but the troubles of France were too deep-rooted to fade in her absence. Already the black shadow of Bismarck flickered on the eastern horizon. The Second Empire sensed uneasily that it might be dancing to its close.

Across these last tinseled scenes of the old Tuileries and of the Chateau de Compiègne the figure of a dazzling American girl flits like a bird. Miss Clara Jerome, in a cloud of tulle, besieged by proposals of marriage, and in love with the one man her mother had forbidden, could be seen wringing all possible delight from a first season. The dark old palace with the statuesque *cent gardes* in their glittering blue and silver uniforms standing rigid at every door provided a background that no young person could forget. Devoid of shyness, she enjoyed an occasional waltz with the schoolboy prince, who to improve his ease of manner was allowed to attend informal soirees at the palace.

She herself has described one of the *petits lundis* when her mother being unable to attend had arranged for her to be chaperoned to the Tuileries by a married couple.

"As usual you know how impossible I have always found it to be punctual. I was late in meeting these friends, and they departed without me, leaving a message they would wait at the top of the big palace staircase. I flew back to the carriage with Dobbie, our devoted Negro nurse, at my heels. She came from the old South and had very definite views on the importance of chaperoning young ladies. For nothing on earth would she allow me out of her sight until I could be handed over to my official duenna. We drove post haste to the Tuileries, and there she descended beside me with an indomitable expression on her black face: 'Ah'm not going to leave you until Ah sees you safe.' You can imagine the surprise of the palace guards who lined the great staircase as a young girl fluttered up the marble steps closely pursued by a large Negress wearing a green turban on her head and a red shawl around her shoulders.

" '*La jeune Américaine!*' gasped guests at the top of the staircase, and then my friends stepped forward and Dobbie smiled, curtseyed, and took her leave, satisfied that the conventions had been upheld and that no impropriety could now befall her young mistress."

Among the outstanding hostesses of Paris to whose *salons* the Jeromes were regularly invited was the Princesse Mathilde, cousin of Louis Napoleon and formerly his fiancée. Jennie wrote: "The most intelligent and brilliant woman of the Second Empire, she used to give cotillions at her first house in the Rue de Courcelles at which the *collets montés* and aristocratic families made their appearance in greater numbers than in the Tuileries: the noble *faubourg* (pre-Napoleonic nobility), satisfied that her mother was a Princess of Wurtemburg, while her uncle was the Czar Nicholas I, did not look upon her as a parvenue and an interloper.

"The Princess loved to surround herself with those possessing wit and talent, and sought to make her *salons* compare with those of the 18th Century. . . . That these sacred portals were opened for anything so frivolous as a dance, was to please the Prince Imperial and the Empress's nieces, the Mesdemoiselles d'Albe."

Princesse Mathilde had not always been a royal highbrow, however. At the famous *bal masque* at the Hotel d'Albe a few years earlier she had astonished the diplomatic corps by appearing at the party in extreme undress with her body dyed dark brown. She survived this scandal, however, and also the misfortune of being sister to the unutterable Plonplon who, until the birth of the Prince Imperial, had damned Bonapartism by being its heir. It was in the Princess's house that Miss Jerome, a delicious featherwit of eighteen, had the pleasure of meeting Dumas, Sardou, Theophile Gautier, and Daudet, the intellectuals of Paris whose names she recorded in a diary without comment, save for beguiling descriptions of her own dresses from which posterity supposedly must deduce the impression *she* must have made.

When he had been a young man with but faint prospect of becoming Emperor, Louis Napoleon had courted Mathilde. Their engagement lasted until his second attempt on the throne failed. Then her father, the "old roué of Westphalia" * had broken off the betrothal and insisted on a more remunerative match with a Russian count. This gentleman exceeded the bounds allowed to Muscovy bears by slapping his wife's face in public. The Tsar stepped in, ordered his unmannered subject to donate a large share of his fortune to the Princess, and she retreated to Paris, secure behind the barricade of a legal separation but unable to remarry. The city respected her intellect and liberal views. Mathilde became the leading patron of writers and artists, and her lions were of the highest grade. If she entertained more than cousinly feelings for her former financé, none could guess it. That unhappy domestic interlude was never mentioned and, carrying her head high, the Princess contented herself with the creation of a brilliant *salon*. If she suffered afresh when Louis Napoleon, looking for an empress, had to pass her by on account of her unannulled marriage, no one was kinder than Mathilde when Eugenie mounted the throne. Now in a time of increasing stress she became a political pivot.

---

* King Jérôme of Westphalia, the last surviving brother of the great Napoleon.

In January, 1870, while the Empress, basking in Egypt, was lulled by blue skies and the strains of Verdi's *Aïda,* Louis Napoleon flung the last of his famous country parties, and Leonard received the intimation that *une élégante* would need twenty new dresses for a week's stay at the chateau. When she had supervised her maid's unpacking, young Clara spared some observation for the Emperor, who "seemed to be in bad health and beset by political worries." As was usual in Eugenie's absence, the Princesse Mathilde did the honors. Hunting and shooting and local sight-seeing were always provided to amuse the guests, and for those who could totter by the time night fell, there would be dancing.

The house parties of Compiègne were intended to resemble English country entertaining, but no one was left alone to dream or to amble or to read by the fire. Visitors groused at being dragged out from the hothouse atmosphere of the great drawing rooms on perpetual organized excursions. But not so the young. Miss Clara explored all she dared of the chateau and missed no possible amount of activity.*

"There was a *grande chasse,* or stag hunt, on the first day, at which all the guests appeared, riding or driving. Those who hunted wore the royal colours, the men in green coats and the gold hunt buttons, the ladies in flowing green habits and three-cornered hats. The stag on this occasion was brought to bay in a lake, the Prince Imperial giving him the *coup de grâce.* At night there was a *curée aux flambeaux* in the courtyard of the chateau, the whole party assembling on the balconies in the glare of the innumerable torches. The carcass of the deer lay in the centre covered with its skin; the *hallali* was sounded; at a signal the

---

* After the First World War, as old Mrs. Moreton Frewen, she took her daughter Clare Sheridan to Compiègne to see "the room I slept in as a girl." The guide who accompanied them stared unbelieving as she identified the guest rooms: "And here I stood in front of a mirror in white tulle before going down to dinner."

CLARA HALL 1825-1895
WIFE OF LEONARD JEROME
BY SCHIAVONI

Portrait of Clara Jerome, by Schiavari. *Courtesy of Sir Shane Leslie.*

Right: The Empress Eugenie. *Courtesy of Captain Oswald Frewen, R.N.*

Left, above: Wall Street in 1854. *Courtesy of the Bank of New York.* *Left, below:* Leonard Jerome in his coach. *Courtesy of John I. Leslie.*

Right: Minnie Hauk as Carmen.

Above: Jennie Churchill.
Below: The Duc de Persigny. *Le*
by Clara Sheridan.

The Marquis de Tamisier. *Lent by Clara Sheridan.*

Jennie Jerome.

Leonie Jerome.

William Travers. *Lent by Cl*
Sheridan.

Above: Lord Randolph Churchill.
Below: Leonie Leslie.

Jennie, Clara, and Leonie. *Courtesy of John I. Leslie.*

Clara Frewen.

hounds were unleashed, and in a moment every vestige of the stag had disappeared."

Clara thought it savage and cruel, but she admitted herself impressed by handsome Castelbajac, director of the hunt. *"Il était tellement beau."* Her mother did not object so long as the girl's attention was diverted from Tamisier.

"The next day an expedition was organized to see the Chateau de Pierrefonds, a distance of nine or ten miles; the party went in *chars à bancs* [the old-fashioned horsed version, literally "benched chariots"] under the guidance of the architect who had just completed its restoration. . . . The day ended with tea in the beautiful armory of the castle from which the Emperor presented each lady with a souvenir in the shape of a small weapon.

"One day there was a Cabinet Council, and the guests were exhorted to be discreet in their amusements and not to disturb his Majesty. Who knows what fateful questions were discussed. Times were disquieting and *pourparlers* with Prussia had proved anything but pleasant. The Government was in direct conflict with the Opposition."

Napoleon had, in fact, decided to invent hurriedly a new kind of constitution and parliamentary cabinet. Remaining absolute himself, he strove to create a liberal empire, which would win over the opposition. Small wonder his guests were asked to refrain from noisy games!

Among the ministers summoned to this council at Compiègne was the Maréchal Bazaine accompanied by his Mexican wife. The Emperor's guests seem to have been less astounded at the Maréchal's idea of disciplining the Chamber by using troops than at the evening toilette of Madame la Maréchale. At a time when all evening dresses were white or pastel this lady appeared in a gown of vivid scarlet with gloves to match. "This was thought *très anglais,* as no one in France wore such brilliant colors.

"Every night from sixty to a hundred guests sat down to dinner, the Emperor never permitting it to last more than three quarters of an hour. Sometimes magnificent gold plate adorned the table, sometimes precious *biscuit de Sèvres*. Before dinner the company assembled in two long lines. The Emperor took in Princesse Mathilde, sitting opposite her at the centre of the table, a few seats of honour being reserved on each side, while the rest placed themselves as they wished, the ladies choosing the gentlemen to take them in, according to the custom of Compiègne. After dinner there was dancing, in which the Prince Imperial, then only thirteen, was allowed to join till ten o'clock, when his tutor would approach him, saying *"Monseigneur, vôtre chapeau,"* which meant he must go to bed. At the close of the visit there was a grand lottery and in which all tickets won prizes. The Emperor stood near two great urns from which the numbers were drawn, and as each guest received one he wished him *'Bonne chance.'* Some little juggling must have gone on, for my mother and the American minister, Mr. Washbourne, won valuable pieces of Sèvres china, whereas the presents for the younger people were less costly." Young Clara received from the Emperor's hand an inkstand shaped like a knotted handkerchief filled with gold Napoléons. As his Majesty gave it to her, he remarked, *"Mademoiselle, n'oubliez pas les Napoléons."*

She never did.

THE SPRING OF 1870 CAME WITH unusual warmth and beauty. Leonard knew he ought to return to Wall Street, but he could not bear to depart, and besides he had just taken a fine new house in the Boulevard Haussman, in which his picture collection could be hung to advantage. He was, in any case, finding New York exceedingly fraying. Old Commodore Vanderbilt had now become besotted by two sisters, whom he had set up as lady brokers. They communed with "the other side" and gave spookish advice concerning stocks and shares. They also aroused considerably earthy impulses in the gentlemen who visited their office for astral financial help. "Spirits are the last straw, and Tweed runs the city. I dread going back," Leonard told his wife. And off he went for a ride with the Prince de Sagon who, never having heard of bears, save as animals, made a refreshing companion. And in the evenings he had his daughters' piano playing to listen to and Minnie Hauk's progress to appraise.

There were a few political excitements this spring. Louis Napoleon, hot from the reconstruction of his new liberal empire, launched a plebiscite, asking one question only. Did the people assent to his reforms? Many were puzzled how to answer. Must their approval of reform be tantamount to approval of Bonapartism? Paris and the great cities cried, "No," but to the amazement of other countries seven million Frenchmen answered, "Yes."

This undeniably proved a triumph for the Emperor, but in May his old friend Lord Malmesbury wrote home, "I thought him much altered in appearance and looking very ill. . . . I naturally began by congratulating him on his plebiscite which was just counted up, but I found that he was not satisfied as some 50,000 of the army had voted 'Non.' He, however, explained that 300,000 soldiers had voted for him. This struck me as strange, for I imagined his army was in number 600,000 and I made the remark, to which he gave no reply, but looked suddenly very grave and absent."

Throughout the early spring there were rumors of war but not of a very serious kind, for Prussia was just a cocky little state and King Wilhelm had *so* enjoyed the Fair.

Jennie finished her studies and began to talk of the following season when it would be her turn to be presented at court. To Mrs. Jerome's relief the idea of becoming a musician instead of a great lady was fading away. The glitter of the Tuileries had won over artistic aspiration.

"Did your teacher truly say you could attain concert standard?" asked Leonard.

"Yes," Jennie stared up, her dark eyes flashing, her cheeks and lips rosy with the natural color of her tremendous health, "if I continued to work hard. But then he looked at me and sighed and said, 'But you won't.'"

Jennie, a more vigorous and dynamic character than her elder sister, could hardly wait to make her mark in the world. Clara brought home what fragments of interesting conversation she could remember, and the inmates of the Jerome schoolroom regarded the palace as a stage on which they would each be allowed to shine in the train of brilliant Pauline Metternich and bewitching Melanie de Pourtales. No one with Leonard's blood in his veins ever proved remarkable for modest aims.

Meanwhile the Duc de Lescera, a Spanish relative of the Empress, visited and made advances to the elder Miss Jerome, who was sufficiently amused to encourage him until her mother, who wanted no Catholic alliance, however aristocratic, ordered him from the house. However, with the connivance of Clara and Jennie, he came back through the drawing-room window. Mrs. Jerome burst in, and her trembling daughters expected a scene, but she, somewhat near-sighted, mistook the Duke for their servant and said, *"Pierre, commandez le déjeuner pour sept heures."* *"Oui, Madame"* replied the Duke and, as he left the house, he passed the message to the cook.

During this year only one slight shadow was recorded. It occurred after a particularly animated *petit lundi* when Count Hazenfeldt, Secretary to the German Embassy in Paris, who was a frequenter of the Jerome salon, drew Mademoiselle Clara into a window embrasure and remarked, "I never saw their Majesties in better spirits than they were last night, but God knows where they will be next year at this time."

When Clara recounted this to her sisters, both Jennie and Leonie frowned.

What *could* he mean?

The court removed to St. Cloud in early summer and there the fourteen-year-old Prince Imperial, and the Empress's nieces the Mesdemoiselles d'Albe played happily throughout the long golden days.

Old timers, unamused by excesses of artless innocence, grumbled that the vast chateau now resembled "a boarding school," or worse still, "a nursery."

June passed. After throwing off the Bourbons, Spain offered its throne to Bismarck's stool-pigeon Leopold of Hohenzollern. France (and all Europe for that matter) screamed with indignation. Leopold withdrew, and war seemed to have been averted. Bismarck, determined to establish German supremacy through conflict, scowled while the population of France trembled with disappointment, for they also were determined to have a war—not to pause and prepare, but to have it out now, immediately, while the blood pounded hot in their veins and the marching songs had not grown stale. Only the Emperor seemed relieved when he could murmur, *"C'est la paix."*

Leonard hesitated as to whether he should remain with his family or sail with James Gordon Bennett, Jr., in England in what was to prove the first international Atlantic yacht race, a two-boat tussle fated to become as famous as the Great Race of Sixty-six.

Bennett had embarked on a fiery and somewhat boastful correspondence with an Englishman, James Ashbury, Commodore of the Royal Harwick Yacht Club and owner of a beautiful schooner. His *Cambria* was 188 tons, 108 feet over all, and had a mainmast sixty-one feet high above which she could carry a main topmast of another thirty-five feet.

Ashbury challenged his yacht against any in the world and Bennett (now Vice-Commodore of the New York Yacht Club), had sailed his *Dauntless* over in 1869 to winter at Cowes, refit in the spring for a transoceanic race, and contest the Atlantic run with her. *Dauntless* was 120 feet over all, spreading seven thousand square feet of canvas. It took a crew of thirty-seven men, expending their utmost, to keep her at best sailing speed.

"*Dauntless* was among the best in 1870, and Bennett had as good reason as Ashbury to believe that in a transatlantic race his schooner would fly the winning colours." The prize was a set of silverware valued at 250 pounds, and the start was dated for July 4 off Daunt Rock, Queenstown, Ireland.

Lawrence had come over to join the crew of the *Dauntless,* and Leonard could hardly resist joining him. Charles Longfellow, son of the poet, was the other amateur to sail with Bennett. Of the professionals, who numbered thirty-four, Captain Bully Samuels and the Browns, Lyons, and J. Taylor "constituted a brain trust as formidable as any that modern times have known."

July 4 found a large collection of British and French yachts assembled at Daunt Rock to cheer in a fresh westerly, which soon brought fog and rain. The two yachts began the race. . . . At 2:30 P.M. *Dauntless* cast off her tug and stood away on the starboard tack.

The 1870 race has been so hotly debated in the sailing world ever since, that it is irresistible to quote from Alfred Loomis' classic descriptions in *Ocean Racing.*

"Three o'clock saw *Dauntless* drawing ahead and weathering *Cambria,* which tacked inshore to escape. *Dauntless* followed her in and at 4:30, after another tack, her crew had the satisfaction of seeing the British schooner safely tucked away under the

American's lee. An hour and a half later *Cambria* stood in near the Old Head of Kinsale, and *Dauntless* maintained a starboard tack offshore. Here the two yachts parted company. . . ."

They were not to see each other for three thousand miles. In this hard-fought start *Dauntless* had proved the better boat. Among *Cambria's* brain trust "there was evidently one who knew that a boat which cannot go to windward with her competitor, must break with her and seek a different slant of wind."

From this night on, *Cambria* battled straight across the Atlantic, while *Dauntless* made the great mistake of taking a southerly route. For July 7 her log reads: "At 3 A.M. took in gaff top-sails. At 6½ housed top-mast. At 7½ wind and sea increasing, took in flying jib. In furling it, two men—Charles Scot and Albert Demar—were washed off the boom. Hove to the yacht for two hours, lowered foresail and got out boat, but failed to see anything of the missing men. At 9½ the wind increased to a gale, we reluctantly gave them up, took the boat on board, and kept on our course. Double-reefed mainsail, and took bonnet out of foresail. Ends in a fresh gale, thick, rainy weather, and short high sea."

They had already lost the race.

Loomis continues, "Better favored by the fates, *Cambria* had worked north to 54–59, her highest latitude, and from the seventh she slanted slowly down, taking what current there was on her port beam until she came within the helpful influence of the Labrador current."

By the time three weeks had elapsed, the interest of all New York was centered on Sandy Hook, "hoping against hope that the *Dauntless* would justify the faith of the American patriots."

Gentlemen of the press were scanning the horizon to eastward, and the New York *Times* relates: "The operator's room at the station was filled with half a dozen active newspaper reporters, who were constantly consulting Mr. James Farrell, the bronzed and veteran ship-news reporter, who, with telescope in hand, was keeping a vigilant watch seaward. His keen eye swept the water for miles and miles in every direction, but failed to make out anything resembling either of the two anxiously expected vessels. Precisely at 3:05 P.M. (on July 27), he turned from his glass and announced that a yacht was coming up toward the Hook, but that her colors were not discernible.

"The speck rapidly approached and assumed plainer proportions until it was discovered to be the sails and spars of a schooner. Nothing was visible of her hull, which seemed to be a part of the sea on which it floated. Exactly forty-one minutes elapsed, according to Mr. Farrell's calculations, before she passed the lightship, seven miles outside of Sandy Hook. Her outlines were then fully and clearly distinguished. The wind was blowing off her port quarter due east, and she scudded along under full sail. The flags which she carried at her ensign, together with a private pennon, contained the letter C in the center. She was at once pronounced to be the *Cambria*.

"A sigh of disappointment swept over America. *Cambria* had sailed from Ireland to Sandy Hook in twenty-three days, five hours, and seventeen minutes. It was only one hour and forty-three minutes later that *Dauntless* passed the finish line. Only one hour and forty-three minutes in a race of three thousand miles! It had been a good try, but in the end it had to be conceded that *Cambria,* a slower boat, won the first international yacht race because of faster head work."

As soon as he got ashore, Leonard wrote an excited letter to his daughters, but they scarcely read Papa's account of the fatal decision to sail a southerly route, the loss of the two men, or the shift of wind that favored *Cambria* at the finish. Very different events filled their heads, for the Franco-Prussian War had broken out, Paris reverberated to the "Marseillaise," and cries of *"Vive l'Empereur"* echoed on the boulevards all through the night.

THE EMPEROR NAPOLEON III stood by with leaden heart while his people shouted for blood. Through early July Wilhelm of Prussia was tormented by the French to give impossible guarantees that no repetition of the Hohenzollern episode should ever occur. Bismarck saw the war, for which he had so long schemed, once again materializing.

Never had a country shown more enthusiasm for battle, than France in 1870, a year in which she had neither a trained army nor a plan of action. The country worked itself into a patriotic frenzy. Only the Emperor made an attempt to assess possible results, and he was dubbed spoil sport. It might have been wise of the Chamber to investigate the Army's efficiency before hysterically voting unlimited war credits, but the nation's enthusiasm exceeded the bounds of sanity. Cafés and cabarets were packed with elated crowds. Over three thousand people danced around the Place de la Concorde. Someone counted them. It was all *très émotionnable*. And, of course, the weather was just right.

No preparations for a major war were made, but songs echoed through the streets. The Emperor, sick and pessimistic, aroused the indignation of patriotic journalists by his cautious rejoinders. But although sensing catastrophe, he knew himself unable to stem the tide. The horror of battlefields never left his mind. He loved his fellow men and the realistic visualization of conflict tortured him. They scorned him for this. The French expected a Bonaparte to be martial.

Minnie Hauk, who was at the opera with her mother on the night war was declared, wrote this vivid description:

"I spent the summer of 1870 in Paris, to get new dresses and to see my numerous friends again. While I was there, Auber came one day and invited me to a performance of his opera *La Muette de Portici,* to be given the same evening at the Imperial Opera. He said the Imperial couple had announced their intention to be present. It was to be a gala night. I readily accepted, Auber himself came to fetch me, and when we arrived at the theatre, all the *crème de la crème* of Paris society was already present. He pointed out to me all the notabilities, the Ministers of State, the Duc de Gramont, Rouher, Maurice Richart, also many of the duchesses and princesses, all in most beautiful toilets and bedecked with sparkling jewels; but Napoleon III and the Empress did not put in an appearance.

"The curtain went up, but to my great surprise, instead of the first scene of *La Muette,* I saw on the stage the prima donna of the opera, Marie Sasse, dressed in white, with a long mantle embroidered with gold bees thrown over her shoulder, carrying in her outstretched right hand the French national flag. The conductor raised his baton, but for several minutes he was prevented from beginning by the most deafening applause.

"In a box opposite ours sat the beautiful young Duchesse de Mouchy, dressed in the French colours, frantically waving her handkerchief. Suddenly she and the other occupants of her box rose from their seats, and at the same time we heard a ringing voice shouting *'Tout le monde debout.'* It was Émile de Girardin, the well-known journalist, who, from his box on the grand tier had invited the whole audience to stand up. Everybody stood, while the orchestra crashed into the inspiring strains of 'La Marseillaise'!

"I could not believe my ears! The battlesong of the Great Revolution at the Imperial Opera! What had happened? Had war against Prussia been declared? Why, then, the Republican 'Marseillaise' and not the Imperial hymn?

"When, after the prelude, Marie Sasse, in her beautiful voice, began to sing the first verse of the 'Marseillaise,' the whole audience joined her, finishing up with such hurrahs, shouting, clapping of hands, stamping of feet, and waving of hats, sticks, and handkerchiefs as I have never witnessed again in any theatre. Throughout the deafening tumult I heard people shout, '*Vive l'Empereur!*' '*Vive la France!*' followed with ever increasing enthusiasm by shouts '*À Berlin! À Berlin!*'

"Auber had excitedly left the box and run on the stage. I followed him, and in the narrow passage we met Jacques Halévy, the composer of *La Juive*.

"Halévy appeared most agitated and shouted to Auber, 'Who has done this? Surely not with the Emperor's consent?'

"Auber replied, 'No, it was Maurice Richart [the Minister of Fine Arts], but the Emperor must have been informed beforehand!'

"Halévy shook his head and exclaimed quite in despair, 'Where are we drifting to? The song of the Revolution at the Imperial Opera!'

"In reply Auber pointed towards the raging audience and said, 'He just hit the right thing; only listen how they acclaim the Emperor!' It was the last time the French did so, for a few months later the Empire had fallen and the Republic was proclaimed!"

From New York Leonard started to cable frantically to his wife, begging her to move to London, but Clara possessed no sense of danger. She allowed her girls to walk the boulevards with their governesses while the crowds roared for victories and ceaselessly repeated, "*À Berlin!*"

Leonard calmed down on receiving his wife's description of passing events. She seemed to be enthralled by the general delirium, and was most advantageously placed to receive gossip, for Persigny brought her the latest news from court daily. Eugenie had been named regent during the Emperor's absence at the front, and with suitable dramatics the fourteen-year-old Prince was dressed up as a lieutenant and sent out to cheer the fighting men. "Do not worry, Leonard. It will soon be over," Clara insisted. "The French must reach Berlin within a few days; *everyone* says so!"

Leonard, having hardly washed the salt spray from his face, did not wish to return to Europe, except in case of urgent necessity. His New York *Times* had launched a powerful attack on William Tweed (state senator, "boss" of New York City, and kingpin of Tammany) and was employing Thomas Nast, greatest cartoonist of the day, to expose the Tweed ring in brilliant, satirical drawings. It would be very inconvenient for Leonard to leave New York for a few months. Moreover, Paris seemed so safe and so far from the guns.

Jennie recorded: "Exciting incidents crowded on us. One day we saw Capoul, the celebrated tenor, and Marie Sasse of the Opera made to stand on top of an omnibus and sing the 'Marseillaise,' an ever-growing crowd joining in the chorus. One night we went to the opera in walking dresses, with our hats in our hands in case there was any trouble and we might have to walk home, which proved to be the case. It was a strange performance, as the singers were constantly being interrupted and made to sing patriotic songs. We found the greatest difficulty in getting home, owing to the streets' being filled with huge crowds marching to the cry of *des chassepots, des chassepots.*' Poor fellows, they soon had them, and all the fighting they wanted."

It was very moving, especially for American girls, singing the "Marseillaise" in the dusk and moving paper flags over schoolroom maps. They saw decorations run up with each rumor of victory. Then blinds were pulled down as stark truths filtered through. The Parisians were high-strung, nervy, and hot-tempered. They had shouted for war, but not for this kind of war.

The Duc de Persigny came to call almost every day after his visit to St. Cloud. He gathered shattering information from the Empress. Louis Napoleon's first letter to his wife read, "Nothing is ready. We have not troops enough. *Je nous considère d'avance comme perdus.*" This was followed by an astounding series of defeats. As is usual in such circumstances, the army commander had to be dismissed. His replacement happened to be Maréschal Bazaine, that soldier of small talent and large words. The country clutched pathetically at this new name, as if by the touch of some wand Bazaine could unmuddle the depots, provide guns for the artillery, turn the bewildered raw recruits into trained troops, and make the whole military machine work efficiently.

On August 6 Eugenie returned to the Tuileries where, camping among the dust sheets, she worked wildly to dispel the country's chaos. She took the responsibility of illegally forming a new cabinet headed by General de Paliakao, an old imperialist who was disgruntled at having been made a count instead of a marshal. As minister of war he saw his chance. His plan for the disorganized armies reached the bewildered commanders just as Bazaine's army suffered its appalling triple defeats around Metz.

The tension in Paris increased. Foreigners drifted away, some not because they feared the Prussian cannon might come within striking distance, but because there were better playgrounds elsewhere.

Only the Jeromes lingered on, riveted to their battle maps. Why, because of a rude, but obviously temporary, invasion should they desert their chosen city, their chosen court? "Our house was the rendezvous of the few of our French friends who had not gone to the front," wrote Jennie.

The Duc de Persigny's daily visits became more distressing, his news more unbelievable. Yet just five days before the regime floundered he found time to write the following note accompanying a gift of note paper:

PARIS

30 août 1870

Ma chère petite Jenny,
Je vous envoie le papier marqué à vôtre nom, comme je vous l'ai promis. Vôtre nom est gravé sans ornement parce qu'il ma paru convenir davantage par sa noble simplicité au caractère de vôtre jeunesse et de vôtre beauté. La première lettre de vôtre nom ne se prête pas d'ailleurs au caprice des combinaisons que comporte celui de vôtre sœur dont le C ambitieux pourrait embrasser l'univers.

J'espère que tel qu'il est ce chiffre vous plaira et qu'en écrivant vos lettres de jeune fille vous penserez à vôtre vieil ami. Mille compliments affectueux et dévoués à votre excellente mère et à Clara, sans oublier bien entendu vôtre chère petite sœur.

Persigny.

On the following day compliments ceased. The Duke arrived grave-faced to explain that the armies did not seem to be linking up as intended. (They were in fact retreating on Paris.) Mrs. Jerome had just fallen and sprained her ankle; her foot could not be put to the ground. Although admitting it might be wiser to depart, she still refused to believe the Prussian advance could continue; she was quite sure they would overstretch their supply lines!

"Maybe you are right," agreed Persigny unhappily. Next morning he rushed in before they had finished breakfast crying, "*Tout est perdu; l'armée n'est pas concentrée. Les Prussiens sont à nos portes.*"

His alarm was so genuine that Mrs. Jerome dragged herself to her feet and told the girls to pack as quickly as possible. They could hardly believe their ears—what, leave their home and belongings with only an hour in which to prepare? Clara retired in consternation to her bedroom, wrote a brief message for the Marquis de Tamisier, and started to sort her ball dresses, but Persigny was insistent. Within an hour they must leave; few trains were running and even now it might be too late to reach the coast. No cabs were functioning, and Mrs. Jerome would have to be carried all the way to the station by whomever they could hire in the streets.

While the Duke gesticulated and entreated, the girls ran around tying up jewelry and treasures in tablecloths and sheets. They created bundles far too heavy for their strength, and by the time they reached the station they were completely exhausted. So were Mrs. Jerome and her maid. But the Duke found them places on a train—any train would do as long as it got them out of the capital and this one was due to head north shortly. Amid the general commotion Clara could not decide if her maid should return for "the heavy luggage" or not. In the end it was decided that dear Marie should walk home, pack up all their clothes properly in large trunks, and hire a cart to bring them to the station next day. The Prussians might be at the city gates, but to be stranded in Deauville without one's hats—really, that would be too much!

Unknowingly they had boarded the last train to leave Paris for months. Poor Marie endured the siege half-starved in the Jerome house, looking after her mistress' gowns which, unfortunately, were edible only to the moth.

At Deauville, over-crowded by dumbfounded refugees, the three girls were lucky to procure rooms for themselves and their lame mother in the Palace Hotel. Tearful and exhausted, they had flung themselves down to sleep till morning when a tap sounded at the door. There stood Monsieur de Garonne, a chamberlain of the Empress, begging for concealment "owing to state reasons which they would know later." Clara unenthusiastically assented. This meant she could not leave her daughters unchaperoned for one minute.

All day de Garonne waited nervously, leaping to hide behind the curtains if anyone came, and greatly intriguing the girls, who remained too well brought up to venture questions. "After dinner, when it was quite dark, he departed as mysteriously as he had come. Two days later we were thrilled to hear of the Empress's escape from Paris, accompanied by Dr. Crane, Dr. Evans (the American dentist) and Mme Lebreton, our friend M. de Garonne having helped to make the arrangements."

The Empress, whose orders from the Tuileries had flatly contradicted those issued by the Emperor, sailed to England in Sir John Burgoyne's yacht, which encountered a terrible storm. The wild seas appealed to Eugenie's uncrushable sense of the theatrical. After all the stresses of the last two months, she could still summon enough imaginative energy to apprise the dramatic effect if she were drowned *now* in full flight! Perhaps the dangers of Paris had been exaggerated in order to drag her from the capital. The mob there was fickle but not fierce. Although ready to tear down gilded eagles, the people did not demand heads.

The yacht landed safely at Ryde on the Isle of Wight, and Eugenie moved to Hastings to await her son, a chivalrous, highstrung boy of fourteen, who had been subjected to the most shattering of experiences. Brought up to idealistic notions of patriotism and honor, he had traveled around with his sick father, seeing the army he venerated turning into a rabble and the country he loved deriding that name of Bonaparte, which he carried so proudly.

Meanwhile the Emperor remained with his armies and plumbed the depths of human misery. The attendant agonies of his physical illness, that piercing pain of stone in his bladder, were not of the kind to annihilate mental suffering. Stoic, silent, still considerate of others, he remained in his saddle all day at the final terrible battle of Sedan "praying for death in a hail of shells." But shrapnel has a partiality for those who wish to live. The long day drew to its end, and the Emperor, unwillingly, still breathed.

They did not treat him badly, the Germans who led the weary prisoner off to Cassel. Such resignation and despair created a mute respect in his captors. He had not led his country into war; he had struggled as far as he dared against popular fervor. And now, when its troops were reduced to bleeding heaps and its frontier was lost, the country turned to upbraid the one man who had striven to avert the calamity and who was brave enough to lower the standard personally when defeat had come.

He must have been glad to be alone among strangers, among courteous indifferent foes, this pallid, haunted Emperor, this little man of courage and good will, this unromantic, most gallant failure.

MEANWHILE, THE JEROME ladies, hatless, maidless, governessless, wondered where in the world to go next.

After a miserable September they accepted with docility Leonard's cable from New York ordering them to depart for England. As the German ring closed around Paris, Mr. Jerome had been frantic with worry. For days he did not know that his family had escaped to the coast. When their Deauville address finally reached New York, he wondered what to tell them while he searched for the first available passage back across the Atlantic.

With difficulty Clara and her daughters obtained places on a cross-channel boat, and they sailed away sadly, seeing France melt into a line on the horizon. On arrival in England they could not decide where to go. For a time they lodged in the Norfolk Hotel in Brighton, hating the gray stony beach, the gray autumn sky, the brisk winds, and above all hating "exile."

When their father reached England, the girls clung to him as their one remaining rock in a dissolving world, but his practical approach to the summer's disasters disturbed them. He stated bluntly there was no possibility of returning to France. Then Mr. Jerome took his family to London and settled them in Brown's Hotel off Piccadilly.

"We may have to spend the winter here, so the girls must pick up the threads of their studies and forget about the treasures they've left in Paris."

"But Papa, the Republic can't *last?*"

"It might," said Mr. Jerome.

Their faces grew long. Midwinter came, and the siege of Paris continued. Leonard bought them new frocks, but still they hung their heads. Lessons had to be improvised and a special room, taken for piano practice. The girls played for hours every day, hammering their moods of tearful anger into the ivory keys.

It was not long before the Duc de Persigny came to call.

"Your last visitor in Paris. Your first in London, I fear!"

Leonard welcomed him with open arms. "If it were not for you, my wife and daughters might yet be caught in a starving city." Persigny brought all the latest imperial refugee gossip. There was much talk of the Emperor (a prisoner at Wilhelmshöhe) abdicating in favor of his son. The King of Prussia could hardly treat with a republican government. A royal restoration, either imperial or Orleanist, could be taken for granted. The girls pouted: *They* did not want a Bourbon back on the throne; they wanted a Bonaparte.

Then, as Persigny called often, each time more forlorn and a little hungrier, it dawned up them that "broken-hearted, ill, and penniless, our poor friend was put to many straits to eke out a living, selling his plate and the little he had been able to bring away with him." Having served as ambassador in London during most of the sixties, he had many friends who should have been eager to help, but this made him all the more ashamed of letting people know his plight. Leonard, rendered sharp and sensitive by the financial difficulties of his own youth, was the only person who came to the rescue in practical fashion. He insisted on taking a room for the Duke at Brown's Hotel and paying all his bills.

This exactly suited the Misses Jerome who, thoroughly home-sick for Paris, wished to see only those French friends with whom they might discuss a speedy return of the Empire. Jennie could not get over the Prussian affront. The most scintillating of courts had disappeared like a mirage just as she was preparing to step into it. Now she found herself ordered back to schoolbooks and music lessons with inadequate English teachers. Girls were not so intensively educated in England as on the continent; Jennie and Leonie scorned the tutoring now offered. Every day they walked in Hyde Park with a German governess (*German,* not Prussian) making dull conversation. However, they both wished to become expert in this tongue, if only to be able to appreciate Wagner's great operas which Princess Metternich had been thrusting on baffled Parisian audiences for the last nine years. From their early years the three girls were worshipers of *Tannhäuser,* and even Mrs. Jerome, like many unmusical people, could grasp Wagner's tremendous recurring motifs.

Jennie wrote: "A winter spent in the gloom and fogs of London did not tend to dispel the melancholy which we felt. Our friends scattered, fighting or killed at the front; debarred as we were from our bright little house and our household goods it was indeed a sad time."

Her mother could not help a certain relief at having her girls in a Protestant country for she had always feared a Catholic marriage. During the first year, however, they made few English friends. Young Clarita was very quiet during these days, being more in love than ever with the Marquis de Tamisier, who, caught in besieged Paris, was managing to send her messages by balloon. But even the thought of the hunger and danger that young man must be enduring did not soften Mrs. Jerome's views. Under the formidable pressure of her mama's displeasure, Clara grew forlorn and sickened as if purposely. Finally she developed a fever that was said to be typhoid; but forever afterward she insisted it had been due to frustrated love.

Leonard saw his hotel suite established as a rallying point for imperialists, and he grew weary of his daughters' sighs. He had good reason to try to reach Paris, for he carried some private proposals from Washington concerning the mitigation of the suffering. Moreover, he wished to discover the fate of his best paintings. After some delay he received a diplomatic passport to visit Paris with Generals Sheridan and Burnside who were going as military observers.

They were all led blindfold through the Prussian lines to American Minister Washbourne, who had remained in the city throughout its ordeal. Washbourne received them warmly and spoke with emotion of the individual acts of human courage and despair he had witnessed. The Washington proposals were unofficial but important enough for General Burnside to accompany Leonard to Bismarck, who was quartered in the neighborhood of Paris. Unfortunately Leonard kept no diary, and Bismarck's secretary merely recorded the visit of the American gentleman dressed "as if hurriedly in a flannel shirt with paper cuffs." (All the soap of Paris had been eaten.)

Shortly afterward, the city capitulated and the Parisians, who a year before had been shouting *"À Berlin,"* retreated behind shuttered windows while the victorious Prussian columns strutted up the Champs Élysées. Even Leonard and the American generals writhed with sense of insult as they watched. "The masses of infantry, most of them wearing spectacles, marched by the Arc de Triomphe, which was barricaded, and through the deserted streets of the once-gay city singing *"die Wacht am Rhein."* Had Leonard's daughters been present, they would have wept.

With some trepidation Mr. Jerome examined his house in the Boulevard Haussman. Its cellar had been blown open by a shell, but his art collection remained untouched. And Marie, the faithful maid, still waited with her mistress's packed trunks. Horrid scraps and minced rats had been her fare during the siege.

On his return to London Leonard found his daughters continued to mope at the tragedy of France. Clara, languid on a sofa recovering from fever, could not bear to listen to the stories of suffering that he had heard in Paris. Only one pastime restored her spirits. For Christmas Persigny had presented her with an autograph book, a fine volume, bound in green leather with her name in silver letters. His courtly note accompanying it read:

LONDON, *Xmas Day, 1870*

Dear Miss Jerome,
Knowing that you desire to form a collection of autographs of distinguished persons whom you have known in France, I am sending you this volume which is suitable for receiving autographs. I am adding a certain number of letters, the only ones I possess here, from which you can choose those you wish for your collection. Dear Miss Clara, this modest Christmas present brings the best wishes of your old friend.

Persigny.

Dear Miss Clara got busy with her pastepot. Her first entry was a note from the Prince Imperial. "Will you please forgive my negligence in the last few days? I am suffering from a slight indisposition. I got measles from a young lady with whom I danced a mazurka, and I really should not dance with any other girl."

In the hopes of stimulating Clara's return to health "the dear Duke" added various other letters to amuse her. Some of these seemed surprisingly indiscreet. Apparently Persigny could see no reason why he should not hand over to this young girl his own correspondence with Bismarck concerning the possible establishment of the Prince Imperial on the throne if the Emperor would consent to abdicate. Clara, as guileless as her old admirer, showed the collection to all and sundry, with the result that a mysterious envoy from the Emperor arrived at the hotel and asked for an interview with Mr. Jerome. Leonard then learned to his surprise that the girls he left innocently poring over their scrapbooks were playing with papers "dangerous to the Imperial dynasty."

Leonard was half-amused, half-annoyed. Collecting autographs had seemed impeccable as a young ladies' pastime. He strode into his dovecote and demanded that the special letters be torn out of the book and handed to his perturbed visitor who vanished forthwith. Clara remained pouting, with her lovely collection spoiled.

The Duc de Persigny then received a personal rebuke from the Emperor, who, from his secretary *le petit Piétri,* had obtained a full account of the contents of Miss Jerome's album; but the Duke offered other less compromising letters to replace these confiscated. Such was his infatuation with the Jerome household that he actually handed over the Emperor's letter scolding him for unauthorized attempts to come to an understanding with Bismarck. Written on fine paper with the imperial crown over a large *N,* this letter survives with its envelope, covered with German stamps on which the humiliating postmark *Wilhelmshohe* is plainly visible:

WILHELMSHOHE,

le 7 janvier 1871.

My dear Persigny,

I have received your letter of the first of January, and thank you for the prayers you offer for a better future. Without desiring to enter into a discussion of the ideas you express, I will say to you that nothing good can come from the confusion which is the result of individual efforts, made without discretion, and without authority. In fact I find it somewhat singular that any one should busy himself with the future of my son without taking account of my own intentions.

I know you have written to M. de Bismarck, who naturally has asked me if you have done so with my authority and in full accord with me. I have answered him that I have authorized nobody to busy himself with my interests, or those of my son, without first obtaining my consent.

Believe, my dear Persigny, in my friendship.

Napoleon.

Another slip of paper in the Emperor's handwriting showed a rough copy of the surrender at Sedan.

But Clara had learned prudence, and she never showed any more letters. They rambled on, the gentlemen with their crested note paper and their wishful thinking and their absolute sureness concerning an ultimate restoration. The King of Prussia might bring France to her knees, but he couldn't be cad enough to allow a *republican* government to remain in power!

Of all the letters that Clara retained for her scrapbook, the most interesting is from General de Paliakao, whom Eugenie had made head of her government and who consistently had given her the worst possible advice:

143

My dear Duke:
   I arrived in Ostend four days ago and found your address. Since our separation on the 7th I have remained in Belgium. I seize the opportunity to have a few words with you.

   Being threatened with arrest on September 4, I departed that evening and sought refuge at Namur, where twenty-four hours later I was joined by my wife and daughters.

   My chief aim in journeying to Namur was to be near Sedan, that I might learn the fate of my son, for whom I had great anxiety. After several days of inquiry, I at last learned that my son, after having been wounded at Sedan (a horse having been killed under him), was a prisoner at Cologne, as he would not accept the capitulation.

   I left Namur for Spa, and a sojourn there not being very comfortable in the winter, I established myself at Ostend, where I await events, the issue of which I cannot foresee.

   How I wish, my dear Duke, that my pen were clever enough to convey to you all the impressions I have received since the fatal Sedan. I have come to the point of asking myself how a disaster of such dimensions could be produced without the principal author of this lugubrious drama being buried under the corpses of his army.

   I had thought that it was easier to die than to suffer dishonour.

   The death of the Emperor at Sedan would have saved France, as well as his son; the capitulation has lost everything.

   Now that France has become the prey of foreign and domestic Vandals, how can this desolation of our unhappy country be brought to an end?

   Unless there should be a general war creating a division in Prussian politics, I do not see what side we can turn to. England appears to have abandoned us, and however the circumstances which cemented our alliance of 1856 might be reproduced for her, even then she could not count on our help, we have fallen so low.

I had offered my services to the government of the National defence, but I withdrew my offer as soon as I saw the government, to the eternal shame of France, call a Garibaldi to defend her.

On the other hand, accusations of treason threaten the generals who have served the Empire, and I am not willing to have my name bandied among all these ignominies.

Adieu, my dear Duke. If you will be so good as to send me news of yourself, my family and I will be happy indeed . . . for our hearts are full of gratitude.

Ever yours,
Général de Paliakao.*

This came well from a firebrand who had led the cry for war and been among those most responsible for the debacle. Having sent out an impossible order for MacMahon's army to join hands with that of Bazaine, Paliakao, in August, 1870, had been the first to perceive how expedient it would be if the Emperor "died at the head of his troops." No one realized that somber fact more clearly than Louis Napoleon himself and no one could have tried harder. But inconvenient as it might be, he still breathed, and neither Paliakao nor any of the other imperialists who insisted that it was good taste for an emperor to die when his cause failed seemed to think the same noble demise might have applied to themselves.

The Jerome girls felt strongly about this letter. Next to it in her scrapbook Jennie took care to quote General Changier who, although hostile to Napoleon III, said: "And he has been called 'coward.' When I remember that this man, tortured by a horrible disease, remained on horseback at Sedan an entire day,

---

* The title of Paliakao was derived from a town in China. The General had presented Eugenie with a string of black pearls from the summer palace.

watching disappear the prestige of France, his throne, his dynasty, and all the glory reaped at Sebastopol and in Lombardy, I cannot control myself."

The Emperor and his heart-broken, fourteen-year-old son had been discarded by history.

IN LONDON THE SUMMER OF 1871 was a sad one for imperial refugees: "Last year when the chestnuts came to flower we were at St. Cloud, as if one could have foreseen . . ."

Meanwhile, France passed through a period of bitterness. Civil war flared easily in the ashes of defeat. The peasants cried for peace and termination of chaos, but the Parisians, exasperated by the hunger, cold, and suffering they had been forced to endure, wanted a real revolution that would allow them to revenge themselves on the generals responsible for their incompetent defense. From fear and lack of understanding between capital and country grew up the sinister episodes of the Commune. The hysterical element of Paris tried to salve its own wounds by practicing massacre and pillage. Revolutionaries turned overnight into thieves and incendiaries. Leonard hurried back to Paris in order to pack up those Italian paintings that he had been collecting ever since Trieste. Clara insisted on accompanying him, and together they sorted their favorites, which were shipped to New York just before the riots of May 23, when a crowd set fire to the Tuileries. On the following day Clara hurried forth to see with her own eyes if the the rumors she had heard were true. The old palace where she had attended so many balls crumbled in smoke and flame while a rough crowd threw furniture out of the windows and held auctions on the lawn. To her amazement Clara saw Napoleon's dining service (of white porcelain with the golden *N* surmounted by an imperial crown) being sold in lots to the highest bidder. Without a moment's hesitation she joined the fray and raised her voice for one stack of plates after another. *Ah, ces Américains* . . . they had more money than anyone else. Who could bid against them? The crowd let her have them. There were better bargains than these old plates in any case; look, there were bolsters and feather beds being thrown from the top floor—and blankets and fine eiderdowns!

Clara was left alone, with her purchases lying around on the grass. Cinders floated through the air, blinding her eyes, and crash after crash marked the end of those old walls that had housed so many generations of French kings. The mob ran and roared in its hunt for household goods. For a time she watched the frenzy. So this was the Commune—a scramble for bargains! Then she looked around for some practical method of transporting the china back to her house. Men with wheel barrows were in much demand. Hiring one of them, she stacked the imperial dinner service on board and turned her back wistfully on the smouldering ruins. She never would dance there again. Better not to look.

Meanwhile, Leonard, in the Boulevard Haussman, anxiously awaited Clara's return. To his surprise she finally appeared in a state of disarray, blackened by cinders and accompanied by a small man pushing a large barrow from which stacks of plates seemed about to topple.

"What on *earth* have you been doing?"

"Look," she said, "the poor dear Emperor's best dinner set, handed out of the window, auctioned in the garden. . . . I got it, but don't ask me how."

She'd got it and she kept it. Leonard felt it would be embarrassing to allow the imperial monogram to appear at his table, but years later the set came into the possession of a grandson who had no need to entertain such scruples. French ministers and generals could not help evincing curiosity when they saw the unmistakable N on the dinner plates.

"How did these come into your possession?" they would inevitably ask. They could hardly have guessed the answer.*

Returning to London, the Jeromes cheered their family with promises for the following year, and when the heat grew intense in August Leonard took them all out of town. He chose a charming seaside village where he had long intended to spend a summer. This was Cowes, the yachting base on the Isle of Wight where the *Henrietta* had been received after her noble drive across the Atlantic. "In those days," wrote Jennie, "it was delightfully small and peaceful. . . . The Royal Yacht Squadron Club lawn did not resemble a perpetual garden party, or the roadstead a perpetual regatta. Yachts went in and out without fear of losing their moorings, and most of them belonged to the Royal Yacht Squadron. . . . Royalties could walk about and amuse themselves without being photographed or mobbed."

The Jeromes took a cottage and proceeded to enjoy expeditions to Shanklin Bay and Freshwater. One day a gentleman called when they were all out and left a card saying he would come again. "Le Comte de Pierre-fonds," they read. Who could it be? Next day the Emperor's secretary informed them that Napoleon and Eugenie had arrived on a visit. Pierre-fonds was the pseudonym that Napoleon generally used when he left his house at Chislehurst to travel around England.

"Shortly afterwards we were asked by their Majesties to go for an expedition around the Island. The party consisted of the

---

* This dinner service is used today by Sir Winston Churchill at Chartwell. The golden crowns are hardly scratched.

Emperor and Empress, the Prince Imperial, the Empress's nieces the Mesdemoiselles d'Albe, Prince Joachim Murat, the Duc d'Albe, a few Spaniards, and the suite, which was composed of one or two faithful followers. The expedition was rather a failure owing to the roughness of the sea, most of the party seeking 'the seclusion that the cabin grants.' The Mesdemoiselles d'Albe were desperately ill, and lay in a state of coma. But the Empress enjoyed the breeze. The Prince Imperial, full of life and spirits, chaffed everyone, some of his jokes falling rather flat on the Spaniards, who were feeling anything but bright, and evidently thought it no laughing matter. I can see now the Emperor leaning against the mast, looking old, ill, and sad. His thoughts could not have been other than sorrowful, and even in my young eyes, he seemed to have nothing to live for."

After Sedan, nothing indeed . . . except the precious future of his gallant little son; for him whose fourteen years were bright with honor and love of France, for him alone the Emperor would struggle a little longer.

Eugenie's spirits revived in a gale, while her pea-green followers wilted and drooped and the young Prince recovered for a few hours from the terrible brooding knowledge of his country's failure. He had charm and wit and dash. Leonie, three years younger, fell desperately in love.

Before returning to Chislehurst, his Majesty again called on the Jeromes. After this visit, with pity and distress the three girls watched him walking away down their garden path, a stumpy little man with a halting step, who walked as if in pain.

They never saw him again.

IN THE AUTUMN OF 1871 TENSION in Paris eased sufficiently for Leonard to bring his wife and two elder daughters back to Boulevard Haussman while little Leonie (to her intense displeasure) departed to school at Wiesbaden. With funereal exclamations the two Claras delved through their luggage, which had been packed up eighteen months previously. Out of date were the tulle ball gowns and the flowered bonnets intended for garden parties at Compiègne! It would be months before their interest in clothes could be revived. Meanwhile, Jennie finished off her education with an intensive study of music and languages in the continental fashion. Leonard repaired and restocked his shelled wine cellar and opened his house to dispense what hospitality he could to friends of prewar days, but French people were too weary and bruised to show much interest in sport.

Persigny, their "dear old Duke" (who was to die of depression and disappointment within the next year), also returned to Paris and spent long hours commiserating with his friends in the Jerome *salon*. To tell the truth he was becoming rather a bore, as people do when obsessed with a vanished past, but he had saved them from a most unpleasant experience in the siege and the Jeromes were loyal friends, even if they no longer ran quite so eagerly to meet his carriage at the door.

They all found life extremely *triste*. Jennie wrote: "Ruins everywhere: the sight of the Tuileries and the Hotel de Ville made me cry. St. Cloud, the scene of many pleasant expeditions, was a thing of the past, the lovely chateau razed to the ground.

And if material Paris was damaged, the social fabric was even more so. In vain we tried to pick up the threads. Some of our friends were killed, others ruined or in mourning, and all broken-hearted and miserable, hiding in their houses and refusing to be comforted."

Jennie, who had dreamed of playing a star part at the imperial court, now stood in the Place de la Concorde where the statue of the lost city of Strasbourg was swathed in crepe and felt the melancholy of baffled youth surge through her heart. Clara's attempts to renew her romance with the Marquis de Tamisier were still frustrated by Mrs. Jerome, and the only interesting visit paid seems to have been to the Duc de Praslin at his beautiful Chateau de Vaux-Praslin.

"Our host took us all over the huge building, pointing out everything of historical interest, until we came to an ornamented door, before which he paused, but did not enter. 'La chambre du feu Duc de Praslin,' he said in a grim voice, and then passed on.

"This was the room of the late Duke, his father, who had murdered his wife. . . . The Duchess's unfounded jealousy of the governess drove the Duke to this terrible act. On the way home we discussed the details with bated breath . . . how the Duchess had been first stabbed, then smothered under the canopy of the bed, which the Duke pulled down on her; how the Duke was tried by his peers and sentenced to death, but the night before the execution, was found dead in his cell, friends having smuggled poison to him." *

---

* It has since been established that he was smuggled out of his cell and lived for years in England supported by his family. Greater fame fell on the governess than on the much pitied Duke, for at the trial she pleaded her cause so eloquently that she left the court a brave attractive figure without the slightest aspersion on her character. Eighty years later she was brilliantly portrayed in Rachel Field's *All This and Heaven Too* (New York, The Macmillan Company, 1938). The Praslin descendants suffered severely, however, from this scandal. For eighty years they were, a Frenchman told me, "depreciated" and made no big marriages.

When in the early summer Leonard swept his daughters back to the carefree atmosphere of Cowes, they could not but rejoice at leaving their once loved Paris in her period of gloom and disillusion.

Having established his family in their "sweet little cottage" with its trim garden facing the sea, Leonard departed for New York. He traveled by steamboat now, and was teaching himself to use the weeks spent each year on the Atlantic as work periods in which he could study and invent new schemes. His financial flair was fading; the effort to make money bored him more and more. Only the fight to keep horse racing on a high level had his interest. He had to withstand attacks from the dishonest, who were eager to make a racket out of the sport, and from anti-gambling Puritan and Quaker elements. "I fight one side with my right hand, and the other more persuasively with my left."

Meanwhile the New York *Times* was reaching the climax of its battle with the Tweed ring. People long considered invincible were being systematically harpooned.

Briefly events had run thus: Throughout 1870 and 1871 a consecutive attack had been maintained accusing Tweed of using his official position to loot the citizens of New York. Tweed answered the *Times's* allegations that he had scraped some fifty million dollars into the ring's private money box by arranging for six well-known New Yorkers to undertake an inquiry and make a public report. This eventually read: "We have come to the conclusion and certify, that the financial affairs of the city under the charge of the Comptroller are administered in a correct and faithful manner." John Jacob Astor III, supposedly the richest heir in America, headed the committee and added his name to the impressive signatures at the foot of this document.

It had looked as if Tweed must remain established in power and piety forever. Six months later, in July, 1871, just at the time when Leonard was sailing back across the Atlantic in the yacht *Dauntless,* a small revolt occurred in Tammany Hall. One Sheriff O'Brian was refused his expenses, and after an unsuccessful attempt to dislodge Tweed from leadership, O'Brian deserted into the enemy's camp. He delivered to the *Times* a mass of transcripts from the account books of the Comptroller, which flatly contradicted the Astor report and finally revealed that the Tweed ring had embezzled not fifty, but about seventy million dollars. The figures were so vast that all the chartered accountants in New York City could hardly work them out.

At Tweed's trial the jury disagreed. They argued that one man could not be responsible for such grand-scale extortion. Thousands of respectable New Yorkers must have tolerated, if not condoned, the ring or it could hardly have reached such dimensions, but no names were published. At a second trial Tweed was sentenced to twelve years in prison. One million dollars of the vanished seventy was retrieved, and returned to New York City. The *Times* knew it had won the greatest victory in newspaper history.

August Belmont never blinked an eye or said a word concerning his appearance on the Tammany platform. It was better perhaps to forget such associates, when Tweed had been placed in jail and Jim Fisk had been shot to death in the Grand Central Hotel by the lover of his beautiful, faithless mistress. Mr. Belmont found more pleasurable memories in his art collections, in the patronage of opera, the running of Jerome Park, and the surveillance of that famous chef whom he commanded to cook a splendid meal every single day to keep the fellow's hand adroit.

Leonard had not been able to put his full energies into the Tweed battle but he felt proud that he had owned a quarter of the *Times* for over ten years.

A final commentary on the affair has been written by Lloyd

Morris * ". . . it could be surmised that John Jacob Astor III's acquaintance with accounting had merely suffered a temporary lapse when, with his distinguished associates, he certified to the sound condition of the city's finances. The death of his father, William Astor, in 1875, left him the wealthiest man in the United States. He often rewrote telegrams to save one word, and in many other ways was known to keep his vast fortune in excellent repair." Ways which, alas, were unknown to Leonard Jerome.

LEONARD ALLOWED NO HINT OF fresh financial troubles to reach his family. Their happy summer days remained intact. Cowes was, in fact, "delightfully small and peaceful" in the manner most likely to please Mrs. Jerome, who since the fall of Paris had taken to behaving somewhat in the manner of an exiled queen. Her lovely elder daughters were presented to the Prince and Princess of Wales at the Royal Yacht Squadron Ball during Regatta Week and allowed to go to a few exclusive parties. They took it for granted they should head the elite in any country where they chose to alight.

In those days it was usual, when invited out to dinner, for young ladies to take their music with them so that during the evening they could be asked by inwardly groaning guests to play their "pieces." After a few coy refusals they would relent sufficiently to sing a ditty or pick out the tune that some old governess had drummed into their rhythmless fingers for such occasions.

* Lloyd R. Morris, *Incredible New York* (New York, Random House, 1951).

English girls, brought up backstairs in large country houses with the dogs and horses, were usually painfully shy, and the series of tremulous encores necessitated by politeness conveyed their anguish only too adequately to the already squirming audience.

Human nature being as it is, Clara and Jennie could hardly have been expected not to glow with satisfaction when asked for *their* pieces. During the last year they had been concentrating on the mastery of piano duets, so that without a trace of nervousness they would sit down side by side, look at each other for a moment, and with expert precision start on Schumann *à quatre mains*.

"Such a lovely sight it made, those two young heads, one blonde and one dark, bent raptly over the keys," remembered an admirer years later. And the inevitable triumph of the next half hour might have elated any mother save Mrs. Jerome, who wondered if it was ladylike to play *quite* so well!

No such thoughts entered the minds of the guests, who had arranged themselves as comfortably as possible for the customary period of pain. The musical remained riveted; the unmusical (and there were many among English gentlemen) listened openmouthed, unavoidably aware that with all that pounding and so many notes being hit at the same time some kind of jolly good show must be going on at the piano.

At any rate, it seemed impossible not to notice the Misses Jerome. Their American vitality allied with continental culture created an atmosphere at every party they attended. Certainly Clara and Jennie regarded themselves as no mean artists, but so arduous had been the training leading to this standard that they accepted ovation as merely being their due for having practiced four hours a day. For all Leonard's daughters music had become part of the air they breathed. He rejoiced in their gifts, but their mother listened less to chords and trills than to the gasps and exclamations that her girls' performance elicited. Jennie worried her in particular. She played with such fire and abandon; was it really becoming?

Having sought by cold baths and rigorous exercise to impart even greater health to her daughters than they already inherited, Mrs. Jerome found she had succeeded beyond expectations. They now chaffed like race horses in training. Every hour of the day had to be crammed with activities. "The girls are just like Leonard," she wrote "never, never tired . . . what does one do about it?" Perhaps Clara and Jennie became conceited despite their mother's restraining efforts. Certainly these two exotic young creatures did not notice anything extraordinary in their easy entry into that hidebound English society whose portals had so far remained closed to all not born and brought up within its ranks. Accepting their social popularity as natural, neither daughter dreamed that the key which opened this narrow world to them might be Leonard Jerome's reputation as a sportsman. His sailing exploits and his efforts to establish horse racing in America had given him renown in sporting circles throughout the world, but few men receive fair due in their own home.

He had sufficient philosophy not to be hurt by the evaluation of youth, and he did not eat his heart out because now he was regarded simply as a provider of pretty dresses and presents. To the end, he could laugh at his daughters' sense of their own importance.

He let them frolic through the summer along with those poor, hounded royalties all so "eager to throw off ceremony." No hint of his private struggle must reach Clara's ears. "She hates money, or thinks she does," he remarked jokingly. "I've never discussed business matters with her." He had long ago settled various trusts in her name so that she could not be too seriously affected by his own speculations. But these grueling days in Wall Street left him tired, and hungry for family news. He longed for letters, which his daughters with the selfishness of their years were too engrossed with their own pleasures to compose. But alone in his large, empty town house Leonard grew lonely. An exhortation to write more penned on August 7, 1873, used the family pet names pleadingly:

> *Mrs. Clit, Miss Clarita, and Miss Jennie.*
> Dearly beloved, it is nearly two weeks since I had a letter. You must be sure to write me particulars of all that is going on. I have no doubt you will see many nice people and will have Cowes all to yourselves as far as Americans are concerned. Did you get the tent from London? And do you make it lively and have you secured the Villa Rosetta for another year? etc. I rather like the idea of Cowes next summer and a yacht. Don't forget while sitting under your own vine and eating up your own fig tree that I am awfully disappointed if I don't get my weekly letters.

He needed affection to supplement his nervous energy, but only little Leonie remained a diligent, if rather mournful, correspondent from her school in Wiesbaden; and even her pages complained of lack of news from Cowes and guilelessly expressed a hope that her birthday on August 15 would not pass unnoticed.

Leonard, of course, remembered to send a gift. He longed for her now, for her funny little face and impish expressions and quaint remarks. But he had to banish even the image of her from his mind, for a hundred dreary papers lay on his desk and must be read. The demands of finance did not allow time for European holidays, and in any case the Flash Age was ending. Owing to mad speculation and the overbuilding of railways, a commercial depression was setting in.

After the Civil War Henry Clews had wholeheartedly proclaimed the importance of helping the South to recover its lost wealth by diverting foreign capital into Southern investments. He built up schemes for regenerating and revivifying the agri-

157

cultural and manufacturing interests of the defeated states. Leonard, sharing these views, had invested heavily. Now a sudden panic had revealed Georgia securities as worthless, although she had credit abroad. The immense losses caused the failure of Henry Clews' firm, and after months of protest and accusation the whole Southern Relief plan seemed to be a fiasco. Jerome had to add this loss to six hundred thousand dollars invested in Indiana bonds. Mr. Hudson, the official agent, had sometime previously obtained the state's official stamp and used it dishonestly. Eventually Indiana disowned its agent, and Jerome's money was regarded as gilt-edged investment.*

During the financial upheavals of the seventies, Leonard reckoned a man of his standing must be able to stand blows even on this scale without altering his way of life. He was still seen at the clubs and at his race track, laughing, talking to all, quick with flippant repartee; but a description has been preserved of the arrival of the final disastrous news.

"At last, one evening, while he was entertaining some friends at dinner, a telegram was brought to him, which he opened, read, and laid by the side of his plate. When the dinner was over he rose and asked pardon for the impoliteness of reading the telegram, 'but, gentlemen,' he continued, 'it is a message in which you are all interested. The bottom has fallen out of stocks and I

---

* A newspaper clipping states: "In 1862 the agent of the State of Indiana swindled Jerome out of $600,000 by the unauthorized use of Indiana 5 per cent bonds. The agent of the state, duly appointed by the Governor and Senate, having his office at 20 Wall Street, was entrusted with these bonds which were duly executed at Indianapolis, the Secretary's signature countersigned by the Comptroller and bearing the great seal of State. These bonds were then hypothecated until the aggregated sum reached $600,000, the agent assuring Jerome before he made any advance that the bonds were all right. Indeed, so clean apparently was everything about them that the chief place for reborrowing on them throughout the year was Winslaw, Lancier financial agents of the State of Indiana. The state repudiated the acts of its agent and, as an individual is not allowed to sue a state, Mr. Jerome was, and still is, unable to collect the debt."

am a ruined man. But your dinner is paid for, and I did not want to disturb you while you were eating it.' There was a babble of questions; then a sudden scattering, and Mr. Jerome was left with his telegram. He has chosen to remain alone ever since. Only a very few persons are now admitted to his companionship and fewer still to his intimacy." *

"Ruined," as he called himself, Mr. Jerome was still a wealthy man. He had settled a large fortune upon his wife; he recovered a fortune from the wreck of his speculations; he had made a fortune since by his investments. But in Wall Street he no longer ruled, and that to him meant ruin.

At last Leonard Jerome realized that his career as a financier was over. Long ago he had ceased to take the game seriously, and yet the irrevocable knowledge came hard.

In the house where he now lived alone the gas lamps were burning brightly. A letter from his wife lay on the hall table. He took it up to read in bed. But the pages covered with tremulous spidery writing contained no soothing good-night message. His tired eyes deciphered the words "hasty . . . rash . . . headstrong . . . unconsidered . . . impulsive. You must return to England by the next boat."

They had only known each other three days. The young man had not yet started any career, and there were other reasons to be written later underlining the general unwisdom of this impetuous decision.

Jennie, his precious, beautiful Jennie, was engaged to be married.

---

* Stephen Fiske, *Off-hand Portraits of Prominent New Yorkers* (New York, G. R. Lockwood and Son, 1884).

THE PERSON WHOSE ADVENT ON the Jerome horizon had spread this sudden conflagration of feeling has been described by a most adequate filial pen: "Behold him now at twenty-three, a man grown, markedly reserved in his manner to acquaintances, utterly unguarded to his intimate friends, something of a dandy in his dress, an earnest sportsman, an omnivorous reader, moving with a jaunty step through what were, in those days, the very select circles of fashion and club-land, seeking the pleasures of the Turf and town." *

Lord Randolph Churchill had, up to this date, made no particular imprint beyond that of the ardent sportsman admired by his caste.

The younger son of the seventh Duke of Marlborough by Lady Frances Vane, eldest daughter of the third Marquis of Londonderry, he had been brought up in the fashion traditional for boys of the English nobility.

The splendor of Blenheim Palace was his background, a nursery wing in that vast structure meant "home," and the park with its oak trees, which had witnessed the hunting of Plantagenet kings, was his playground. Educated at boarding school after the age of eight, he had, on leaving Eton, made a continental tour before entering Merton College, Oxford. The university lay only a few miles from Blenheim, so that he could often bring his friends home and offer them the sporting delights of an enormous

---

* Winston Spencer Churchill, *Lord Randolph Churchill* (London, Macmillan and Company, Ltd., 1906).

estate. "His nature responded to the glory and romance of Oxford; and in its cloistered courts, so rich in youth and history, he found a scheme of life more varied, tolerant, and real than any he had ever known." For three years he had studied moderately, hunted zealously, and made some lasting friends "not many in number, but staunch and true."

His Eton acquaintance, Lord Dalmeny * often accompanied him on visits to Blenheim where, among other conservative statesmen, the boys met Prime Minister Disraeli, who took a particular interest in the young. "Dizzy" would talk and joke with them by the hour. In such an environment, with this company at their disposition during the formative years, it seems hardly strange that both youths developed almost casually a natural brilliance of expression. These boyhoods contrasted severely with that of Leonard Jerome. Within the precincts of Blenheim Palace no inkling could have arisen of the inducements of that hard American system which encouraged a poor boy to work his way through college, ignoring social status. In England a classical education was dealt out automatically to boys of the upper class. Often they loathed it and scorned scholarship and its fruits forever, but Latin and Greek remained a class privilege. The Duke's son was not likely to find a waiter sitting next to him at lectures.

In the serenity of Blenheim park studded by thousand-year-old oak trees, among its legends and its history the children of the Dukes of Marlborough were raised in consciousness of their heritage. In that vast palace presented to his illustrious ancestor by the English nation, at the table of his parents who formally entertained the eminent Conservative politicians of the day, young Randolph felt the ease of his birthright. A seat in Parliament waited ready for him if he wished. Woodstock, lying practically within his father's demesne would be his whenever he

---

* Afterward Lord Rosebery, Liberal Prime Minister.

cared to stand. His name alone assured that. Against a Churchill no outsider ever had a chance. To the working and middle classes the path of young Lord Randolph must have looked easy; his forbears had nobly fought for England, he inherited the glory of John Churchill's name, and, unless he did "something dreadful" or turned Liberal, he could rest assured his world would regard him as an interesting, distinguished person. He ought to have been happy. But contrary impulses shadowed his mind.

The Duke had determined that Randolph *must* stand for Parliament because it would ensure Woodstock being held for the Conservatives. "No one could possibly have so good a chance as the young cadet, born and bred on the soil, who knew half the farmers and local magnates personally, whose excursions with the harriers had made him familiar with all parts of the constituency, and whose gay and stormy attractiveness had won him a host of sworn allies.

"Yet he had often in words and in letters expressed a disinclination for public life. It is curious to notice how, even in the days of buoyant, unconquered youth, moods of depression cast their shadows across his path."

Such was the situation and state of Lord Randolph Churchill when in August, 1873, he went to Cowes for the pleasures of sea and sailing, then much in vogue.

Among the "little balls" which Mrs. Jerome allowed her daughters to grace with their presence was one in honor of the Tsarevitch and the Tsarevna, given by the officers of the cruiser *Ariadne,* then lying as guardship in the Roads. To this festivity, not unnaturally, "all the pleasure seekers who frequent the Solent at this season of year made haste to go in boats and launches from the shore and from the fleet." Merriest and loveliest of the butter-flies who flitted out to the cruiser that evening were the Jerome sisters in their white tulle frocks adorned with fresh flowers. Both loved to dance and were expert in every step, having been schooled nearly as carefully in this line as at the piano. Their ease and grace, their vivacity and shining eyes, made them the cynosure of the crowded ship's ballroom. Lord Randolph Churchill, usually bored at dances, took one look and began to busily search for a friend who could arrange an introduction. Jennie's dark eyes smiled at him from a host of admirers. He detested dancing of all kinds, but his only chance to further their acquaintance lay in some kind of terpsichorean effort. He led her boldly to the floor.

After a formal quadrille in which he was not quite sure of the steps, Jennie could hardly express sorrow when he asked her to sit out. She soon discovered that he talked better than he danced, and though her eager feet hated to miss one moment of a waltz, some vibrant quality in this young man with the prominent eyes and changeable expression held her interest. Discovering that Lord Randolph was not shy and made no secret of his feelings, she began to sparkle in the effort to parry his wit with her own. Up until this evening men had merely been dancing partners. She welcomed one who was not. That night as casually as possible she asked Mama to invite Lord Randolph to dinner on the following evening, and Mrs. Jerome sent a note—though not without a look of interrogation. She had not seen that look on Jennie's face before.

"The dinner was good, the company gay and attractive, and with the two young ladies chatting and playing duets at the piano the evening passed very pleasantly. . . . That very night Miss Jerome told her laughing and incredulous sister of a presentiment that their new friend was the man she would marry; and Lord Randolph confided to Colonel Edgecumbe, who was of the party, that he admired the two sisters, and meant, if he could, to make 'the dark one' his wife."

On the following day they met again—according to their own account "by accident"—and went for a walk. Once again

Mrs. Jerome was asked by her daughter to proffer an invitation to dinner. "Are we not inviting that young gentleman rather often?" she queried. But he came. "That night—the third of their acquaintance—was a beautiful night, warm and still, with the lights of the yachts shining on the water and the sky bright with stars. After dinner they found themselves alone together in the garden and brief courtship notwithstanding, he proposed and was accepted."

The tiny garden bathed in moonlight, the sea, the stars, Jennie with her flushed cheeks and curved red lips and deep eyes, even more beautiful now that she was in love than before . . . with these intoxications young Randolph lost his head completely. He returned to Blenheim "shaken by alternating emotions of joy and despondency. He had never been in love before, and the force and volume of the tide swept him altogether off his feet. At one moment he could have been preferred; the next he trembled lest all his hopes should be shattered by circumstances unforeseen. Nor, indeed, was his anxiety without reason; for many and serious obstacles had yet to be encountered."

In a letter written on August 20 from Blenheim Palace he sought somewhat lengthily to explain to his father the amazing feelings which beset him and which he was quite sure lovers had never known before.

. . . You won't feel any annoyance with me for not having consulted you before saying anything to her. I really meant to have done so; but on the night before I was leaving Cowes (Friday) my feelings of sorrow at parting from her were more than I could restrain, and I told her all. I did not say anything to her mother, but I believe that she did after I was gone: for she wrote to me just as I was starting (I did not, after all, leave Cowes till the Monday) and she said in her letter that her mother would not hear of it. That I am at a loss to understand.

I told Mama when I got here and should have written at

once to tell you; but I was so wretched and miserable at leaving thus, I was quite incapable of writing quietly.

I now write to tell you of it all, and to ask you whether you will be able to increase my allowance to some extent to put me in the position to ask Mrs. Jerome to let me become her daughter's future husband. I enclose you her photograph, and will only say about her that she is as good as she is beautiful, and that by her education and bringing-up she is in every way qualified to fill any position.

She has an elder sister, and one younger, who is not yet out. Mr. Jerome is a gentleman who is obliged to live in New York to look after his business. I do not know what it is. He is reputed to be very well off, and his daughters, I believe, have very good fortunes, but I do not know anything for certain. He generally comes over for three or four months every year. Mrs. Jerome has lived in Paris for several years and has educated her daughters there. They go out in Society there and are very well known.

I have told you all I know about them at present. You have always been very good to me, and done as much and more for me always than I had any right to expect; and with any arrangement that you may at any time make for me I shall be perfectly contented and happy. I see before me now a very happy future, almost in one's grasp. In the last year or so I feel I have lost a great deal of what energy and ambition I possessed, and an idle and comparatively useless life has at times appeared to me to be the pleasantest; but if I were married to her whom I have told you about, if I had a companion, such as she would be, I feel sure, to take an interest in one's prospects and career, and to encourage me to exertions and to doing something towards making a name for myself, I think that I might become, with the help of Providence, all and perhaps more than you had ever wished and hoped for me. On the other hand, if anything should occur to prevent my fondest hopes and wishes being realized (a possibility which I dare not and cannot bring myself to think of), how dreary and uninteresting would life become to me. No one goes through what I have lately gone through without its leaving a strong impress and bias on their character and future. Time might of course, partially efface the impression and recollection of feelings so strong as those I have tried to describe to you but in the interval the best years of one's life would be going, and one's energies and hopes would become blunted and deadened.

I will not allude to her. I believe and am convinced that she loves me as fully, and as strongly if possible, as I do her; and when two people feel towards each other what we do, it becomes, I know, a great responsibility for anyone to assist in either bringing about or thwarting a union so closely desired by each.

Goodbye. I have written to you all I have done, all I feel, and all I know.

Anxiously wishing for an answer from you,

I remain,

Ever your most affectionate son,

Randolph.

"The Duke was very seriously disturbed at the news of his son's intention and declined to commit himself to any expression of approval until he had made searching inquiry into the standing and circumstances of the Jerome family. He deplored the precipitancy with which the decision had been taken. 'It is not likely,' he wrote upon August 31, 'that at present you can look at anything except from your own point of view; but persons from the outside cannot but be struck with the unwisdom of your proceedings, and the uncontrolled state of your feelings which completely paralyses your judgment.' His rebuke was supported by his wife, who urged affectionate counsels of caution, patience, and self-restraint, and was pointed up by a set of witty and satirical verses from his brother, Lord Blandford, setting forth the unhappy fate of those who 'marry in haste and repent at leisure.' " *

---

* Winston Spencer Churchill, *Lord Randolph Churchill* (London, Macmillan and Company, Ltd., 1906).

Meanwhile, Jennie contended with the difficulties raised by her own family. Randolph's surprise that Mrs. Jerome "would not hear of it" sprang from his ignorance of that lady's character. Quite as firmly as the Duke and Duchess of Marlborough she distrusted love at first sight, and the violence with which these two young people had, after three days, affirmed the *eternal* aspect of their feelings only caused her to fear the opposite. Concerning marriage proposals she had always maintained a most cautious outlook. No one seemed good enough for *her* daughters, and as a younger son Lord Randolph did not appear a tremendous catch when the peers of France had circled around her eldest girl. He was at least a Protestant, but for the moment neither party appeared able to express more than a vague hope of allowances from fond parents which would allow the marriage to take place soon.

Mrs. Jerome did all she could to cool her hot-headed daughter, but when she realized the Duke and Duchess were hesitating to give consent to their son's marriage, her indignation knew no bounds. She wrote furiously to Leonard, and her letter crossed one of his giving a conditional assent to Jennie's engagement. Leonard had long experience of human nature. He deplored the daily scenes and storms and tears that he knew must be engulfing the previously contented little household at Rosetta Cottage. Not daring to leave New York for financial reasons, he had sat back and given the matter that calm consideration of which mothers are often incapable in matrimonial matters. He wrote advising her to soothe Jennie and let things take a slow course. But the moment he heard of the Duke's opposition he angrily cabled, "My consent withdrawn."

In the midst of his scattered fortune, with long days of work necessary to retrieve a few hundred thousands, Leonard Jerome rose up in fury. *He* might put questions to a future son-in-law, but none had the right to query his daughter! The great name of Marlborough left him cold. Leonard had, in his time, known many European dukes and duchesses and on the whole found they impressed him less than they impressed themselves. While the pride of a haughty Yankee flared in New York, chill bewilderment descended in Blenheim Palace. What exactly *were* Americans? And did one *marry* them?

At the end of August, 1873, Mrs. Jerome shut down the Villa Rosetta and took her daughters back to Paris. She forbade Jennie to answer Randolph's letters, and the Marlboroughs learned to their surprise that American mothers can be extremely high and mighty. As a result of Clara's high-handed action Randolph seethed for two weeks without news and created an atmosphere of tension so intolerable to his own parents that the Duke was soon only too glad to acquiesce to a formal engagement of one year. At Randolph's request he wrote a soothing letter to Mrs. Jerome and she, holding smelling salts in one hand and writing cables with the other, decided to ask Leonard to cancel his cancellation of the original conditional assent.

Jennie had been threatening to lose her looks; Randolph, his mind. Now they became normal people again. With the serene superiority of triumphant lovers, they took up pens.

"In this field, the young lady had a great advantage. The placid succession of the duties and amusements of country life, the round of shooting parties, the varying totals of slaughtered hares and pheasants, the mornings on the Woodstock bench, and descriptions of relations and county folk, however vivacious, were inadequate materials to set against days spent in Paris during the autumn of 1873, when the gossip of the world was reviving after the gag of the war, when Bazaine was on trial for his life, when Gambetta declaimed in the Assembly, and when the drawing rooms, even of foreigners, were full of Royalist and Bonapartist whisperings. For the most part, his letters were strictly confined to the subject of main importance. They told over and over again, in the forcible, homely English of which he was a natural master, the oldest story in the world. Indeed, but for the contributions of Miss Jerome, the correspondence would certainly have lacked variety." *

On September 23, 1873, Randolph wrote joyously from Blenheim:

> . . . I cannot tell you what pleasure and happiness your letter gives me: it makes me feel quite a different being, so you really must not threaten me with a long silence. You certainly have great powers of perception, and I cannot but own that there is a good deal of truth in what you say about my being one moment very despairing and another moment very sanguine. I cannot help it: I was made so.
>
> My father has been away for a few days, and yesterday I got a 'piece' from him on the subject of his consent. After a good deal of unnecessary rigmarole and verbosity he says:
> "The great question is still unsolved, whether you and the young lady who has gained your affections are, or can be, after a few days' acquaintance, sufficiently aware of your own minds to venture on the step which is to bind you together for life. What I have now to say is that if I am to believe that your future is really bound up in your marriage with Miss Jerome you must show me the proof of it by bringing it to the test of time. I will say no more to you

---

* Winston Spencer Churchill, *Lord Randolph Churchill* (London, Macmillan and Company, Ltd., 1906).

on this subject for the present, but if this time next year you come and tell me that you are both of the same mind we will receive Miss Jerome as a daughter, and, I need not say, in the affection you could desire for your wife."

Now these are his words, but I do not mind telling you that it is all humbug about waiting a year. I could, and would, wait a good deal more than a year, but I do not mean to, as it is not the least necessary; for though we have only known each other a short time, I know we both know our own minds well enough, and I wrote a very long and diplomatic letter to my father yesterday, doing what I have done before, contradicting him and arguing with him, and I hope, persuading him that he has got very wrong and foolish ideas in his head. You see, both he and my mother have set their hearts on my being member for Woodstock. It is a family borough, and for years and years a member of the family has sat for it. The present member is a stranger, though a Conservative, and is so unpopular that he is almost sure to be beaten if he were to stand; and the fact of a Radical sitting for Woodstock is perfectly insupportable to my family. It is for this that they have kept me idle ever since I left Oxford, waiting for a dissolution. Well, as I told you the other day, a dissolution is sure to come almost before the end of the year. I have two courses open to me: either to refuse to stand altogether unless they consent to my being married immediately afterwards; or else, and this is still more Machiavellian and deep, to stand, but at the last moment to threaten to withdraw and leave the Radical to walk over. All tricks are fair in love and war. . . .

A month later he was writing to Miss Jerome with still more confidence:

    . . . I was so happy to see your handwriting again: it is the next best thing to seeing you. As you will have seen from my letter of Friday, we have no cause now to be disappointed or to be in bad spirits; everything goes on as favourably as we could expect, and my father does not wish for a moment to prevent my seeing you as often as I can, and has promised to give his consent to our marriage when he is sure we are fond of each other. As to the year, I have every right to say that I do not think they will insist on it. . . .

The clouds have all cleared away, and the sky is bluer than I have ever seen it since I first met you at Cowes. It is exactly six weeks tomorrow since we met on board the *Ariadne,* and I am sure I seem to have lived six years. How I do bless that day, in spite of all the worry and bother that has come since; and I am sure you will not regret it. I have not had a further conversation with my father since I wrote to you, for I think it is best to leave things for the present as they are. Our early golden dreams of being married in December won't quite become realised, but still it won't be very long to wait; and I shall be able to see you from time to time, and write as often as I like; in fact, we can be regularly engaged, and all the world may know it. . . .

It is curious what an effect books have on me; I have two old favourites. When I feel very cross and angry I read Gibbon, whose profound philosophy and easy though majestic writing soon quiets me down, and in an hour I feel at peace with all the world. When I feel very low and desponding I read Horace, whose thorough epicureanism, quiet maxims, and beautiful verse are most tranquillising. Of late I have had to have frequent recourse to my two friends, and they have never failed me. I strongly recommend you to read some great works or histories; they pass the time, and prevent you from worrying or thinking too much about the future. Novels, or even travels, are rather unsatisfactory, and do one no good, because they create an unhealthy excitement, which is bad for anyone. I wonder whether you will understand all this, or only think me rather odd.

There are three new elections to come off, owing to death vacancies; and if they go against the Government, as they very probably will, we are sure to have a dissolution, and then I shall become member for Woodstock. But, after all, public life has no great charms for me, as I am naturally very quiet, and hate bother and publicity, which, after all, is full of vanity and vexation of spirit. Still, it will all have greater attractions for me if I think it will encourage me to keep up to the mark.

I hope your sister is quite well, comforts you, and sticks up for me when you abuse me to her or doubt me. . . .

Meanwhile the Jerome sisters followed their intent and interesting life. Together they went to the trial of Maréchal Bazaine at Versailles, which took place in "a long low room filled to suffocation with a curious crowd many of whom were women. A raised platform, a table covered with green baize and holding a bottle of water, a few chairs arranged in semicircles, completed the *mise-en-scène,* which seemed rather a poor one for the trial for life or death of a Marshal of France."

Clara had not set eyes on Bazaine since that far-off country house party at Compiègne three years before, when his wife's red gown had caused deeper sensation than the rumors of war with Prussia. Now she saw him, a disgraced commander-in-chief, led in to face the Duc d'Aumale, president of the accusing court. Jennie writes, "All eyes turned on him, and some of the women jumped on their chairs, levelling their opera glasses at the unfortunate man. This was promptly put a stop to by the gendarmes present, who pulled the offenders down unceremoniously by their skirts. *'Fi donc!'* I heard a gendarme say, *'Ce n'est pas gentil';* nor was it."

Bazaine sat impassive, even while Maitre Lachaud, his advocate, making a curious defense at one moment, pointed with a dramatic gesture to the accused, exclaiming, *"Mais, regardez-le donc! Ce n'est pas un traître, c'est un imbécile!"*

The trial lacked the elements of reality. France was only chasing the most obvious scapegoat. Bazaine, found guilty, received a death sentence which was commuted to twenty years' imprisonment, and the authorities permitted him to escape some months later. It seemed unbelievable he had ever been a real marshal or commanded a real army, but perhaps the dead slept better in the knowledge that a fool, rather than a traitor, had led them. The trial gave sharpness to Jennie's facile pen, and soon she received a scolding for using the verb *prorogue* incorrectly. Instead of submitting with meekness to this reprimand, she hurried to a young friend, Count de Fénelon, whose name should have made him an authority on word usage, and secured his backing.

This was not the manner in which Lord Randolph, hot from the chase of foxes over Oxfordshire fences, expected his future wife to receive literary instruction. He wrote:

> . . . Hang *le petit* Fénelon, little idiot! What do I care for him? He may be a very good authority about his own beastly language, but I cannot for a moment submit to him about English. . . . To prorogue means to suspend something for a definite time, to be resumed again in exactly the same state, condition, and circumstances. Therefore, to talk about proroguing the Marshal's powers would mean that they were to be suspended for a certain time and then resumed again exactly as before. Parliament is prorogued, L'Assemblée is prorogued; that does not in the least mean that the powers of either are lengthened or increased in any way, but that they are temporarily suspended.

"What a very English letter!" commented Mrs. Jerome, while Jennie, confused but valiant, maintained her point and continued to quote the Count.

By December Randolph had won a consent from both sides to visit his betrothed. He ended a letter with:

"I am looking forward particularly to utterly suppressing and crushing *le petit* Fénelon. We must really, tho', drop this argument when I am with you, as it is likely to become a heated one, I fear. We will therefore 'prorogue' it."

Lord Randolph intended to arrive in Paris with a ring, not a dictionary.

During the months of Jennie's courtship Leonard remained glued to his responsibilities in New York. The times were bad for speculators. The Vice-President of the United States, cabinet officers, and a future President had been involved in the misappropriation of forty-four million dollars from the Union Pacific Railroad through a setup called the *Crédit Mobilier*. Since the Union Pacific was sponsored and financed by the United States, the whole country suffered from the crash of its stocks. Five thousand other commercial enterprises collapsed, and panic rocked the nation.

All financiers lost heavily during 1873, and Leonard Jerome was among them. President Grant summoned a conference of great business brains to give him advice. "Building railroads from nowhere to nowhere is not a legitimate business," remarked old Commodore Vanderbilt. Five bleak years followed.

After long deliberation Leonard decided to pack up his art collection and ship it back to Clara, who appeared to be permanently settled in Paris. He could not run the house in Madison Square without her, nor did he wish to. The Raphael and early masters they had bought during the fifties in Italy were crated and shipped back to Europe. On November 22, 1873, the *Ville de Havre,* in which they had been consigned, met with a collision at sea off the Azores. The ship went down with large loss of life, and no treasures could be salvaged. The Jerome collection, which had received scant appreciation in New York, sank uncatalogued and uninsured. Clara had been longing for her paintings: "They were like old friends, but one must think only of the poor people who died."

Leonard wrote sadly, but the girls were immersed in other interests, in music and politics.

Jennie showed her capacity for maintaining the urgent pace that had once been characteristic of her father. She kept up her studies, attended concerts, read avidly in three languages, and, as Leonard said, "formed original, if arrogant, opinions."

"Oh dear, with what haste Jennie does things," complained her mother. "I do not mind her practicing from eight until eleven every morning, but one would think all those other activities would wear her out. They wear *me* out."

Only Jennie's elders however, suffered from a depletion of nervous energy in her proximity. To the younger generation, she imparted her own enthusiasm and vitality.

Lord Randolph Churchill had a rapierlike mind and brittle nerves.

"Although possessed of unusual nervous energy his whole life was a struggle against ill health. Excitement fretted him cruelly. He smoked cigarettes till his tongue was sore, to soothe himself. Capable upon emergency of prolonged and vehement exertion, of manifold activities and pugnacities, of leaps and heaves beyond the common strength of men, he suffered by reaction fits of utter exhaustion and despondency. Most people grow tired before they are overtired, but Lord Randolph Churchill was of the temper that gallops till it falls. An instinct warned him of the perils which threatened him in a life of effort." * Instinct led him toward Jennie. The stamina and strength he lacked would be her gift to him.

---

* Winston Spencer Churchill, *Lord Randolph Churchill* (London, Macmillan and Company, Ltd., 1906).

175

Two unexpected impediments prevented Randolph's December visit to Paris. First, he had to spend a month in Ireland awaiting the death of his aunt, Lady Ely, and then Mr. Gladstone suddenly dissolved Parliament. This latter event placed a weapon of considerable power in the ardent suitor's hands. The Duke regarded the local borough of Woodstock as his family heritage. The Conservative member wished to resign, and who but the Duke's younger son was the candidate most likely to succeed? Marlborough did not fear his boy's political views, but he did fear losing the seat to a Liberal. If Randolph could be persuaded to stand, a Conservative victory would be certain. The Duke had always wished to see this talented son embark into public life; and Randolph, knowing his father's hopes, could rejoice that the moment had arrived to strike a bargain.

"All tricks are fair in love and war," he had written Jennie three months before. The noble Duke learned this with rapidity, for when the General Election dealt Randolph the ace of trumps, he did not hesitate to use it. Rather than risk thwarting his son just as the Conservative electors of Woodstock were dispatching a formal entreaty to him, Marlborough agreed that the marriage might take place "within less than a year."

Having gained this point, Randolph showed no small alacrity in carrying out his side of the bargain. No longer intent on fighting his own family, all his efforts could be diverted against the Liberal opponent. Although loath to cancel again that visit to Paris, he hurried back to Blenheim where the annual coursing meeting happened to be taking place in the Great Park. To Jennie he wrote:

BLENHEIM: Monday.

. . . All the farmers were there and, as they had a day's sport, were all in great spirits. I took the chair at their dinner at the Bear Hotel, and you cannot imagine how enthusiastic they were for me. They all go as one man. I hear nothing certain to any opposition; there are no end of rumours, but no one as yet has appeared publicly; I suppose we shall know for certain tomorrow.

I am now off to a part of the borough four miles distant to see more people, and have a large meeting of my committee at four in Woodstock. I think I may say that for the present everything is satisfactory. There are 1,071 voters, and I do not think more than eight hundred will poll; out of these I calculate at least on 460, which will be enough. But this is, of course, mere guesswork; it is still very uncertain, and I am glad I lost no time in arriving.

BLENHEIM: Tuesday.

The Radical candidate, Mr. Brodrick, arrived this morning; I made his acquaintance, and we shook hands and were very friendly. The contest will be a hard one and the result doubtful; it is impossible to say how the labourers will go. However, I have made a very good start, and have nothing to complain of as yet.

BLENHEIM: Saturday.

I am sure it is not necessary for me to excuse myself for not writing to you; you would not believe what work it is. We had a great meeting last night, which was very successful; we had a good speaker down from London, and I made a speech. How I have been longing for you to have been with me? If we had only been married before this! I think the reception you would have got would have astonished you. . . . My head is in a whirl of voters, committee meetings, and goodness knows what. I am glad it is drawing to an end, as I could not stand it very long; I cannot eat or sleep.

I am now off again, 10:00 A.M. to see more people.

BLENHEIM: Sunday.

At last I have a pretty quiet day; but I have been very busy this afternoon, and, in spite of its being Sunday, I have been active among several little odd fellows whom it is important to pick up. How this election is going I really can form no opinion, and the excitement and uncertainty of it make me quite ill. Yesterday I was canvassing all day in Woodstock itself. People that I think know better than anybody tell me it will be very close. You see, with the ballot one can tell nothing; one can only trust to promises, and I have no doubt a good many will be broken. Our organisation and preparations for Tuesday are very perfect, and the old borough has never been worked in such a way before. You have no idea how this election gets hold of me. One can positively think of nothing else except voters and committees, &c., till one's brain gets quite addled and in a whirl. I have a presentiment that it will go wrong. I am such a fool to care so much about it. I hate all this excitement. . . . I saw my opponent to-day in church. He looks awfully harassed. I feel quite sorry for him, as all his friends here are such a dreadfully disreputable lot; and as I have got the three principal hotels in the town, he had nothing except a wretched, low, miserable pot-house to stay in. . . .

Unfortunate Mr. Brodrick! The result of the election in no way belied the quality of his accommodation.

. . . Ever since I met you everything goes well with me, too well; I am getting afraid of a Nemesis. I always hoped I should win the election, but that under the ballot and against a man like Brodrick I should have that crushing overwhelming majority (of 165 out of 973 voters) never entered into my wildest dreams. It was a great victory; we shall never have a contest again. The last two contests, '65 and '68, were won only by 17 and 21 majorities; so just conceive the blow it is to the other side. You never heard such cheering in all your life. The poll was not declared till eleven, and the hours of suspense were most trying; but when it was known, there was such a burst of cheers that must have made the old Dukes in the vault jump. I addressed a few words to the committee and so did Blandford and was immensely cheered; and then they accompanied us, the whole crowd of them, through the town and up to Blenheim, shouting and cheering all the way. Oh, it was a great triumph, and that you were not there to witness it will always be a source of great regret to me. . . . There is nothing more to be done except to pay the bill, and that I have left to my father.

Never could a new Member of Parliament have felt more triumphant. Not only had he won his seat: he was free to marry the girl he loved.

The Duke admitted himself out-played, traveled to Paris to meet the Jerome ladies, and succumbed completely to their charm. Jennie played him Beethoven's "Sonata Appassionata" with violence and appeal. He had to acknowledge that Randolph had chosen a very surprising as well as a very beautiful bride.

Randolph stopped smoking cigarettes all night and relaxed quite happily. In a few months he had contrived to win over his own parents and his prospective mother-in-law. Only Mr. Jerome had yet to be conquered.

AFTER A HARASSING WINTER IN New York, Leonard sailed for France, determined to see Jennie's emotional predicament for himself.

A storm of excitement met him. It was all settled. Mrs. Jerome found the Duke of Marlborough a "perfect dear," and Jennie had taken to holding forth with astonishing confidence on English party politics. All that Papa need do was to settle a dowry, and the marriage could take place.

Lord Randolph had never troubled about money. Having written glibly that his political bill would be paid by his father, presumably he expected a large allowance to follow. In England, gentlemen did not "earn" money. If they inherited no estates, they served the State or the Army. Younger sons had to be endowed or they left the country.

Leonard hesitated. He was an American. He wished his daughter to be well provided for, but in his opinion her husband was the proper man to do it.

In his own struggling youth he had felt it unchivalrous to marry until he could support his wife in the accustomed manner. The material inefficiency of European nobles seemed to him supine, even despicable. No one could call the English aristocracy effete; their boys were rigorously brought up, but to be leaders, not workers. Randolph would be given a suitable house in London and an income sufficient to carry him along on his career, but there would be little left over to deck one of the most spectacular beauties in Europe. No way of "making money" could ever be open to him. Jennie would have to dress and entertain on the settlement made by her father.

"Mr. Jerome had strong and, it would seem, not unreasonable views, suggested by American usage, about married women's property and made some propositions which Lord Randolph considered derogatory to him."

Once again the house in Paris reverberated with heated discussions. The "padded" furniture proved itself more useful than ever when Clara fell into vapors (secretly she was strong as an ox), or Jennie wished to succumb to those tears so especially becoming to long dark lashes.

Meanwhile, Lord Randolph, walking among the flowering chestnut trees, which have intoxicated many a lover, announced a firm determination to earn his own living "in England or out of it." And Jennie romantically acquiesced. Back in his palace the Duke read an exalted letter concerning his son's new chosen course "in which I am bound to say she thoroughly agrees with me," while Mr. Leonard Jerome found himself faced with an ultimatum. Together Randolph and Jennie were a formidable pair, their very faults of impetuous youth and exuberance making them the more winning.

Randolph's temperament allowed him to suffer moments of painful despondency. Not so his lady. She possessed a vigorous optimism that no parental opposition could daunt. Despite her feminine beauty, Jennie alone had caused her father to say, "She ought to have been a boy." Now she devoted her vibrant energy to a man far more high-strung than herself, imparting an immunity to fear of defeat, which had been his only lack. Dear, dear, kind papa! He soon capitulated. The daily torrent of verbiage on the nobility of impecunious love, capped by a vision of these two scintillating innocents setting forth hand-in-hand "to earn a living anywhere—any country will do" was more than he could stand.

Randolph offered his name, a parliamentary career, a town house and a couple of fine horses (carriages could probably be borrowed from Blenheim). Jennie should have six thousand pounds a year settled on her without delay. Mr. Jerome hoped it would prove sufficient. He certainly could afford no more.

Randolph, growing hourly more impetuous and prolific in his arguments, now insisted he had waited long enough. Life was short, and parliamentary duties loomed ahead. If the marriage did not take place soon, there would hardly be time for a honeymoon. Romance triumphed. Melted by a veritable pandemonium of emotion his elders and betters ceased to offer unheeded advice. It was announced that on April 15, 1874, Lord Randolph Churchill and Miss Jennie Jerome should be married at the British

Embassy in Paris. The Duke could not leave England but he sent his blessing, and the Duchess rejoiced that her favorite son had chosen her birthday for his wedding.

Fifteen-year-old Leonie left Wiesbaden to be a bridesmaid with Clara. In careful schoolgirl script she listed the wedding presents, beginning with the gold Russian *coffre* and a locket of pearls and turquoise which arrived from the Prince and Princess of Wales. This list and a letter describing the wedding, which she evidently thought too interesting to post, were tucked away in her desk and discovered some eighty years later.

Randolph's three sisters, his brother Lord Blandford, and his aunt Lady Camden arrived in Paris with Francis Knollys, the Prince of Wales's private secretary, who was to be best man. After a large family dinner came an inspection of Jennie's trousseau of "twenty-three very pretty dresses, six or seven bonnets, and some very fine linen."

On the following morning Clara and Leonie, in pale blue silk with white embroidery and wearing crystal bridesmaids' lockets around their necks, attended their sister. The bride's dress was of white satin, with a long train and flounces of Alençon lace. A long tulle veil "covered her entirely."

Leonard clasped a pearl necklace around his daughter's neck and drove her to the ceremony. Mrs. Jerome in "a gray silk dress with street trimmings" followed with the girls in another carriage.

During the wedding breakfast Randolph and Jennie ate in a little drawing room by themselves. Then after a brief visit with the guests Jennie changed into "a very pretty, dark blue and white striped dress for traveling, and a white hat with a white feather."

It was a fine day, and an open carriage with four gray horses and two postilions waited at the door. When his daughter left the house, Leonard gave her a second present, a parasol of Alençon lace mounted on a delicate gold and tortoise-shell handle. "It's the loveliest thing I've ever seen!" said Jennie. Papa felt his heart melt.

As the carriage moved off through the spring sunshine, the young couple turned to wave good-by. Jennie looked unbelievably lovely clutching the parasol, her eyes sparkling against its foam of lace. "Dear, dear papa." "Why, Mama, don't cry. Life is going to be perfect . . . always." Leonie and Clara were busy throwing old slippers. After four they both departed on a country visit and that evening Leonard and his wife sat alone in their house in the Rue du Roi de Rome. They found the room unexpectedly sad and the piano "terribly silent."

THE CONTINENTAL HONEYMOON only lasted two weeks, for Lord Randolph wished "to return in triumph with his bride to receive the dutiful laudations of the borough of Woodstock." In early May the pair arrived at Blenheim. Cheering tenants unharnessed their horses and insisted on dragging the carriage from station to palace. The old oak trees of the park were in fresh foliage. As they passed the entrance archway, Randolph cried out with that adoration which Englishmen develop for their family homes, "This is the finest view in England!" Jennie admitted herself impressed, but, being an American, at the sight of Vanbrugh's immense pile she gathered her wits sufficiently, or says she did, to tease her spouse with Pope's famous lines on Blenheim Palace:

> "See, sir, here's the grand approach;
> This way is for his grace's coach:

183

There lies the bridge, and here's the clock,
Observe the lion and the cock,
The spacious court, the colonnade,
And mark how wide the hall is made!
The chimneys are so well design'd
They never smoke in any wind.
This gallery's contrived for walking,
The windows to retire and talk in;
The council chamber for debate,
And all the rest are rooms of state."
"Thanks, sir," cried I, " 'tis very fine,
But where d'ye sleep, or where d'ye dine?
I find by all you have been telling,
That 'tis a house, but not a dwelling."

The Duke and Duchess were waiting on the wide steps to greet her with kindness slightly tinged by condescension. She felt them watching closely to see what an American daughter-in-law would be like.

In this house criticism would always be easy to arouse. Jennie soon enjoyed the small malice of showing herself better educated than their own daughters, reared in the background by elderly governesses. In vain had Leonard tried to teach this ebullient daughter not to show off; to one so young and lively the temptation proved irresistible. And for a pupil of Stephen Heller, who had been Chopin's own pupil, it was only too easy. She trilled on the piano until the Churchills were prostrate; she played the great silver-piped organ (this she had studied in St. Sulpice) until their ears rang. And then she wrote mischievous, mocking notes to Mama. The Marlboroughs knew nothing of fashion! They used funny, frumpy old table mats and kept water decanters with ordinary thick tumblers, "the kind we use in bedrooms," before each place at dinner, and their shoes were the wrong shape.

"How strange life in a big country house seemed to one who,

until then, had been accustomed only to towns!" she wrote. Every day followed a formal routine. Even breakfast proved ceremonious, the ladies appearing in long velvet or silk trains. At luncheon the Duke and Duchess themselves carved up joints for the entire family, including tutors and governesses, and the remains were carried off to poor cottagers by the children on afternoon walks. Jennie took in every detail concerning the great house that would henceforth be her continual background, but apart from the splendid architecture nothing impressed her. She fidgeted to be off to the small house in Curzon Street that the Duke had provided.

"The London season of thirty [now eighty] years ago was far more prolonged and its glories more apparent than they are now. It was looked upon as a very serious matter which no self-respecting persons who considered themselves 'in society' would forego, nor of which a votary of fashion would willingly miss a week or a day." Certainly not the young Lady Randolph, who, according to the fashion of the day, appeared appropriately clad on Gold Cup Day at Ascot in that exquisite wedding-dress of white satin and point lace. She wore a bonnet of nodding roses and Papa's parasol created a filmy cobweb behind her head. Lady Randolph's deep eyes flickered around the Royal Enclosure and made quite a sensation.

At that time newly married couples seldom appeared at large gatherings for two months at least, but the Season had opened on May first, and the young Churchills could not resist attending a ball in honor of the Tsar Alexander II at Stafford House.

When Jennie was presented and the Tsar learned she had only been married a few weeks, he fixed a cold gray eye on her, remarking, *"Et ici déjà!"*

What trivialities occupied the minds of the powerful! A man who held the destinies of all Russia could be troubled to express disapproval because a bride went dancing a few days earlier than was usual.

On May 22 Randolph delivered his maiden speech in the House of Commons, and Disraeli wrote to compliment the Duchess on her son's successful debut. "But the course of the session, and of the years that followed, offered few opportunities to young members for winning Parliamentary distinction. The waters of politics flowed smoothly and even sluggishly."

For the moment Randolph had time to accompany his glamorous wife to every function she wished to attend.

With frankness Jennie writes of that first season which she enjoyed

> . . . with all the vigor and unjaded appetite of youth. After the comparatively quiet life of Paris, we seemed to live in a whirl of gaieties and excitement. Many were the delightful balls I went to, which, unlike those of the present day, invariably lasted to five o'clock in the morning. Masked balls were much the vogue. Holland House, with its wonderful historical associations and beautiful gardens, was a fitting frame for such entertainments, and I remember enjoying myself immensely at one given there. Disguised in a painted mask and in yellow wig, I mystified everyone.
>
> My sister [Clara] who was staying with us, had been walking in the garden with young Lord ———, who was a *parti,* and much run after by designing mothers with marriageable daughters. Introducing him to me, she pretended I was her mother. Later in the evening I attacked him, saying that my daughter had just confided to me that he had proposed to her, and that she had accepted him. To this day I can see his face of horror and bewilderment. Vehemently he assured me that it was not so. But I kept up the farce, declaring that my husband would call on him next day and reveal our identity, and that meanwhile I should consider him engaged to my charming daughter. Deficient

in humour and not over-burdened with brains, he could not take the joke, and left the house a miserable man.

Generally speaking, there is no doubt that English people are dull-witted at a masked ball, and do not understand or enter into the spirit of intrigue which is all-important on such occasions. One reason may be that both sexes are masked in England, whereas abroad this is not the practice, nor would it be understood. The licence a man might take if his identity were to remain unknown would never be tolerated. Besides, it stands to reason that unless one of the two remains unmasked there cannot be much mystifying. Some women refuse to say anything but "Yes" and "No" in a falsetto voice, and think they have had a glorious time as long as their disguise is not discovered. "You don't know me. You don't know me," was the parrot cry of one lady. "And I don't want to" said Lord Charles Beresford, fleeing from her, "if you've nothing else to say."

Randolph was particularly intolerant of bores, a trait that did not add to his popularity. On one occasion when buttonholed at his club he listened halfway through an interminable story and then rang the bell for a footman who he instructed to "listen until his lordship finishes" while he himself slipped away.

The Conservative party had been swept to power with a *majority of fifty*, which allowed Disraeli to be generous toward the Liberal opposition. While Randolph steered an untempestuous course through the new government's first uneventful year, his wife impressed society as "the most beautiful dark woman anyone had set eyes on." The first American to enter the portals of this small exclusive world, she took all bastions by storm. The side of fashionable London that amused her most was Rotten Row, where she rode or walked from twelve to two every day. "It was a brilliant and animated scene which filled the foreigner with admiration and envy, no capital in Europe being able to compare with it. . . ."

Clara soon came to stay, and after their afternoon of piano

practice together (when lesser spirits were resting on chaise longues), the sisters ventured into the Belgravia of Disraeli's novels. In the freshly-painted, flower-bedecked mansions, which English gentry threw open each spring, "dinners, balls, and parties succeeded one another without intermission till the end of July, the only respite being at the Whitsun recess. A few of the racing people might go to Newmarket for a week, but the fashionable world flocked only to the classic races, the Derby, Ascot and Goodwood. . . . We used to drive down on coaches in Ascot frocks and feathered hats, and stay to dinner, driving back by moonlight."

A July letter from Clara to her mother describes the end of the season when too many parties had caused tempers to get frayed.

CURZON STREET.

Thursday

My darling Mama,

What a letter I got from you this morning. Such a sermon! However you will be happy to hear that we had already thrown over the Murietta's dance.

Jennie got a letter from [Oliver] Montagu yesterday saying that he was charged to arrange the Quadrille for the Fancy Dress Ball and that H.R.H. [the Prince of Wales] wanted Jennie and I very much to dance in it. Jennie is to be Queen of Clubs according to H.R.H. and will dance with the King of Diamonds being the Duke of Atholl, and I the Seven of Hearts to dance with Lord MacDuff as Seven of Spades, but Randolph is furious that the Prince should send us word through Montagu and not Francis Knollys besides which he says it will be a great expense as the dresses can't cost less than £15 apiece. R. says he won't let us go. I think it is too bad as it will be very lovely. Only 24 ladies had he asked. My quadrille is M., Princess Christian and

188

Pcss. Louise. I do hope R. will change his mind but he is so obstinate. The Duchess is going to have a small party at Blenheim for the last week in July, and had asked Jennie and I and Randolph. I think it is to bring on the dr Grey affair but I don't know. We went with the Duchess to pay some visits yesterday, to Mme. de Bulow and Mme. de Brilaccias who has asked us on Saturday to meet the Prince and Princess. To-morrow night we are all dining at Lady de Rothschild, a grand dinner. To-night dinner at the Square [the Marlboroughs] and going to Lady Carnarvon's afterwards. And there is a charming garden party at Hatfield, two hours from London. R. is going to ask for an invitation for me, and as the Duchess of Buccleugh is a great friend of his, I am sure to go. We are to make a nice party to go down there together. They say there are going to be 3 other fancy balls, but if we don't go to Marlborough House we shan't be able to go to any. Jennie and R. have quite decided to come to Deauville after Blenheim, and R. after depositing Jennie and I with you, will go off for a cruise with the Duke in his new yacht. It wd be very nice if you could be at Deauville 3 days before us to get the rooms. Do bring dear Leonie, I don't think Deauville will be too gay for her, will it? You will feel as if you still had three daughters to look after. You must not think that we are at all fast. In fact we are very humdrum and stay a great deal at-home. Jennie, you see, can't go out really very much. Goodbye my darling mama, you will soon have us again to bother and worry you!

Yr. loving,

Clara.

I have seen some charming little tables for 5 pounds *dans le genre* of those *l'impératrice* had only much prettier. I do think you shd. let me get a few things for the house, dear Mama. It would make my blue Salon look so pretty, and the things here are fascinating.

August and September were devoted to yachting or stalking. Then the gentry dispersed to their country homes where they hunted the fox, shot game, and entertained the statesmen and sportsmen of all lands. Big London houses closed down from October until February when the winter session brought members of Parliament back to town. Scanning Jennie's memoirs, this country respite seems perhaps fortunate, or a small Churchill might have arrived with scant dignity in Rotten Row or during a moonlight coach ride. Events were to prove sufficiently inconvenient as it was. Jennie, with her health and prowess undiminished, was actually dancing at a small party at Blenheim Palace when she had to hurry away past the endless suite of drawing rooms, through the library, "the longest room in England," down the longest corridor in the world, the quarter-mile of dark red carpet that led to her bedroom.

She never got there. It was all such a surprise! Just when the party was at its height!

Next morning the bells of Woodstock Church rang a peal to celebrate the arrival of a possible heir; * and soon afterward the *Times* printed among birth notices: "On the 30th of November at Blenheim Palace, the Lady Randolph Churchill, of a son."

The baby had been born in a small room on the ground floor, a room which had once belonged to the first duke's chaplain and retained the name of Dean Jones. It was not even a bedroom, but had been converted for the evening into a lady's attiring room and was strewn with velvet capes and feather boas which made a merry, gipsy-like setting for the new arrival. "Most unconventional," said the Duchess.

Leonard and Clara telegraphed their delight from Paris. The first grandchild! A little boy, who would be called Winston

---

* He remained an heir presumptive until 1897, when Consuelo, granddaughter of the famous old Commodore Vanderbuilt, produced a son for the ninth duke.

Leonard Spencer Churchill; Winston after an ancestor, Sir Winston Churchill, father of the great Duke, Leonard after a grandfather from the New World.

THE PARLIAMENTARY SESSIONS OF the next few years offered scant opportunity for any young man to make his name. Lord Randolph and his wife moved to a larger house in Charles Street and there began entertaining their own political circle. At first Jennie, whose upbringing had been artistic and impractical, could not realize that food did not grow on trees exactly as her mother's French cook had always produced it. She found housekeeping terrifying. Happily Mr. Disraeli and Randolph's college friend, Lord Rosebery, who often came to dine, were too busy talking to criticize the cooking.

Mr. Disraeli possessed a singular flow of effusive language quite peculiar to himself. One evening he refused Randolph's offer of liquors with, "My dear Randolph, I have sipped your excellent champagne, I have drunk your good claret, I have tested your delicious port, I will have no more." Jennie, sitting next to him at dinner, could not help being amused, for she had noticed he drank nothing except weak brandy and water.

Before long, the Randolph Churchills had become the most sought-after young couple in England. They set each other off dazzlingly. From the first moment he saw them, the Prince of Wales coveted the company of the Jerome sisters to enlighten the heavy snobbish boredom of his famous "set."

Jennie learned from her husband to use her ready wit as an

adornment rather than a torment; and Randolph prepared himself quickly in the company of older statesmen for that career which he had needed such persuasion to enter.

Every party that included the young Churchills proved a success. Although Randolph read continuously and deeply, cooling his fevered nerves and easily ruffled mind with the classics, he could, within two minutes of shutting a volume, flippantly amuse any drawing room. His wit sparkled through the dull atmosphere of Victorian house parties, lighting small fires of laughter and consuming the tedium that so often grows among those who eat too much and have not enough to do.

One evening when "thought reading" had become the rage, pretty Lady de Clifford insisted on dragging Randolph, who was reading in a corner, to join the game. Snatched from the cool depths of Gibbon, he found himself blindfolded in the middle of the drawing room. Lady de Clifford said, "Don't resist any thought that comes into your head; do exactly as you feel." Without hesitation he embraced her before the whole company.

Henceforth Jennie noticed her husband was left in peace with his book.

Several months each year were spent with the Marlboroughs, and Jennie tried to live in harmony with her austere mother-in-law, at the rustle of whose silken skirt the household trembled. "When the family were alone at Blenheim, everything went on with the regularity of clockwork. So assiduously did I practise my piano, read or paint, that I began to imagine myself back in the school-room. In the morning, an hour or so was devoted to the reading of newspapers, which was a necessity if one wanted to show an intelligent interest in the questions of the day, for at dinner conversation invariably turned to politics. In the afternoon a drive to pay a visit to some neighbour or a walk in the gardens would help to while away some part of the day. After dinner, which was a rather solemn full-dress affair, we all repaired to what was called the Vandyke room. There one might read one's book or play for love a mild game of whist. Many a glance would be cast at the clock, which sometimes would be surreptitiously advanced a quarter of an hour by some sleepy member of the family. No one dared suggest bed until the sacred hour of eleven had struck. Then we would all troop out into a small anteroom, and, lighting our candles, each in turn would kiss the Duke and Duchess and depart to our own rooms."

There is scarcely any mention of young members of the family. Victorian chatelains did not emphasize their children. Jennie luckily procured a wonderful nurse for Winston. Dear, fat, kind Mrs. Everest created an atmosphere of cosiness and affection which the grownups in their tail coats and boned silks were too busy to know about. The summer session, the winter session, the hunting season, the London season, Cowes Week, the house parties in beautiful old mansions . . . all this routine, which it was imperative to follow, left little time for the upper classes to pay even fleeting visits to the nursery.

The following spring very plump Mrs. Jerome came to stay in Charles Street, crackling in stiff dark silks and wearing a bonnet. She inspected baby Winston, listened to Randolph rehearsing a short sharp speech on the release of Irish state prisoners, outlined the Parisian trends to Jennie, and departed "quite exhausted."

Young Clara then spent the London season with Jennie. Her first letter to her mother after leaving France survives in its heavy monogramed envelope:

Monday morning,
48 CHARLES ST.

My darling Mama,
I never had such a nasty drizzling odious crossing! It was so rough, and we never got to London till half past 8!

193

Jennie and R. just going off to a charming little dinner at Lady Dufferins which had been arranged for *me*, but I went straight to bed. I just got your letter this minute and am so sorry about the bonnets but I can get on with some old ones until they come. R. has got my invitation for this Court ball next Thursday at Buckingham Palace through Francis Knollys which will be very jolly; and also one, he thinks, for the Dudleys for Wednesday. To-morrow Jennie thinks I ought to wear the white crepe with sequins as it will be my very first appearance, and it is everything to look well.

Poor Rosamond is ill in bed to-day with a cold, feverish, but they hope it won't be anything serious and that she will manage to get up to-morrow for the ball. We have just come from the Row where we walked with Col. Edgecumbe and Mr. Farquhair. I got up so late that I had no time to write first. However, I will do my best to write every day and tell you everything. R. is in very good humour as he made two hundred pounds at the Derby, and Jennie £20 on her own book.

Goodbye my own darling Mama. I love you so much, but I hope you don't miss me much as you have Leonie. I will soon be home again. Love to Leonie.

Clara.

Apparently Mrs. Jerome must remain in Paris, studying bonnets for her daughters who considered Parisian modes infinitely more beguiling than those of London, while Mr. Jerome's role was to earn sufficient in New York to pay for extensive wardrobes. In return the loving parents were to receive plenty of news.

A letter dated June 16, 1875, reads:

Darling Mama,

I got your cross note this morning, and cannot understand how it is that you have not got my Saturday letter at least. Really my darling Mama if you had known what a hurry and bustle it was, and how tired I was too at Ascot you wd not be so cross about it. Besides you say it is 10 days since you heard from me and that cannot be as I wrote the minute I got home. We had a most charming dinner last night. I wore the blue chosen by Leonie and Jennie her black gauze and Mrs. Standish her black. Vogüé * gave me a most charming bouquet. Blount gave one to Jennie and then we went to the play where Vogüé would sit next to me. And then dressed and went to the Marjoribanks ball. Jennie wants me so much to be nice to Sir William Gordon Cumming and wants him to make up to me. I think *entre nous* that it wd take very little to make him devoted to me, although he is a young man who never speaks to a young girl and only flirts with married ladies. He began *très sérieusement à faire la cour* to Jennie but last night he would not leave me in the hall. But I could not think of him at all as he is very very poor ** and awfully conceited and not *sympathique.* I don't think I could really like a man like that. Vogüé has just asked us to dine at his house in John St., Berkeley Square should I stay longer, but he leaves the end of the week for Switzerland and he told me he would come back by way of Germany and look us up at Ems, but Frenchmen have such a way of saying things they don't mean.

To-night there is this dreadful dinner at the Square [the Marlboroughs'], which will be such a bore. Rosamond [Randolph's younger sister] has been a week at Brighton and is looking very well so perhaps they will ask some "choice young men" for her. I can't tell you how jealous Randolph says the Duchess is of Jennie and I. She is always very kind and amiable but *une certaine aigreur* in the way she talks. Poor Jennie doesn't know what to do while we are at Ems as she thinks it very expensive to come with us and it would be considered very fast for her to stay here

---

* Vicomte de Vogüé, a charming, erudite Frenchman, well known in racing circles and a friend of the Prince of Wales.

** Not at all. He was a rich Scots landowner. The other charges probably were true.

by herself without Randolph. What a pity it is she has not more money. . . .

Leonard could hardly allow his daughter to make the "fast" choice—which happened to also be the economical one—and stay alone in her London house. A large check arrived by the next post.

Clara's digs at the unfortunate Rosamond continued in most uncharitable form as relays of exquisite tulle gowns were dispatched from Paris. We hear of her flaunting pale cream lace with rosebuds, white satin and chiffon with blue bows and forget-me-nots, while Rosamond looks "rather pasty" and the Duchess frowns. This may have been a telling method of adding to her list of proposals, but it did not gain invitations to houses where there were marriageable daughters. And a whispering campaign that the Jerome sisters "painted" soon caused considerable distress to Jennie and Clara.

The lost letter of which Mrs. Jerome complained eventually reached her and was placed in a trunk of family papers.

Saturday June 12th,

My darling Mama,
    We have just come home and I sit down immediately to write you *with my hat on.* I wrote you from Ascot a tremendously long account of all we were doing but I found out afterwards the servant I gave it to preferred going to the races and never posted it at all. We were a cheery party. Although the men were not particularly *sympathique,* but every day there were a crowd of outsiders to tea and dinner. My party consisted of Sir William Gordon Cumming (who is charming), Captain Oliphant, Davidoff Etc. The first day we all were down to breakfast at ten, then played lawn tennis in the garden, then dressed for the Races which were awfully jolly as the Prince and Princess were there. I never saw such wonderful *toilettes* and the Royal Enclo-

sure was very swell and select. Lord Hartington took me to lunch in a private room with the royalties, the Prince himself giving his arm to Jennie and altogether the day was *très réussi!* Vogue and Halley Blount were a great addition as of course they were all devoted to us and as Halley and Castlereagh etc. were stopping with the Prince they were considered big swells. I can't tell you how much I like Vogüe. I always thought I would if I ever knew him and I think he likes me. All the Frenchmen came home with us piled up on the coach and had tea on the lawn. Hardwicke also making his effect in his wonderful Master of Buckhounds costume. Each lady found a charming little bouquet every night at dinner, the men boutonniers and afterwards some of them played billiards and the rest of us danced! *Voilà mardi!*

Everyone dragged in one after the other for breakfast, then we dressed for the races. I wore Leonie's blue silk which was thought very pretty. The Princess was not there, but the Prince flourished and won a lot of money and did like the other day. I walked about with all the men and then took lunch with Mr. Delane, editor of the *Times*. He has a charming house on the other side of the course and we only had chic people. Mrs. and Miss Stephens * were there, and Mrs. Stephens told Mrs. Farquhar it seems that she "hoped little Lady Randolph had better manners than she had last year." Such a common vulgar creature she is. Vogüe, Hardwicke and Blount came to dine. I wore my white muslin and pink roses and Jennie wore her dark blue low dress. Lady Dudley kept seats for us every day at the races and was most kind so handsome too. Lord B—— walked a little with me but he was very distrait throughout the meeting as he had horses running every day. Jennie took her Sir William Cumming all to herself, he being the swell of the party and does not let anyone else talk to him but I don't think him as nice as Carrington and Vogüe who are my *cavaliers particuliers!* The Prince is very kind to us and takes us for a little walk every day. Thursday was Gold

---

* Americans of great fortune. Miss Stephens became Lady Paget.

Cup Day. Jennie wore her wedding dress with new crepe de Chine trimmings and I my pale blue with marguerites *au corsage* and my new marguerite bonnet, which is very pretty. We managed to have lots of fun after the races as Oliver Montagu invited us to take tea at the "barracks of the Blues" at Windsor. So we all crowded on top of the coach and Oliver and Col. Williams (Col. of the regiment) received us in grand state with tea on the lawn, the band playing. Oliver felt fine with his uniform on. He *has* been kind to me and I hear he goes about telling everyone how nice I am! We got home tired after a long dusty drive and gay although some of the men who had lost were rather cross. *Friday.* A bad day but I never enjoyed myself so much. I wore my pink foulard and Jennie her dark blue and the men were all *very* nice to us. After the Races, Hardwick took us all with the coach to see the Queen's hounds in their Kenels (which I don't know how to spell), and then we went home and as more of the men have won back their money the dinner was more cheerful. Jennie wore her pale blue tulle with silver and I my white tulle with jet and then went to the Ball at Chiswick (the Prince and Princess's place) which was a great success. Carrington and Vogue were there and looked particularly dashing. I never enjoyed a dance so much although I think Lord E. a humbug. The Princess had on a brown tulle and looked very well and we did not get home till 5 o'c. Old Lord Westmorland (that is he is about 45) took a great fancy to me, but he is a bore I think although he is considering something wonderful this evening. We all made a point of being down to breakfast together and then all came down to London by the 2 o'c. train . . . then on to Windsor for the cricket match and danced on the lawn in tents, the Prince and Princess being there but she gave it up. I ran up to see Baby Winston a minute and here I am writing you my journal . . . Jennie sends her love and is writing too. Kiss Leonie.

Your loving,
Clara.

What eons of time these great ones had to waste and how important the "dressing" seems. They were being pulled in and out of their clothes all day. A lady could not go to a play except in black or dark blue; this accounted for the scampers home at 11:00 P.M. to "dress" for a ball. And breakfast! Then it consisted of two hours' conversation in velvets while in formal houses the men had to don morning coats before re-attiring themselves in shooting jackets.

Our heads spin, and yet the very frivolity of these letters rings so true a note. After all her expensive education, Clara can't spell *kennels* but she knows how to dress, quote French and German, and play the piano. Her mother has taught her correct tactics with that mob she refers to as "the men"; these she used to show in pantomime as a coy beckoning, followed by hands held up in shocked reproach.

Evidently she still preferred Frenchmen, and lucky it was for her that Sir William Gordon Cumming failed to please or her fair name might have been tarnished with his at Tranby Croft a few years later.*

---

* Sir William's friendship with the Prince of Wales combined with his Colonelcy of the Scots Guards seems to have made him odiously conceited and rude. His contemptuous remarks to ladies in particular made him enemies who rejoiced in his final downfall. When Gordon Cumming was introduced to my grandmother Leonie, then a lively sensitive girl of nineteen enjoying her first walk in Hyde Park at the fashionable hour, he snapped: "Over here husband-hunting I suppose?" Even more unforgivable was his remark in a drawing room to Louisa, Duchess of Manchester, before she married Lord Harrington (later Duke of Devonshire). "When is Harty-tarty going to make an honest woman of you?" Louisa turned pale and bided her time. When Gordon Cumming was eventually caught cheating at Mrs. Arthur Wilson's famous country house party given for the Prince of Wales at Tranby Croft, Louisa Devonshire made certain that every club in London knew. A party of men had in fact noticed Cumming's tricks in Jennie's own house where he had flared up at poor Leonie, snapping: "Why do you stand behind my chair?" but Randolph refused to allow a scandal to break under his roof and merely desisted from ever inviting him again. The Wilson sons suspected Cumming and unwisely laid a trap during the royal visit. When caught he was led to the Prince's bedroom by General Williams where he signed a paper swearing never to play cards again. H.R.H. kept the paper and secrecy was assured him. But the men

199

Jennie's letters of the seventies are unfortunately brief; she merely mentions having the Prime Minister to dine or Lord Rosebery and Lord Salisbury as accompanying her at the opening of Parliament. Knowing the clear forceful mind she showed in later years, and her powers of expression, knowing her to have been surrounded by interesting personalities, by ambassadors and statesmen and kings, one regrets that in the only surviving epistle of length to darling mama she delineates but a single person: "I do like him Mama. He has such a lovely moustache."

Leonie, meanwhile, with furrowed brow and smoldering ardor, was practicing longer hours than either of her sisters had ever known. She hated being the youngest sister, chained to governesses while Jennie and Clara enjoyed the gay world. Music was her only compensation, and under the tuition of Stephen Heller, Chopin's friend and pupil, she became the best pianist of the three sisters. Mrs. Jerome fussed because she was not going to be pretty like the others, but Leonard called her his "funny little thing" and she began to be his favorite.

---

of the party had wives and lady loves who could not resist blatting at Doncaster Races next day. When Cumming returned to London he drove straight to his club. As he entered, every man there deliberately turned his back. Shame forced him to bring an action; the newspapers took it up and sensational publicity resulted. Not only did Cumming have to resign his regiment and accept exile in Scotland for ever, but tension reached such a pitch when the Prince of Wales appeared in the witness box to give evidence, that Queen Victoria suggested to her son that he had better consider relinquishing his succession to the throne. The Kaiser leapt at this chance of wounding his royal uncle by a letter expressing horror that the Honorary Colonel of a German regiment should be involved in a cheating case. For a generation the name of Tranby Croft signified not a house but a scandal.

THE FOLLOWING YEARS REQUIRED continued hard work for Leonard Jerome. Because of his daughters' manner of life, a diligent concentration on financial matters became increasingly essential. Being more interested in horses and yachts than in royalty, the doings of Jennie and Clara could not enthrall him to the extent they enthralled the American newspaper readers. Jennie's beauty had a quality that could "knock your eye out." She became for countless hard-working housewives the idolized symbol of what an American girl could achieve.

Meanwhile Mrs. Jerome had, in plump middle age, developed into a patroness of cultivated unfortunates. Unpublished poets, ousted prime ministers and sacked diplomats stumbled over the outmoded, inlaid, eighteenth-century French furniture of her *salon* in the Rue du Roi de Rome. Her sympathy, withheld from the "fast set" of the Prince of Wales, into which her daughters ventured with trepidation and delight, flowed lavishly toward "the poor dear Empress," that "unfortunate archduke" and those minor ex-kings who strolled Europe in search of good dinners and consoling phrases.

From Leonard's point of view the most companionable member of his family had become the sixteen-year-old Leonie, practicing the piano with iron will up to eight hours a day. Stephen Heller taught her to play Chopin better than impatient smoldering Jennie ever could, but Leonie spent much of her time at that "hateful finishing school" at Wiesbaden, the smartest in Europe, where the girls, polished within an inch of their lives, were given an education suitable for the curator of a museum. The pupils who issued forth all made spectacular marriages and remained impractical intellectuals all their lives. (Her best friend there, Sophie Chotek, was to marry the Archduke Ferdinand and be assassinated beside him at Sarajevo in 1914.)

In 1875 Leonard decided to spend the winter at Pau with his unmarried daughters, and in the spring he snatched a couple of months to visit Ems and Bayreuth. Leonie had discovered Wagner and made Papa take her to the first production of the *Nibelungen-Ring*. In Budapest Leonard heard Minnie Hauk rehearsing the roles of Senta (*Flying Dutchman*) and Elsa (*Lohengrin*) at the Royal Court Theater.

Once or twice Mr. Jerome paid a visit to London, met the Duke and Duchess of Marlborough, played with his little grandson, and observed what he could of the activities of his busy, breathless daughters. The storm of preparation and entertainment which took place daily in Charles Street ("boxes of hats and gowns seem to arrive every hour"), drove him out to clubs and racing stables. Once more he visited his old friend Mrs. Ronalds. Having spent a period improving her delicate lungs as a guest of the Bey of Algiers who regarded her as a "divine being," Fanny Ronalds had now settled permanently in London. Her musical *salon* in Cadogan Place offered something quite new to English society. Visitors came to tea, made highbrow conversation, and listened to those struggling musicians whom Mrs. Ronalds considered worthy of launching. For the unmusical who disliked long hours on hard gilt chairs, a snobbish consolation might be scraped from meeting His Royal Highness the Duke of Edinburgh, a violinist of no small merit, for whom Fanny played accompaniments. The love of her life "dear, dear Sir Arthur Sullivan" was nearly always present. One day his bars of music engraved on her tombstone in Fulham Cemetery would give a clue to the conventional epitaph "Forever thine." And those who had the score would know to whom Fanny finally left her heart.

Leonard accompanied "sweet Mrs. R." to Covent Garden Opera, where she owned a box. She glanced at him sideways with those brown eyes which so many men apoplectic with emotion had tried to describe. "Your daughters must all marry Englishmen," she said, "and bring their children to my tea parties to learn to care for music." (They did, but none of Leonard's grandchildren had a note in them.)

With distressing frequency Mr. Jerome had to break off amusing commitments in Europe, sail back to New York, and earn sufficient for the upkeep of the several large houses.

If he grew lonely during these family separations, no trace showed in speech or letter. He wrote, "The strict old Union Club, although shabby and sombre, remains my favourite haunt." Here gentlemen of leisure could discuss horses, prima donnas, and yachts in solemn whispers, and now James Gordon Bennett was planning to introduce polo to America. Having learned this Indian sport from retired army officers in England, he had just shipped the first polo mallets, balls, and ponies to New York. With Frank Griswold he began to teach the rules to teams of oddly mounted friends in a riding academy. August Belmont, aging but still game, joined in, and Leonard cursed the old strain, suffered in that weight-lifting contest, that made it impossible for him to attempt this new game. The first American polo match was played at Jerome Park in 1876, Bennett's and Jerome's coaches transporting the players. The sport proved so entertaining to spectators that it was decided to inaugurate matches after the races, and polo began to flourish under the selective influence of smart club. Nothing could be called a real success unless a number of people who were dying to get in were kept out.

While Leonard, aged fifty-eight, fretted at his inability to participate in the matches, he received a letter from which fell the spark of a new idea. Jennie wrote that Randolph's brother, the

Marquis of Blandford, was driving his own coach as a public vehicle between London and Dorking. Leonard roared with laughter: "If I can't earn indoors in Wall Street, I'll earn outdoors as a coachman."

He had already founded the Coaching Club along with Colonel William Jay and De Lancey Kane, who were brilliant masters of four-in-hand driving, and now he started excursions to all the taverns and inns within fifty miles of New York City. The first public parade of the Coaching Club had taken place in Fifth Avenue during the spring of 1876. Horns blew, and Colonel Jay, in bottle-green coat, yellow striped waistcoat, and silk topper and boutonniere, led the smartest array of turnouts New York had ever seen. Rules had to be strict; every horse must have artificial flowers on its throatlatch, the driver's apron must be folded outside when not in use, and only the most elegant ladies were invited to perch behind the driver. Their feathered hats and lacy parasols caused almost as many gasps of interest as the be-ribboned horses.

Minnie Hauk and her mother returned briefly during this summer and let Leonard listen to excerpts from Bizet's *Carmen*. "What do you think of it?" she asked, and he replied, "I like it, but will the public accept anything so new?"

"I'll make them," said Minnie, "I'll make them like it."

"L'amour est un oiseau rebelle," caroled Minnie in her strange voice with its thrilling range, and before the refrain had had time to fade, Jennie and Randolph arrived with a long breathless story. Randolph and his brother had quarreled with the Prince of Wales and split London society into warring factions. Queen Victoria was sorely distressed, and an unprecedented number of people could never speak to each other again.

Jennie said that her father seemed to be the sole person who could listen without becoming ruffled. Walking over to the windows that overlooked Madison Square, he pulled back the red plush and white lace curtains to let what little breeze there was blow into the room.

"Tell me quietly," he ordered.

The tale poured forth. Randolph's brother, Lord Blandford (he who had written those sarcastic lines on hasty marriages) had himself wedded a daughter of the Duke of Abercorn and become the father of several children. Despite a propensity to describe in verse how marriages ought to go, he did not prove a model husband but Lady Blandford never noticed anything, and when he openly courted the pretty Countess of Aylesford, she merely copied that lady's dresses.

Lord Aylesford was a famous man to hounds, a heavyweight who made a brilliant reputation for cross-country riding in the Shires. Eventually the Prince of Wales (himself entranced by Lady Aylesford) went to India, taking Lord Aylesford in his company. Lord Blandford indiscreetly seized this moment to move his horses to a hunting inn adjacent to the Aylesford house.

When Lord Aylesford returned, he started a case that caused the whole structure of society to tremble. The Prince of Wales insisted that, having compromised the lady, Blandford should ask for a divorce and marry her. This Lord Blandford refused to do. Meanwhile the only person in England who knew nothing of her husband's predicament was Lady Blandford. He had always enjoyed practical jokes, and one morning when Blandford came down to breakfast late and lugubrious, reflecting on the recent arrival of a child for the Countess of Aylesford, she innocently devised a joke which, by coincidence, excelled all the others. While awaiting her husband's arrival, she replaced his poached egg with a small pink baby doll. She thought it would be such a surprise when he lifted the cover! It was. Lord Blandford choked, fled the room, and disappeared abroad for several weeks. His wife could not think why.

Meanwhile Randolph furiously championed his brother against the Prince and actually threatened to reveal certain love letters written by the Prince, which Lady Aylesford had for some reason entrusted to him. Hot words flew, and finally H.R.H. sent Lord Knollys to challenge Randolph to a duel, suggesting Rotterdam as a suitable place. Even Jennie's iron nerves began to fray. She passed sleepless nights until Randolph appointed Lord Falmouth as his second and dispatched him with a message to say he would fight any nominee, but could not lift a sword against his future sovereign.

At this stage Queen Victoria heard of the quarrel and expressed grave displeasure. Society divided, and the London season broke up among acrimonious arguments.

Such was the tension that as Jennie tactfully put it: "Randolph felt in need of solace and distraction." This had been sought in a hasty trip through Canada with Lord Ilchester which may have cooled tempers, but so pitiless a heat wave was in progress that "we seemed to spend most of the time eating melons and having cold baths."

Leonard listened carefully.

"Forget it," he said. "It was really your brother's affair. And now we will all go to Newport to sail and drive and see what I have left in the way of horses."

Off they went to the haven of Jennie's childhood, which was throwing up a plague of Roman temples and Loire Chateaux in place of the country villas she had known. The August Belmonts entertained them with ten-course dinners while liveried footmen held candelabra on the stairs and young Mrs. Henry Clews, "Newport's best dressed lady," confided that each year she set aside ten thousand dollars for "mistakes in clothes."

At Saratoga, where Leonard took them to the races, "the beauty of the ladies and gorgeousness of their dresses astonished the Englishmen of the party." Lawrence Jerome arrived. "For heaven's sake, keep them diverted" asked the brother. Lawrence suggested a visit to the Philadelphia Exhibition. Jennie describes her uncle as one of the wittiest men of his day, who kept them in transports of laughter. Stopping at various stalls, he would accost the rest of the party as though they were strangers and, taking up some new invention, would produce such a comic flow of salesman talk that crowds collected to buy the article while a delighted shop assistant tried to slip Lawrence a commission. Soon Randolph ceased to brood over the injustices of royal personages, and according to Jennie they all returned to England "refreshed."

Randolph now took an increasing dislike to the vapid society portrayed by Clara's guileless pen. As his son has written, without this trouble over Blandford he might have "wasted a dozen years in the frivolous and expensive pursuits of the silly world of fashion."

Disraeli had often asked the Duke of Marlborough to accept the appointment of Viceroy to Ireland. Now that his two sons had quarreled with so august a person as the Prince of Wales, the Duke acquiesced. Blenheim Palace was to be closed down and its entire household transported to Dublin Castle.

In December, 1876, the Viceroy made his state entry riding in uniform among a glittering staff. The family, including Randolph and Jennie with baby Winston, followed in carriages with postillions and outriders.

All official entertaining had to be conducted in the somber old castle, but the viceregal lodge, a Georgian house in Phoenix Park, was put at the Duke's disposal as private residence. For Randolph, who was to act as unofficial private secretary to his father, there was a charming little white house five minutes' walk from the lodge.

The Viceroy's son and daughter-in-law naturally assisted at all official functions. Jennie's presence threw a curious glamour over the most formal and austere of ceremonies. Lord d'Abernon (then considered England's most handsome young man) has paid no mean tribute to her especial quality:

"I have the clearest recollection of seeing her for the first time. It was at the Viceregal Lodge, Dublin. She stood at one side to the left of the entrance. The Duke was on the dais . . . but all eyes were on a dark lithe figure, radiant, translucent, serene. A diamond star was in her hair, her favourite ornament—its lustre dimmed by the flashing glory of her eyes. More of the panther than of the woman in her look but with a cultivated intelligence unknown to the jungle. Her desire to please, her delight in life, and the genuine wish that all should share her joyous faith in it, made her the centre of a devoted circle."

Lord Justice Fitzgibbon, the "law adviser" to Dublin Castle describes his first meeting with Randolph after the presentations in the throne room. Lord Randolph hurried in hot-headed, to ask legal advice regarding the sacking of a disgruntled footman. The Lord Justice dispelled Randolph's illusions regarding possible methods of dealing with those servants who "did not like the look of the castle." And there began, so Fitzgibbon wrote later, "a friendship which, although full of constant anxiety and apprehension, is one of the dearest memoirs of my life. How it grew so fast I can hardly tell. I suppose electricity came in somewhere. . . ."

When a panther is married to a gentleman emitting electric sparks, their dinner table is likely to be stimulating.

During the four years that she lived in Ireland, Jennie has said she never met one really dull man. Mr. Butt (leader of the Irish party in the House of Commons, and tame forerunner of Parnell), Professor Mahaffy, the most erudite wit in Dublin, and famed Father James Healy dined frequently in the miniature lodge, hurling forth argument and anecdote.

Venturing away from Dublin, Jennie studied with amazement the strange poetical peasantry. She accompanied Randolph on shooting, fishing, and hunting expeditions and knew great happiness, for the natural charm of the Irish people hung like a smoke screen over a country simmering with bitterness. Each autumn the Duke rented a sporting home, Lord Sligo's in Mayo where the snipe shooting led to fantastic walks through Connemara or Knockdrin Castle in Westmeath where the foxes were as wild as the people. Now Jennie's prowess as a horsewoman could be shown to advantage. "Hands, hands! Light hands!" Leonard had drummed into her. The greatest sin for a woman, except singing a false note, was to jerk a good horse in the mouth. She wrote, "Hunting became our ruling passion. Whenever I could beg, borrow, or steal a horse, I did so. We had a few hunters of our own which we rode indiscriminately, being both of us lightweights. Some of my best days with the Meath and Kildare Hounds I owed to a little brown mare I bought at Oxford, who negotiated the 'trappy' fences of the Kildare country and the banks and narrow doubles of Meath, as though to the manner born. Many were the 'tosses' I took, as the Irish papers used to describe them, but it was glorious sport, and to my mind, even hunting in Leiscestershire later could not compare with it. With the exception of the Ward Union Staghounds and the Galway Blazers, I think we hunted with nearly every pack of hounds in Ireland."

In view of later happenings it may be of interest to record Jennie's impressions of the west of Ireland. "In our walks we had many opportunities of seeing the heart-rending poverty of the peasantry, who lived in their wretched mud-hovels, more like animals than human beings. Alas! I fear these deplorable conditions must ever prevail in Ireland, where neglect and misery have rooted the people in their shiftless and improvident habits." During these four years of tramping the bogs and galloping after hounds, her husband was forming a firm conviction. Lord Randolph Churchill appears to have been one of the few Englishmen in the nineteenth century who realized that an Ireland, misgoverned for five centuries and burning to revolt, might prove the most urgent problem, indeed the greatest danger the British Empire could face in calamity's hour.*

In 1877, while still a minor member of the Tory party, though no longer an uncritical admirer of his chief, he made a speech which created considerable consternation: "I have no hesitation in saying that it is inattention to Irish legislation that has produced obstruction. There are great and crying Irish questions which the Government has not attended to, and as long as these matters are neglected, so long will the Government have to deal with obstruction from Ireland."

The press gave much publicity to these unconventional utterances, the *Morning Post* observing in its lead: "It is no exaggeration to say that neither Mr. Parnell nor Mr. Butt could have used stronger language in support of their respective lines of action. But it is not an Irish Home Ruler, or Irish Obstructive, who has used it. It is the Conservative representative of an English borough and the son of the Lord Lieutenant of Ireland."

Sir Michael Hicks Beach deplored Randolph's outbursts to his father, and the Duke (who may have been excused for thinking he had suffered enough from his sons for one year) replied:

GUISACHAN: September 25, 1877.

My dear Beach,
   The only excuse I can find for Randolph is that he must either be mad or have been singularly affected with local champagne or claret. I can only say that the sentiments he has indulged in are purely his own; and, more than this, I was as much amazed as you in reading them, and had no conception that he entertained such opinions. The conjunc-

---

* Neither he nor any other statesman of that century could have foreseen the day when lack of the Irish ports would almost lose Britain a war against Germany.

ture is most unfortunate and ill-timed; but at the same time it must be remembered that though my son, and occupying by leave P. Bernard's house, he is not in any way officially connected with me, and the assumption therefore that he represented my opinions would be both unwarranted and unfair. I quite appreciate your consideration in making no allusion to his remarks, and perhaps, unless it should be absolutely required, the less notice drawn to them the better. Should you, however, feel it to be necessary to correct mis-apprehensions consequent on his speech, I conceive you are perfectly entitled to do so. I can only repeat that I am extremely annoyed at the folly of his utterance, which I believe on reflection he will regret himself. Perhaps, if I might suggest, a letter from yourself to him in your official position and responsible for Irish business in Parliament might be the best way of dealing with the occurrence.

Yours very sincerely,

Marlborough.

Tension between the viceroyal lodge and the white doll's house at its garden gate grew acute. Jennie distracted herself by planting rose trees and playing with her son on the tiny lawn. When the Duke and Duchess strolled along to suggest she reason with this uncontrollable rebel whom all of them loved so dearly, she assumed evasive tactics. Randolph knew his own mind, she countered, he could not be persuaded to admire a Conservative policy he found wanting, and who was she to scold him for having Radical and Liberal friends? Surely it was unwise for wives to argue with their husbands?

Then came the famine of 1879. The Duchess of Marlborough issued an appeal for the starving poor in their wet hovels and collected one hundred fifty thousand pounds for food, fuel, and clothing. Jennie and Randolph hurled themselves into this work and grew steadily more appalled at the nightmare problem of this ill-treated, angry, unbowed nation. But what could one do? After four hundred years of harsh and stupid rule, how could it suddenly be changed? The Duchess' charitable efforts could be but a palliative; blankets and soup kitchens would not affect the tragedy of many thousands of evictions in the following year and the retributions wrought by desperate peasants, turned out of their squalid cabins because they could not pay the rent. No personal contribution, not even five hundred pounds from the Queen of England, altered the hard fact that grain was being exported from a country suffering famine. And the efforts of certain landowners, chiefly in the north, who helped their tenants in the time of distress proved negligible in the general misery.

One of these landlords, a Sir John Leslie, of Glaslough in Monaghan, brought his son to the viceregal lodge at about this time and held discussions with the Duke concerning measures which could be taken for the protection of tenants in these hard days. During the previous famine of 1847 a five-mile wall had been built around his own demesne as a temporary method of giving employment and now no evictions were dreamt of and food was being distributed. For some reason there were no absentee landlords in Monaghan. Unchaperoned and unfearing in a land where hate and ambush and murder were becoming rife, Sir John's four young daughters drove out daily in dog carts to bring help to far-flung bog cottages. Sir John's son, a quiet, blue-eyed youth of twenty, stayed to dinner and was invited to attend the small dance being held in the viceregal ballroom. Being the youngest guest, he naturally danced several times with the debutante of the house, Miss Leonie Jerome, just out of the super-schoolrooms of Wiesbaden and Paris, a connoisseur of things artistic, an arbitrator on things fashionable, with no knowledge at all of the woes of bogland. He sat out with her behind a pillar, and in the precipitate fashion of those days, as if fearing he might never see her again, suggested marriage. The lady reacted according to the books on etiquette; she was shocked rather than flattered, and delivered a pretty little sermon.

Then Jennie interrupted. "What *are* you two talking about so seriously? Politics, I'm sure." And the conference was broken up, or *prorogued,* to use a favorite family word, for young Leslie did not take no for an answer (if, indeed, he really got no) and four years later, having at intervals resumed the subject, he succeeded in obtaining a different reply.

In the spring of 1880, when the hunger had abated but the evictions were about to begin, the Duke of Marlborough resigned his viceroyalty and returned to Blenheim, where many complaints awaited concerning the running of his estates during his absence. A General Election took place just before his return and Randolph, who had spent March touring his constituency and listening to the laborers' grumbles, managed to keep Woodstock for the Conservatives. But Disraeli's government was out. Old Gladstone had rumbled forth from retirement and was now returned to power with a large majority.

Describing Lord Randolph at this time, his son has written, "Starting with many advantages, he was still, at thirty-one, obscure. . . . His party was now humbled in the dust. . . . Grave and violent dangers beset the State, and no one troubled to think about an undistinguished sprig of the nobility. Nevertheless, his hour had come."

THE FACT THAT LIFE COULD NEVER remain calm in the proximity of Lord Randolph Churchill grew more apparent every day. He had set London society sizzling and left it because hostesses had to choose between him and the Prince of Wales at every smart party, at every dinner and ball and gathering. He had ventured an independent political opinion, and already his father and the excellent Sir Michael Hicks Beach, a family friend, appeared to reel from shock. Whatever path he chose, a buzz of criticism arose. Indignant comment would be the daily butter to Jennie's bread. She had better learn to like it, to thrive on the turmoil inevitably attendant on genius. For this would be her portion through all the years to come.

While in Ireland she had tasted that peace which accompanies cross-country riding and sport. She had seldom accompanied her husband to London on his political visits, for the strain of wondering if she might suddenly meet the Prince, who had once been a friend, drained the pleasure from all social activity, but Randolph insisted she come over for the famous Peace with Honour Banquet (peace with Russia over the Dardanelles being the issue), where she heard Disraeli accuse Gladstone of being "inebriated with the exuberance of his own verbosity," a famous epithet he might well have applied to himself. Later she attended a reception given for him at Stratford House * by Lady Constance Leslie, the mother of John Leslie, the shy Grenadier Guard officer "who would follow Leonie around and then just stand and turn pink." As she went up the stairs, Disraeli was bowing low and making fulsome compliments to Lady Constance regarding her brocade dress. "From Damascus I presume?" And then, turning to observe the drawing rooms lit with flickering chandeliers, he continued in that strange flamboyant manner which intrigued the reticent English, "What vistas!"

The brocaded hostess beamed until she noticed John hurrying toward Jennie. Inarticulate but desperate, he whispered, "Is your sister over?" "No," answered Jennie curtly, for she knew the Leslies were planning a grand English marriage for their only son. And Mrs. Jerome was planning an even grander French one.

Meanwhile Leonard shepherded his protégée, Minnie Hauk.

---

* Now Hutchinson House.

At last she had succeeded in inducing a manager to present *Carmen* in London. She left New York full of Leonard's encouragement, for she had sung it over till he knew each bar by heart. One of her few surviving letters reads:

LANGHAM HOTEL, London

April 22nd, 1879

My Dearest Friend!

The first to whom I write is you after arriving on the old side of the Ocean again. For somehow I have not ceased to think of you during the whole voyage. I cannot tell you my friend how disappointed I was in not seeing you again before leaving New York. I made so sure you would call the last day of my stay that only late in the evening after I found you had not come, I wrote you a hasty line.

We had a miserable time of it crossing for we were sick the whole way, it being so stormy and rough.

I longed so to thank you with *viva voce* for your more than friendly interest and advice given to me as from a father to his daughter—which to my utmost ability I followed and obeyed.

I hope you will not disappoint me by not coming to London for you said you would, and I am looking forward to this with great pleasure. We arrived on Sunday at Liverpool and came to London. I am announced to open Her Majesty's on Saturday, April 26th, with *Carmen* so you see not much rest for me.

Please give my very sincere regards to your dear family —and for yourself my most affectionate love and esteem.

Please write to me,

Yours

Minnie Hauk

When the controversial new opera opened, the three Jerome sisters were in a box together, and for days after they were leading the arguments aroused by hammering out phrases on their pianos in London, Dublin, and Paris. When Leonard did arrive in Europe he grew rather tired of *Carmen*.

Randolph's letters to Jennie at this time are almost entirely concerned with politics. He had abandoned forever that dream of a country gentleman's existence. It was a mirage in any case. He did not carry within himself the possibility of quiet living. "I am sure the debate will be very stormy," said one letter. "I am in great doubt what to do. I think I could make a telling speech against the Government, but old Bentinck got hold of me to-day and gave me a tremendous lecture. Of course I have my future to think of, and I also have strong opinions against the Government policy. It is very difficult. I shan't decide till the last night of debate, which won't be till next Monday or Tuesday, so my departure for Ireland will be postponed.

"Northcote made a very feeble speech to-night, and the country every day gets more and more against the Government. Russia's terms of peace are monstrous, but after all it concerns Austria so much more than us, and if she won't move we are practically powerless.

"I had a pleasant evening last night at Kilke's . . . Harcourt, G. Trevelyan, Dicey, editor of *The Observer,* and Sir Henry Maine. Harcourt was very amusing. You need not be afraid of these Radicals, they have no influence on me farther than I like to go, but I hate the Government. . . ."

And another, written casually enough: "I dined with Lord Wharncliffe last night, and took in to dinner a Mrs. Langtry, a most beautiful creature quite unknown, very poor, and they say, has but one black dress."

Jennie little guessed that a rival in the history of beautiful women had been heralded upon the scene. A year or so later crowds were standing perilously on chairs to catch one glimpse of the "Jersey Lily" as she walked through Hyde Park.

Furniture removal cost little in those days, and it was with

Jennie. *Courtesy of Seymour Leslie.*

My dear mama
I am so glad
you are coming
to see us I had
such a nice

bathe in the
sea to day.
love to papa
your loving
winston

Above: Winston Churchill's first letter. *Courtesy of Seymour Leslie.*

Leonard Jerome
at the age of 69.

X WINSTON! 1888

Above: The three generations: (first row, left to right) Oswald Frewen, Shane Leslie, Clara Sheridan, Hugh Frewen, Norman Leslie, and Leonie Leslie; (second row) Clara Frewen, Mrs. Leonard Jerome, Jack Churchill; (third row) Lady Randolph Churchill and Winston Churchill. *Courtesy of Sir Shane Leslie.*

Right: Leonie Leslie, with her nephew Winston Churchill, in Dublin, 1880. *Courtesy of Seymour Leslie.*

Winston Churchill, at right, with his brother John. This picture was taken in 1884. *Courtesy of Seymour Leslie.*

Brede Place. *Courtesy of Roger Frewen.*

Above: Castle Leslie, Glaslough.
Left: Clara and Jennie.

Blenheim Castle.

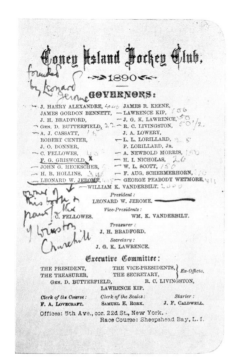

Above, left: Leonard Jerome's last race card.
Below: His last letter to his wife. The engraving on the letterhead shows Jerome Park.

pleasure that Jennie established herself in a London house while large horse drays unloaded what Randolph called "the stage props" on the doorstep. Inheriting her mother's unrestrainable impulses to buy "18th century junk quite *démodè*" in dusty antique shops, Jennie had enjoyed "antique-ing" in Dublin, where the perpetual "selling up" of the large houses of improvident Irish gentry brought Georgian furniture on the market at low prices. "Such a clutter of horrid old-fashioned bits and pieces going off to furnish the new house" aroused sniffs among the housemaids and footmen who thought they knew what was what in *English* households.

While waiting for the decorators to finish, Jennie wrote her mother an illuminating account from a London Hotel. The whole family had been worried over Leonie's beau, Charlie Fitz-william:

> July 12th 1880,
> LONDON.
>
> *Dearest Mama,*
>   I owe you all letters but the time flies and life here in London is such a "hurry scurry" that even when I have a quiet moment it is with difficulty that I settle down. Old Everest got a cold and I had to give her a holiday—and she is still away. Luckily I found a very good monthly nurse who looks after the Baby. Winston is a very good boy, and is getting on with his lessons, but he is a most difficult child to manage— So much for the infants! You will be glad to hear that R. has been covering himself with glory and I'm told he has made himself a wonderfully good position in the House. Last Monday he spoke on an Irish Question which interests all the landlords at the moment, and he made a *really* splendid speech—everyone says so—and Gladstone got up and answered him for an hour. I am sending you Vanity Fair. It is a capital caricature I think. When this Govt. goes out (which they say will be soon) I fancy R.

217

and his boon companion Sir Henry Drummond Wolf must be given something. I am only so afraid of R. getting spoilt —he wd lose half his talent if he did. I keep reminding him of it. London is very gay just now. I haven't been to many balls; as I simply cannot afford to get dresses and one can't wear always the same thing. Besides I was not bidden to the one I wanted to go to (because of the Prince) and I did not care about the others. This week I am going out every night, to-morrow to the opera—I was sent a box so I called Natica and Johnny Kaye. We were thinking of going to Dinard for August but they say Parliament will not be up till September. I shall send Winston and John to Ventnor for a month. Money is such a hateful subject to me just now don't let us talk about it. So glad to hear the Races had come off so successfully but I agree with you in everything you say about Fitzwilliam. I never thought it was a good match in a money point of view but if they had as much to live on as we have they wd do well enough. As far as position goes nothing cld be better, and last but not least Leonie cld *never* find a nicer man. At the same time I clearly see all the objections and no one feels more than I do all you say of her being worthy of something better from the worldly point of view—but when I look around here it seems to me the chances for *any* girl, are very small—there are so few parties, and when I see a girl like Georgie, with everything that money, dress and position can do for her, hanging on year after year! and she is not the only one—there is one of the Duchess of Newcastle's daughters Lady Beatrix Clinton a nice looking girl, very well educated, and with a large fortune, they say £12,000 a year. Well this is her first season, and she insists on marrying Johnny Kaye's brother, Mr. Cecil Kaye a sick tiresome youth. I'm only telling you this to show you what nonsense it is trying to arrange marriages and how difficult it is to marry *at all*.

. . . Of course if you ask me not to encourage Fitz-william I won't. At the same time I am *dreadfully* prejudiced in his favour . . . Give my best love to Papa and

Randolph's who wants me to say that he is delighted at the success of the Races he takes the *greatest* interest in it all.

Ever yr. loving,
Jennie.

Leonard disapproved of the European aristocrat's habit of looking for heiresses instead of for opportunities to earn, but his wife had caught the *parti* fever. The period in England that Jennie described was curious, for it prevented natural pairing of the species. Primogeniture had always prevailed in England, but during the nineteenth century a new snobbism arose that prevented the younger sons from going into trade or striking out independently. Although obsessed by the importance of money they could take no action to rectify their own situation. Hanging around on allowances, they were able to better themselves only along the narrow paths of Army, Navy, or diplomatic service. Naturally they tended to eschew marriage and its responsibilities.

While each noble family was able to produce only *one* elder son, it usually furnished a bevy of husband-hungry daughters, not necessarily as well-endowed as the Dukes' daughters mentioned by Jennie but nevertheless reared in a great mansion and accustomed to the grand style. If unable to catch an heir these girls had to decide between remaining on their high shelf or stepping down to share the frustrations of a younger son, thus slipping from the titled heights of the nobility into the vacuum of landless gentry. After nerve-racking intrigues and long waiting, Randolph's five sisters did eventually manage to procure eldest sons, four of whom were peers. The upper class seemed to be mentally paralyzed by its own snobbery. It took an American to bluntly state the situation which made it "extremely difficult for a girl to get married at all."

The Churchills' new house in St. James Street lay next door to that of Sir Stafford Northcote, who had inherited the Conservative party from the failing Disraeli. He was a bland, inoffensive old gentleman, supremely unsuited to lead an opposition; and Randolph, a fighter to the core, writhed at the ineffectual manner in which Conservative affairs were conducted. Combustive force enabled him to form that extraordinary Fourth Party which for five years was to outrage, delight, goad into action and reduce to impotent exhaustion the Whigs and the Tories in turn.

Meanwhile Jennie hung her new drawing room with silk panels and wept when the winter fogs destroyed them. But thick walls were more important than inner hangings. Old Northcote was to grow puzzled and then furious when he learned of the four self-assertive men who were preparing their independent political offensive in the house next door.

The other members of the Fourth party, Sir Henry Drummond Wolff, a witty and respected older member; Mr. John Gorst, an eminent lawyer; and young, charming, incalculable Mr. Arthur Balfour had already been accustomed to sit on the front bench in the House of Commons. Lord Randolph joined them when an elderly Conservative vacated a seat beside them, muttering, "This is getting too hot for me."

The industry of this band in moving amendments and preparing devastating speeches aroused groans among the Liberals, who after their victory at the polls had thought to ride easily. It seemed hardly believable that only four men could conduct such sustained and coordinated attacks. At first the older members of the Tory party, too hidebound and cautious to render constructive criticism or spirited opposition themselves, were delighted to find the job done for them. But when they noticed the Radical tendencies of the Fourth party in regard to the workmen's compensation bill and the like, frowns spread over elderly brows. They realized that the unforgivable sin of original thought was infesting their ranks.

In August, 1880, five months after the election, the Liberals solemnly rebuked the Fourth party for "obstruction." During this short period its four lively members were accused (amid laughter) of having made among them 247 speeches and asked seventy-three questions! Randolph retaliated by quoting from an old article written by Gladstone himself:

"Now if a great party may obstruct, it is hazardous to award narrower limits to the small ones, for it is precisely in the class of cases where the party is small, and the conviction strong, that the best instances of warrantable obstruction may be found."

"This," he cried, "will be our charter!"

In September, when a hot summer and long hours had reduced remaining members to ill-tempered exhaustion, the session closed, and Randolph and his friends in the best of form joined Jennie in the country, where she had retreated with six-year-old Winston and a new baby named John.

Jennie knew that her husband's star was rising fast, that his brain and wit and clarity of expression had no rival in Parliament, but what a pathetic side of her existence is revealed by a letter written at the beginning of winter from Blenheim. Leonard was sending her all he could afford to ease the burden of Randolph's career, but the path of a beauty in an alien country is not necessarily strewn with roses. This is the first American version of life in a ducal palace:

BLENHEIM PALACE,
Woodstock.
Nov. 21st

Dearest Mama,

I was so pleased to get your letter. You know you don't treat me very often to one! I'm so delighted to think that you are coming over in March. It will be great fun going over to Paris together. It is such ages since I've seen you. It is really too long. I quite forget what it is like to be with

221

people who love me. I do so long sometimes to have someone to whom I could go and talk to. Of course Randolph is awfully good to me and always takes my part in everything, but how can I always be abusing his mother to him, when she is devoted to him, and wd do anything for him —The fact is I *loathe* living here. It is not on account of its dullness, *that* I don't mind, but it is gall and wormwood to me to accept anything or to be living on anyone I hate. It is no use disguising it, the Duchess hates me simply for what I am—perhaps a little prettier and more attractive than her daughters. Everything I do or say or wear is found fault with. We are always studiously polite to each other, but it is rather like a volcano, ready to burst out at any moment. Clara and Leonie both know what her ways are like. So it is no use describing *les petites misères* that make up the total of one's existence here. What one can laugh at in the abstract is most bitter when one is living with a person and accepting their hospitality. We've been here more than a month. The children have got charming nurseries and are well looked after. I've got a very nice room and sitting room on the ground floor; I paint and do pretty much what I like. Well! You can believe me when I say that I wd be happier living quite alone in our little house without seeing a soul. However it is not for long, only a fortnight more. I know I am very foolish to mind what can't be changed but it is trying! Now to talk of something cheerier you will be glad to hear R. made a capital speech at Portsmouth. I wish I cd send you the *Morning Post* but I couldn't get it. Of course the Liberal press is furious at his attacks on the Govt. but their spiteful articles are rather flattering than otherwise. How I wish the Conservatives might come in. We could then have a chance. Meanwhile our money affairs are pretty much like everyone else's it seems to me, hard up notwithstanding Papa's most generous "tips."

Randolph is obliged to spend so much in a political way, going to these meetings etc. and this big public dinner in

Woodstock will cost a lot . . . the building alone costing £120. . . . But this demonstration is of great importance to R. and the thing must be well done with Ld Salisbury and a lot of big swells coming. You don't know how economical we try to be. I've not bought but one winter dress, and that was bought in Woodstock for twenty-five shillings and made by my maid—dark red thin flannel. Clara and Leonie would cry fi! of my wardrobe. There is no one here but Ld. Portarlington and Lady Londonderry—the Dowager. They both asked after Clara and said nice things. I've heard no amusing gossip, only a few letters from sporting friends. Best love to all dear Mama.

Ever,

Yr. loving,

Jennie.

P.S. R. Sends his best love— Bye the bye couldn't you send a barrel of American eating apples to St. James Place? I'm so fond of them."

Fi! is the word I fear for a lady who receives £6,000 a year, and only has one red flannel dress and must beg Mama for apples!

WHILE HER HUSBAND DEVELoped into the most notorious, as well as most fascinating, character in London, Jennie reveled in his political tumults. From breakfast until dinner, plots were hatched around her dining table. The Duke of Marlborough, accustomed to entertaining only Conservative leaders, suffered a fresh shock on learning that the more brilliant members of the Liberal party were frequently invited to his son's house. But he chided Jennie in vain. She enjoyed sharp repartee even of Liberal origin. Envious London society abandoned the old whisper that she rouged and charged her instead with tinges of Radicalism!

Mr. Joseph Chamberlain, Sir Charles Dilke, and Sir William Harcourt were the friends whom the Duke found most pernicious. All three begged Jennie to do their portraits. She had taken up oil painting with her usual impetuosity, starting off with huge canvases and dozens of tubes of paint. "It is such fun to let oneself go," she explained to the dubious friend who had mistaken one of her pictures for a brilliant piece of wool work. But she refused to immortalize these Liberals, saying, "I couldn't paint you black enough to suit my father-in-law."

It had not yet become fashionable for young pretty women to attend debates, but, Jennie spent many successive evenings in the ladies' gallery. "As we could not yet enter the same house as the Prince of Wales, much of the vain and foolish excitement of London society was closed to us, and politics became in fact our entire and all-absorbing interest." Mrs. Ronalds came to practice with her and recounted the small anecdotes concerning the Prince of Wales' set which were considered of such vital interest. She had been to the Duke of Portland's first great week end at Welbeck where the Prince had been "kept amused" (they always seem to have found this exceeding difficult) by Fanny's accounts of her adventures in many lands. Other guests present were the Duke and Duchess of Manchester and Lord Hartington "who looked often at Louisa Manchester." No one missed a trick. They had nothing else to do.

A letter from Jennie, written after her sisters had just returned to New York, shows a cool view on matrimony.

May 30th 1880.

Dearest Leoni—

I was so glad to see the arrival of the *Bothnia* last week and to know that you were all safe. I have been very dissipated of late, there seems to be so many things going on. I lunched with Lady Lonsdale, such an extraordinary set she has about her, Consuelo and Natica Delacour, Bertie Balfour, Tyrvoliss (*et v'là un nom*), Allen Young and the youngest Lowther. The house is charming, full of beautiful pictures and tapestry, but no taste. Last Sunday R. and I dined with Philip Currie at his little house on Clapham Common. He made himself so agreeable and gave us such a capital dinner, his house was full of pretty things, and he had *violet* silk curtains and yellow walls in his drawing room! He talked a great deal about Clara and kept asking me 50 times when she was coming over. Tell her, that if Papa agrees, she had much better take him. He is as good looking as ever—and *so* agreeable and clever. R.—— swears by him.

Randolph made a speech the other night about "Bradlaugh" * which was a tremendous success. Everyone was full of it and rushed up and congratulated me to such an extent that I felt as tho' I had made it. I'm told that Tumtum ** expresses himself highly pleased and the result is that we have been asked to meet both him and the Princess to-morrow, at a dance Lord Fife is to give. I suppose he must have been told to do it as he is about the court officially. Friday I went to two balls, both very good.

Such an absurd thing happened yesterday. The Star man *** was here having tea when a very smart carriage drove up powdered footmen, wigs, silk stockings and inside

---

* The famous renegade of the House of Commons who refused to take the oath.
** The Earl of Rutland.
*** Lord Falmouth who had been elected Randolph's second in the famous intended duel.

a very fat old trump. "Who on earth is this old demon?"
I said. "Why, it's my mother!" the Star confessed. Tableau!
There are 2 such pretty girls going out now, the Duchess
of Newcastle's daughters, they dress so well. The other
night they had mauve satin ball dresses, the skirts tulle
with little plisses. Winston and I went yesterday to the
Horse Guards, for the Queen's birthday and nearly came
to grief in the crowd, had it not been for Lord Valentia who
came to the rescue and pulled us out. I've seen nothing of
John Kaye of late. I'm told that Mrs. Candy is in love with
him and much to his ennuie rushed about after him. The
other day she heard him asking me if he might come to tea
—and to my astonishment *she* appeared! I'm glad to say
he did not turn up so she was sold! Consuelo proposed herself to dinner the other night. We had old Chanceller Ball
and Lord Portarlington and she being *enivrée,* insisted on
telling "roguey poguey" stories, which I think astonished
them, they did me! Quite between ourselves I think it
du plus mauvais gout to talk like that before men.

Best love *et à bientôt.*

Yr. loving,

Jennie.

The members of the Fourth party were naturally Jennie's
closest friends. Sir Henry Wolff had admired the Jerome girls
since their early days in Cowes, and John Gorst, as well as Arthur
Balfour, possessed musical tastes so that when the House allowed,
she would sweep "half the Fourth party" off to concerts. Balfour
could play Beethoven and Schumann with her, and she kept a
letter of his dated 1883.

HOUSE OF COMMONS.

My dear Lady Randolph,
    I am groaning and swearing on this beastly beach: while
you are listening to Wagnerian discords, I am listening to

Irish grumblings, there is a great deal of brass in both of them; otherwise there is not much resemblance! I am sitting next ——, I might be sitting next to you! I am an unhappy victim. However, there is no choice. Monday night is a most unlucky one for Richter: the Irish have a talent for turning everything into an Irish debate; and when the Irish speak I must answer, as I have just been endeavouring to do!

Your miserable servant,

Arthur James Balfour

In the meantime, Gladstone's government vainly sought to shelve the stark Irish Question. While the peasants grew more desperate, the crops failed more regularly, and amid scenes of riot and misery evictions continued.

It was upon the subject of evictions that "Lord Randolph delivered the first of those Irish speeches which, in the course of the next three years, were to win him acceptance as an authority upon Irish question." His years in Ireland equipped him "for the discussion of the one vast and predominant question of the day. He took rank almost at once among those to whom Parliament would most gladly or most gravely listen upon Irish affairs."

General Gordon who visited the west of Ireland at the time has left an impartial Englishman's impression, "I must say that the state of our fellow countrymen in the parts I have named, is worse than that of any people in the world, let alone Europe. I believe that these people are made as we are; that they are patient beyond belief; loyal, but broken-spirited and desperate; lying on the verge of starvation in places where we would not keep cattle."

The Liberals had spoken words of sympathy to Irish peasants as to English workers, but having obtained power they seemed unable to act.

In the spring of 1882 Randolph became ill, and Jennie took him to America for a few months' rest. Leonard assessed his son-in-law as "frail but fiery," telling Clara, "I think Jennie is wonderful for him, he draws on her strength. I love having them here. I believe in R."

All through the following winter Randolph assailed Mr. Gladstone on the questions of Ireland and Egypt, but he fought almost as hard within his own party. It had become a firm intention to force the replacement of Sir Stafford Northcote by Lord Salisbury.

Mr. Gladstone was sensitive to the terrible working conditions created by the Industrial Revolution but despite his efforts and promises factory life remained a hell on earth, and the disillusioned workers turned wildly to any new leader. "Randy's" clear-cut views, and sense of reality, aroused roars of acclamation wherever he spoke. Only he and Mr. Gladstone could draw such crowds. Liberals and Radicals raged with fury at the sight of a young aristocrat stealing their thunder with the working men. His own party watched with raised eyebrows, and made what use they could of this "meteor whirling in our midst." But meteors are always regarded with caution and usually with distrust.

"Give it to 'em hot, Randy!" was the cry of the street crowds, and the *Times* and *Morning Post* began to record his speeches verbatim. "Wit, abuse, epigrams, imagery, argument all were 'Randolphian.' No one could guess beforehand what he was going to say, or how he would say it."

The world of rank and fashion watched with annoyance, and yet with respect, when he proclaimed, "I hope before long to see Tory working men in Parliament. . . . If you want to gain the confidence of the working classes, let them have a share, and a large share, a real share, and not a sham share, in your party Councils."

Only Randolph would have used the word *sham*.

In April, 1883, Sir Henry Wolff and Lord Randolph Churchill started a new political society named the Primrose League with the intention of cutting through all classes. Both Jennie and the

Duchess of Marlborough became members. Jennie has recorded that Randolph suffered terribly from nerves before delivering those concise fiery speeches which appeared so spontaneous, adding naively that *she* on the contrary did not suffer from any lack of confidence.

In the autumn of 1883 Randolph took Jennie and little Winston abroad. They explored the Swiss and German mountains, and at Gastein had tea with the Emperor William I of Germany. Randolph wrote: "The Emperor, I must admit, was very guarded in his conversation, which was confined to asking me how long I had been here, and whether I had come for my health. My wife, however, sat by him at tea, and had much conversation which, I have ascertained, was confined to the most frivolous topics. I have reason to believe, though it is humiliating to confess it, that the fame of the Fourth Party has not yet reached the ears of this despot. I must say he is a very fine old fellow, and the Germans seem to love him. There were several other Prussians and Austrians present; but I was rather bored on the whole and so was my wife." Jennie was not too bored to note the Emperor's diet while on a cure. "He began with poached eggs, and went on to potted meats, and various strange German dishes, added many cups of strong tea, and ended with strawberries, ices, and sweet, tepid champagne."

WHEN LORD RANDOLPH RE-turned to London, the Reform Bill, which was to increase the electorate from three million to five million, had started its stormy progress through the House. Randolph's best speech of the time was a withering attack on a member who argued against votes for "Irish peasants who lived in mud-cabins." Randolph was forever trying to exact legislation to better the Irish people's material condition, and to give in to their every demand except Home Rule, which he considered "impossible" and certainly not beneficial to Ireland. "We owe the Irish a great deal for our bad government of them in the past," he said, but then proceeded with this suggestion: "If we are not stingy, there are few injuries, however deep, which money will not cure."

In this case, a sublime error!

From December, 1884, until March, 1885, Randolph traveled through India shooting tigers. When he returned, the excitement of the forthcoming General Election had superseded the dramas of Irish nationalism and Russian aggression. "It is not easy to estimate, and quite impossible to explain, the personal ascendancy which he had by this time, acquired in the House of Commons." "What place will you give him when the government is formed?" a friend asked Sir Stafford Northcote. "Say rather," replied the Prime Minister presumptive, "what place will he give me?"

This passage was repeated to Randolph, who was heading the movement to replace Northcote by Lord Salisbury. With unthinking cruelty he murmured: "I had no idea he had so much wit."

There was danger in Randolph's presumptions on the "indisposition of Sir Stafford for acute party warfare." He often doubted the outcome of his stand, and fell prey to bouts of depression.

To a friend in the Turf Club he said: "I am very near the end of my tether. In the last five years I have lived twenty. I have fought society. I have fought Mr. Gladstone at the head of a great majority. I have fought the Front Opposition Bench. Now I am fighting Lord Salisbury. I have said I will not join the government unless Northcote leaves the House of Commons. Lord Salisbury will never give way. I'm done."

But Northcote was persuaded to retire to the House of Lords and brilliant Sir Michael Hicks Beach became leader of the House of Commons in his stead.

Randolph had triumphed. He accepted the office of Secretary of State for India which, owing to the anxieties caused by Russian moves towards Afghanistan, could be considered the most important post after the Foreign Office.

On joining the government, a member had to seek re-election in his constituency. Overpressed by ministerial work of importance he allowed Jennie, who had always accompanied him on political gatherings, to fight the election for him. She bought a new bonnet, memorized necessary speeches, and hurried to the Bear Hotel, Woodstock, which she and Randolph's sister Lady Georgiana Curzon made Tory headquarters. The seat was uncertain, and in some anxiety Sir Henry Wolff, Lord Curzon, and Sir Frederick Milner traveled down to aid the two ladies. They need scarcely have worried.

Lady Randolph and Lady Georgiana, sure that none could conduct a campaign better than themselves, rose to the occasion superbly. "We were most important, and felt that the eyes of the world were upon us. Reveling in the hustle and bustle of the committee-rooms, marshaling our forces, and hearing the hourly reports of how the campaign was progressing, I felt like a general holding a council-of-war with his staff in the heat of a battle."

There were only a thousand voters in Woodstock and all could be approached personally. Lady Georgiana, a fine driver, brought down her tandem, and they decorated the horses with ribbons of pink and brown, Randolph's racing colors. Together the ladies trotted through the countryside, smiling and waving to the folk they knew, stopping to cajole those who doubted.

Their faces were well known to all around Blenheim, and only
on the very outskirts of Marlborough territory did jeers arise.
But these Jennie turned to good account. Off on her own, out of
earshot of the committee she dared throw aside the usual political
slogans and speak as she liked. Randolph might have winced had
he heard her but, on the whole, she found "Please vote for my
husband; I shall be so unhappy if you don't," accompanied by an
appealing smile more effective than diatribes against Gladstone's
policy. It was a dour fellow indeed who could resist the spell of
Jennie Churchill when she drove into the fields, climbed on a
hay rick, and with flushed cheeks begged for a vote.

At the end of a fortnight everyone concerned had become
worn out except the two ladies. Lord Randolph won by 532 to
405. Jennie's triumphant farewell speech from the Bear Hotel
ended by thanking the electors "from the bottom of my heart."
She returned to London in a state of elation, and wrote her father:
"It must have quite gone to my head, for it seems odd the crowds
in the city streets did not recognize and applaud me."

Certain people wondered if such canvassing could be deemed
entirely fair. Not many members possessed a sister with a saucy
tandem, and none a wife with Jennie's eyes. Jingles on the subject
were printed galore.

But just as I was talking
With Neighbour Brown and walking
To take a mug of beer at the Unicorn and Lion
(For there's somehow a connection
Between free beer and election),
Who should come but Lady Churchill, with a turnout that was
fine.

And before me stopped her horses,
As she marshalled all her forces,
And before I knew what happened I had promised her my vote;
And before I quite recovered

From the vision that had hovered,
'Twas much too late to rally, and I had changed my coat.

And over Woodstock darted
On their mission brave, whole-hearted,
The tandem and their driver and the ribbons pink and brown.
And a smile that twinkled over,
And that made a man most love her,
Took the hearts and votes of all Liberals in the town.

Bless my soul! that Yankee lady,
Whether day was bright or shady,
Dashed about the district like an oriflamme of war.
When the voters saw her bonnet,
With the bright pink roses on it,
They followed as the soldiers did the Helmet of Navarre.

Sir Henry James the Attorney General wrote:

NEW COURT, TEMPLE, 1885.

My dear Lady Randolph,
You must let me very sincerely and heartily congratulate
you on the result of the election, especially as that result
proceeded so very much from your personal exertions.
Everybody is praising you very much.

But my gratification is lightly impaired by feeling I must
introduce a new Corrupt Practices Act. Tandems must be
put down, and certainly some alteration, a correspondent
informs me, must be made in the means of ascent and
descent therefrom; then arch looks have to be scheduled,
and nothing must be said 'from my heart.' The graceful
wave of a pocket handkerchief will have to be dealt with
in committee.

Still, I am very glad.

Yours most truly,
Henry James

233

HE QUARREL BETWEEN THE Prince of Wales and Lord Randolph Churchill had simmered on. An early attempt to rectify the breach ended badly. Lord Randolph received a summons to the Prince's levee. He wished to avoid it, but friends persuaded him to go. By some misunderstanding His Royal Highness had not been alerted of Randolph's presence; he stared in cold surprise at the gentleman who had provoked him to suggest a duel, and Randolph, considering himself insulted, returned home pale with fury saying that he had been "caddishly trapped" and then cut. The friends who had busied themselves preparing this reconciliation did not dare approach, and even Jennie with nerves of iron departed to the country to recover from "such seething and fulminating."

In 1883 Queen Victoria took pains to end the feud, and Jennie attended a Drawing Room at the Queen's special wish. Aware of Randolph's white-hot pride, the Prince started to send messages suggesting that a reconciliation might lie within the dignity of both parties. For seven years society had found itself in a dilemma whenever the two antagonists approached the same house; and, dramatic as this may have seemed at the beginning, it had devolved into a great bore. Now, as Queen Victorian doubtless observed, it might soon prove embarrassing to have a Minister of the Crown who could not speak to his Prince.

After the reconciliation had been effected, Jennie marked the event by giving a dinner party for the Prince and Princess of Wales, at which Mr. and Mrs. Gladstone and Lord Rosebery were among the guests. The conversation proved so animated there was no possibility for awkward thoughts, or looks, or even silences to occur.

In March, 1886, H.R.H. took pains to be gracious to Mr. Leonard Jerome, who was staying near him in Cannes, complimenting him on what he had done to further horse racing in America, on his sailing prowess, and above all on his three remarkable daughters. Leonard copied out the terms of the big American Stakes for the Prince, who was astonished to hear of the large number of nominations in forthcoming years.

While Randolph held the India office, Queen Victoria sent for Jennie, and personally bestowed on her the Order of the Crown of India, a pretty affair of pearl and turquoise which, if it added but vaguely to her prestige, would certainly enhance any evening dress. Jennie traveled down to Windsor Castle by train. Her outfit had been decreed by a card from a lady in waiting:

"The Lady Randolph Churchill:

"Bonnet and morning dress: grey gloves. To Kiss the Queen's hand after receiving the decoration, like the gentlemen to-day. A room will be prepared for her."

The Queen, wearing a long white veil, stood with her back to the window so that an aureole shone around her plump little figure. With a few kind words she tried to pin the Order on Jennie, but alas the best velvet dress embroidered thickly with jet gave no hold, and after some prodding her Majesty ran the pin straight into Jennie's shoulder. With difficulty the honored lady restrained a squeak of pain, but the Queen saw her start and was much concerned at having spiked a loyal subject. Eager as Jennie was to note details concerning this seldom-seen sovereign, Queen Victoria seems to have been equally interested in the most talked-of beauty of the day. Next morning a note arrived:

My dear Lady Randolph,
I hope you got home quite comfortably yesterday, and took no cold. The Queen told me she thought you so handsome, and that it had all gone off so well.

Believe me ever,

Yours truly,

Jane Ely.

This note was proudly placed among the invitations on the mantelpiece of her new drawing room. Number 2 Connaught Place, beside Marble Arch, was now the Churchills' house, and this she had decorated with paneling which the fogs could not destroy.

Shortly after the pinning episode, Lord and Lady Randolph were commanded to Windsor for the night. They dined in a small room hung with Winterhalter portraits. Jennie found the habit of conversing in whispers when in the royal presence was, to put it mildly, "conducive to shyness." When Her Majesty spoke, even the whispers ceased, and the answer to any question had to be given in a silence where one dropped fork would have clattered like castanets. Once more Jennie felt the Queen's cold gray eyes rove slowly over her. Fervently she hoped that her dress was not a shade too low, her color too high, or her answers too pat. "I tried hard to keep my tongue under control," she said later. "You know how I tend to rattle on, and I was terrified of saying a word too much, and arousing that dread 'We are not amused.'"

In December, when the General Election took place, Lord Randolph attacked in the Liberal stronghold of Birmingham. Jennie found the Duchess of Marlborough had now become her ally and had ceased to resent that unfair endowment of beauty. Together they tramped through miles of slums, canvassing house by house and addressing men in factories. It was the first time that women had attempted personal canvassing in industrial slums, and they found the workers resentful. As both parties always seemed more interested in obtaining a majority in the House than actually bettering the wretched industrial conditions this was hardly surprising. When the Duchess, shaken by bad language, retreated from a doorway, Jennie rallied her. She had to put her own wits and courage to the test as never before. Soon she found it easier to cease argument and try appeal. As long as Randolph was not watching, she was ready to use any methods. One day she met sullen silence in a factory.

"Why are you all so cross?" she asked.

A man stood up. "We don't like being asked for our votes."

"But you have something I want. How am I to get it, if I don't ask?"

This raised a laugh.

Jennie's method of approaching "the people," her easy manners with grocer's wife and butcher's lady, permeated the Conservative Primrose League until sedate English peeresses were ready to capture votes by hook or by crook. "Would it not be too vulgar?" gasped a member, when an entertainment was being discussed by the Ladies' Council. Lady Salisbury, wife of England's Conservative Prime Minister, rose up: "Vulgar? Of course it is vulgar; that is why we have got on so well."

Lord Randolph did not manage to defeat the famous John Bright in central Birmingham, but his new Tory democracy obtained considerable success in other working-class centers. Having altered the vote from two Liberals to one Tory to three Liberals to two Tories, Lord Randolph returned to London and was elected for South Paddington, his home district. In the House 335 Liberals were returned against 249 Conservatives and 86 Parnellites. This meant that Gladstone could not swing a majority.

And the Tory resurrection was entirely due to Randolph. The country proceeded to wait for Gladstone's decision on Home

Rule, "the dream of a sun-lit Ireland, loyal because it was free, prosperous and privileged because it was loyal, the crowning glory of an old man's life, all find their place in that immense decision."

On January 26, Lord Salisbury's "Cabinet of Caretakers" resigned, and Gladstone formed his own ministry. Throughout the spring, the confused and divided parties prepared their stand on the Irish bill which was to be the tombstone of the "Grand Old Man." In June, Gladstone brought the Home Rule debate to a close with his splendid speech, which ended with ". . . the ebbing tide is with you and the flowing tide is with us. Ireland stands at your bar, expectant, hopeful, almost suppliant. Her words are the words of truth and soberness. She asks a blessed oblivion of the past, and in that oblivion our interest is deeper than even hers. . . . Think, I beseech you—think well, think wisely, think not a moment, but for the years that are to come, before you reject this Bill."

Protestant Ulster, the nettle which Gladstone had never really dared to grasp, shouted it would fight if the bill went through and the huge Liberal core of industrial England was roaring dissent from its own Prime Minister's view. That night the Liberal party split. Amid tumultuous shouts, the Bill for Home Rule was rejected by 341 votes to 311, and the six-month-old government fell. Gladstone saw that Irish Home Rule had broken his own party in two. "The Parliament so lately returned in his support had destroyed itself, almost before it had lived, rather than follow him further." Parliament was dissolved, and on July 1 the country went to the polls for the second time in six months, with only one issue in mind, to vote for or against parliamentary union with Ireland.

IN THE SUMMER OF 1886 CAME THE most exciting election of the century. Lifelong friends fought each other bitterly in an entirely new cleavage. Between Home-Rule Liberals and Liberal Unionists arose a rift which threw the latter into the Tory camp. Sure of his London seat, Randolph spoke only in Manchester and Birmingham, the enemy strongholds.

The voters of England showed their opinion sharply: Gladstone and the Home Rulers were utterly defeated. Lord Salisbury became Prime Minister and Randolph accepted the responsibility of two high offices, Leader of the House of Commons and Chancellor of the Exchequer.

"How long will your leadership last?" asked a friend.

"Six months," Lord Randolph laughed.

"And after that?"

"Westminster Abbey."

Jennie saw her husband, at the age of thirty-six, entrusted with two of the most important appointments in England. He was the natural leader of his party; the Conservatives did not love him, but they could not do without him: "The double fascination of mystery and success lent him an air of authority, which neither irreverent language nor the impulsive frankness of youth could dispel."

Happily Randolph possessed a very serious side, for as Disraeli noticed, "An insular people subject to fogs and possessing a powerful middle class, requires grave statesmen." Lord Justice

Fitzgibbon wrote, "If I were you I would rather not be obliged to carry as Leader the financial reputation of the State, in addition to the rest of the load. The English are your sheet-anchor and finance is their pole-star; and a middle-aged commercial Chancellor would make them easy in their minds when you could not."

Tackling the Irish question, Randolph proposed monetary drafts to help crew a deep-sea fishing industry, improve railways, and drain bogland around the great rivers. Parnell hurled back these offers of material assistance, and the Irish Nationalists listened in moody silence whenever the Chancellor of the Exchequer rose to speak. "You must find it very hard work," said a friend, "leading the House, and at the same time being at the Exchequer."

"Not half such hard work as it was getting there," Randolph answered.

When the session ended, Randolph kept up a continual correspondence with Lord Salisbury on the subject of Russian angling for the Dardanelles:

"If Russia attacked Constantinople," observed Salisbury, "and all the other Powers refused to intervene, I am rather disposed to the idea that we should have to act in the Dardanelles."

Randolph wrote back fretfully at the Foreign Office: "I feel sure that our present niggling, meddling, intriguing, fussy policy is gaining for us the contempt and dislike of Bismarck every day."

In October "young Churchill" aroused unprecedented feeling when he said in a speech: "I will not conceal from you that my own special object . . . is to endeavour to attain some genuine and considerable reduction of public expenditure and consequent reduction of taxation." Then he proceeded to outline England's foreign policy regarding Russia. "There are other Powers," he proclaimed in the tactful manner of the day, "who betray from time to time a regrettable tendency towards contentious and even aggressive action." England must support the liberty-loving

Powers of Europe "in whose favour our timely adhesion would probably, and without the use of force, decide the issue."

For those days it was plain speaking. Russia would not be allowed a walk-over to Constantinople. Lord Randolph Churchill's name suddenly resounded throughout Europe. No statesman had spoken so clearly for years.

Randolph's career had been swift and dazzling. The House of Commons, a hard school, had molded him, and now it responded instinctively to his oratory and granted him indisputable leadership. Jennie took it for granted that her husband would reach the post of Prime Minister. But in late December, he contradicted the Cabinet concerning the Budget.

After Randolph's disagreement with Smith. the War Minister Lord Salisbury wrote:

"The Cabinet, happily not I, will have to decide the controversy between you and Smith. But it will be a serious responsibility. . . ."

On December 20, 1886, Lord Randolph was summoned to Windsor Castle. He spent the evening with the Queen, who appeared to delight in his company and kept him long in conversation. On this occasion her Chancellor seemed unusually gay and vivacious. He spoke on many topics, but never mentioned that he was ready to pledge his career to reducing armament expenditure. Late that night on Windsor Castle note paper he wrote his famous letter of resignation to Lord Salisbury saying, "I am pledged up to the eyes to large reductions of expenditure, and I cannot change my mind on this matter. If the foreign policy of this country is conducted with skill and judgment, our present huge and increasing armaments are quite unnecessary, and the taxation which they involve, perfectly unjustifiable. . . ."

Lord Salisbury wrote back a long letter ending with "No one knows better than you how injurious to the public interests at this juncture your withdrawal from the Government may be.

"In the presence of your very strong and decisive language I can only again express my very profound regret."

But the Prime Minister did not communicate the matter to the Queen until a second letter arrived from Randolph, formally taking leave of the government. This letter only reached the Prime Minister at half-past one in the morning of December 23. He immediately sent the news to Windsor; but before midnight Lord Randolph had left the theater (where, in a box, Jennie sat, gay and unguessing) to impart his information to the *Times*. The first inkling Her Majesty received of Randolph's resignation was, therefore, when she opened her morning paper. With cold fury she sent an inquiry concerning this breach of etiquette. The fact that his letter of resignation had been written on *her* note paper seemed the last straw.

For some inscrutable reason, Randolph allowed the *Times* to inform his wife as well as his Queen. Jennie came down to breakfast stunned, with the newspaper in her hand.

"Quite a surprise for you," smiled Randolph.

Mr. Moore, a devoted official from the Treasury, rushed in, pale and distracted. "He has thrown himself from the top of the ladder, and will never reach it again!" Moore, who adored his chief, collapsed and died within a month of a broken heart.

Randolph offered no explanation. He had pledged his word to make every effort to economize. He was sure of himself and had gambled all his power on one throw. Jennie felt too crushed and miserable to remonstrate or even to question.

During the next few days, England, and most of Europe, spoke of nothing save "the Resignation." Friends rushed to Connaught Place to bewail this eccentricity, and sycophants disappeared. Queen Victoria intimated her extreme displeasure, and Randolph's letter of apology to her was frigidly received. "How well I remember my bitter feelings in those days!" wrote Jennie. "The political atmosphere round us seemed suddenly full of strife and treachery. It was gall and wormwood to me to hear Randolph abused in every quarter, often it seemed by the men who owed their political existence to him." He certainly ruined Christmas for all his friends, especially for the ministers who had to return from country holidays.

For two weeks the government tottered and then, discovering, perhaps with a sign of relief, that it might hold together without Churchill, appointed a chancellor less crisp and incisive and a leader less wayward. None could show Randolph's brilliance, but was such brilliance necessary or really very safe? The Tories he led to victory had always feared this Radical in their midst. But they thought he was young, that he would learn from a hard lesson and come back to their fold still fiery but chastened.

Only Jennie, watching with desperate anxiety, saw health begin to ebb from that frail, taut body. She knew that, for good or for bad, he had shot his bolt, and that in his own words "with profound regret, but without doubt or hesitation," Lord Randolph Churchill had renounced power forever.

DURING THE YEARS OF RANdolph's rise to fame, Mr. and Mrs. Leonard Jerome had, for financial reasons, lived chiefly in New York. Clara and Leonie had both been married there in Grace Church.

Clara married first. She had hovered between offers in France and England while her mother, fussing like a hen, never considered any suitor quite up to standard. Yet as the years slid by Mrs. Jerome found the daily hours of chaperonage growing tedious. Whenever a gentleman called to see Miss Clara, her mama was expected to sit at the other end of the room pretending to be busy on embroidery, too far to hear what words were exchanged but "within sight." Mrs. Jerome, grown accustomed to her own little coterie of cultured Parisian admirers, found this insufferably boring. "So dull to listen to young people, but even duller to not quite be able to hear." She had always hoped for a big French marriage. With disappointment she realized the unlikelihood of this occurrence now that the girls' dowries were reduced.

No sooner had the Jeromes settled back in Madison Square than romantic-minded Englishmen began to call. Several of them had crossed the Atlantic especially to press their suits, but the one who captured Clara appeared from the West where he had been exploring the buffalo trails of the Big Horn Mountains. Moreton Frewen strode noisily into the New York scene, talking of cattle ranches in Wyoming for British lords, of converting the American government to different financial views, of saving the great herds of wild fauna in national parks, and various other schemes. Senator Jones of Nevada had told him, "It's no good hunting foxes with a brass band," but this was a lesson he would never learn.

Clara took one look at this tall, sunburnt, self-assertive sportsman and fell in love. She learned that he came of an old Sussex family, that he was a famous shot and one of the best gentlemen riders in England. Neither she nor her parents could guess at the strange future she had accepted for herself.

The second son of a squire who considered himself the first commoner in Sussex, Moreton Frewen had been brought up in the grand English tradition by gamekeepers, poachers, and grooms. His boyhood was spent on horseback, hunting in the shires, or riding alone over Salisbury Plain. He could catch salmon and jump double-oxers with art, and he knew every wild bird of England. He also learned to read and write, and at eighteen proceeded to Trinity College, Cambridge, where he enjoyed polo and steeplechasing and lent a kindly hand "nursing friends back to consciousness when they crashed over timber." During an Irish holiday he rode and won the famous midnight point-to-point race in Monaghan against Lord Rossmore, but this did not prevent him from being "sent down." He spent the next six years hunting foxes or racing against sporting lords. At Melton he rode in fine company with Bay Middleton, Whyte Melville, and Lord Lonsdale. The *Cream of Leicestershire* shows him on its cover riding through the railway cut on the day of the great Ranksborough run of January 20, 1877. Men say yet, "Ride straight as they rode it from Ranksborough Gorse."

In 1878 he had to decide between a polar expedition in James Gordon Bennett's ill-fated yacht *Jeannette,* mastership of the Kilkenny hounds, or the career of cowpuncher. With sixteen thousand pounds in his pocket, he set out to explore Texas. "My capital was but a younger son's portion—that and some ability to ride young horses." Across the Red River he saw thousands of buffalo skeletons covering the plains. Three million of these animals had been shot by hunters in the last four years and the Southern herd was almost extinct. Moreton learned that a "bad man" with brown eyes need not be feared, but "the fellow with grey eyes or grey-blue, whose eyes went darker as they looked down a gun—that was the sort of man to reckon with." With a notebook containing this and various other pieces of useful information, he returned to England for the racing season. When he placed all his winnings on a horse ridden by his friend, the famous Fred Archer, "the dear handsome little horse just failed to get home." This decided him to return finally to "the Wild West."

Lord Dunmore, Lord Lonsdale, and Lord Desborough were Moreton's best friends. He advised them excitedly of the wealth of Colorado and Wyoming which he was off to exploit, and suggested they follow with all their immense capital. In his wake the "great silent places between the Yellowstone and the Peace River two thousand miles north," became alive with adventurous English gentlemen.

The Crows and the Blackfeet were growing antagonistic to white invaders, but they used Moreton, who was a splendid shot, to pick out buffalo for them. Seeking to ride in winter over the Great Divide of the Rockies on what once had been a main buffalo trail, "a trail the vast herds of old times used and by which, in their spring migration, they got up from the prairie into the mountains for summer grazing," Moreton and his brother with two other men were caught by deep snow. All would have perished in the mountains had they not been able to head off a section of a huge buffalo herd and follow it over the tightly packed snow, using the animals as a living snowplow. "At one or two deep transverse drifts the leaders plunged in and went clean out of sight, but in a few yards they bobbed out again like porpoises playing through a wave." High in the mountains the buffalo left them. But the narrow path above the canyon was now clear of snow and they rode safely down to Powder River. To south, east, and north they could see two hundred miles— all virgin prairie which was to fill up with settlers and cattle in the next five years, "Of course we had no realisation that we had accomplished a journey that no man in all probability would ever attempt again—the passage of the main range of the Rockies from Camp Brown on the west, to Fort McKinney on the east, in December." Soon, indeed, the attempt would have been impossible, for there were no buffalo or herds of wapiti to keep the canyon trails open.

Moreton and his brother decided the prairies around Powder River would make perfect cattle country. They built a house of pine, and then Moreton started alone on the two-hundred-mile ride to Rock Creek, the nearest railroad. His horse lamed itself at Forty Mile Ranch; so, leaving it there, he proceeded to walk the remaining forty miles. "I was wonderfully well after five months of such conditioning as I had gone through, lean and hard and tough as pin-wire." He started at sunrise but falling into a field of breaking snow, took twenty-six hours to cover the forty miles. "I battled through this snow field nearly all night; the temptation to go to sleep almost irresistible but at about 3 A.M. I seemed to get my 'second wind.' . . . It was truly a great escape, and it is said that old-timers out there still tell the tale of that legendary walk!"

Soon he was on the train to New York, determined to save the great game herds of the Big Horn Mountains. Congress had segregated the Yellowstone Park but, as snow covered up all winter feeding there, the park was worthless for the big wild fauna. In Washington Mr. Frewen pushed forward proposals to include the whole Wind River basin in the park. This area was free of settlers and sheltered fifty thousand buffalo, and twice that number of wapiti. Few listened to him in Washington. "Had it been made a sanctuary for wild life, there would to-day have been a pleasance for the naturalist and traveller; but the fates decreed otherwise and so the great game herds rapidly disappeared."

Frewen had picked up a lifelong passion for bimetallism, and he proceeded to New York, defending free silver as well as buffaloes with his natural gift of gab. Such was the gentleman, lean, strong, opinionated, who caught the eye of Miss Jerome. Leonard naturally took a liking to this original adventurer. "My predestined father-in-law Leonard Jerome, one of the kindliest of men, was the centre for a brilliant coterie to which I had the entree. Stammering and witty Bill Travers, and equally witty Senator Evarts . . . and travelled men blew in from the uttermost ends of the earth, Lord Dunraven, Jones of Nevada, Lords Kintore and Dunmore and 'Uncle Larry.' I doubt if on the earth's surface did such a far-flung group of men ever collect round a single table."

After a brief glance at Miss Clara, and a not-too-modest recital of his exploits in the Big Horn Mountains, Moreton disappeared to Wyoming, where he spent a year driving cattle. Clara returned to England and heard of his prowess as a horseman all during the following winter. She sighed, and the vision of a hard-limbed adventurer struggling through the Rocky Mountains caused her to continue to refuse all marriage proposals, even those which Jennie strongly advised accepting!

In 1881 the social columns of the New York press announced the engagement of Leonard Jerome's eldest daughter to Mr. Moreton Frewen, Squire of England and present owner of a pine-log house on Powder River. The Frewens had inhabited Brick-wall, a large Elizabethan mansion, since the days when Good Queen Bess visited them (and left a pair of satin shoes which still remain). Although among the oldest landowning families in England, their fortunes were depleted, their sons scattering, and the heritage of Brickwall was only for the eldest. Clara did not care.

Moreton spent the day before his marriage in the Union Club with Leonard and Pierre Lorillard waiting to hear the results of the Derby. As well as racing his yacht *Vesta* (which had competed in the great Atlantic Race) Mr. Lorillard kept a stud farm in New Jersey for mares of the Glencoe-Lexington strain so famous for stamina.

Lorillard had entered *Iroquois* in the English Derby. The "ticker" was ticking. Lorillard had the tape between his fingers which slowly spelled out, "Derby Stakes. Epsom. Won by Iroq———"

"Oh," he said, "my horse!"

Moreton exploded. "The first American to win the Derby and he is not there!"

All that night Leonard and Moreton and Lorillard celebrated the great victory. On the following morning, Leonard led his eldest daughter up to the altar of Grace Church. She had arrived very late, for Mrs. Jerome was in tears and Moreton had retreated nervously to the vestry with his best man, Lord Bagot, where, to her amazement, Miss Jerome, waiting in a cloud of white tulle, heard them still heatedly discussing Iroquois.

After the service Leonard fastened a string of diamonds around Clara's throat. Then, when the huge reception had ended, with her trousseau packed in studded trunks and her own French maid (for she was incapable of doing up her own boots), Clara set forth on a honeymoon to be spent cattle ranching! As the train roared westward, her maid's face grew steadily longer. By the time she had seen Madame's wonderful trousseau carried out at the railway point of Rock Creek and driven two hundred miles over a rough trail to the house of pine logs, she was on the verge of hysteria.

"It's quite safe," comforted Mr. Frewen. The last Indian raid had taken place in the previous year when a cattle buyer had been killed on leaving the Frewen ranch by a band of traveling Sioux. Moreton's brother Dick had chased the Indians for weeks but never caught up with them. He found it not unnatural that the Indians should be averse to the decimation of the buffalo herds, their only food supply, by white cattle men.

"They won't come again," laughed Moreton. "If you are nervous, try shooting lessons!"

Clara thought it a pity that her Paris gowns should have to be packed away, but any life her husband planned must be *marvelous*. She was in love. The maid was not.

Young Mrs. Frewen had yet to discover what fate can lie in store for those who marry bronzed Englishmen who emerge from snowdrifts.

$\mathbb{C}$LARA TRANSFORMED THE LOG house. Animal skins covered the floors and walls, and flowering branches were placed on rough tables. The French maid perked up with cowboys for company, and Buffalo Bill himself volunteered to act as Moreton's scout. One dawn shortly after arriving, Clara evinced slight surprise when her spouse sat up in bed, suddenly shouted, "A buffalo at the creek!" and seizing his rifle leapt out of the window in his nightshirt. But she grew accustomed to such occurrences.

Moreton spent all his days driving cattle, camping, fishing, exploring, and hunting. They lived entirely on fresh meat and fish after Sir Maurice de Bunsen stalked and shot their only cow, mistaking it for an emaciated buffalo.

Guests were plentiful, for Moreton's friends, the bucks and beaux of the hunting shires, arrived in droves. In the visitors' book they entered the bears, mountain sheep, and puma they killed, but it was agreed not to touch buffalo or deer, except when meat was needed.

Lord Queensberry (of boxing-code fame), Lord Manners, Lord Caledon, Lord Rodney, and Lord Castletown were sportsmen who enjoyed Clara's hospitality. Less than a day's journey from the house they could camp by Trout Creek and "catch three-pounders by the bushel. Manners and M.F. killed ninety-five wild duck, mallards, shovellers, widgeon, and teal within a mile of the house." This solved housekeeping problems.

Sir Samuel Baker, a famous sportsman, liked to relate his

African stories over the campfire, and discussed with Moreton "the future of our planet, Africa's place in it and our Empire's place." The talk, like the game, was always big.

Clara's life as chatelaine of Powder River ended sadly. When she needed a doctor, Moreton hurried her off to Cheyenne in Buffalo Bill's Deadwood Coach. Her stillborn child was sent to New York to be buried in the Jerome family plot, and some weeks later she herself arrived in Madison Square to be nursed back to health while the French maid horrified the other servants with her stories.

Meanwhile Moreton camped alone in a deep canyon of the Big Horn Mountains. One day while wading about casting he suddenly came on a big bear disporting itself in a pool. He shot the animal through the head and had resumed his fishing when a passing Englishman shouted that Sitting Bull was in a camp nearby. Moreton splashed to the bank, hurried off, and found Sitting Bull squatting behind his camp fire gnawing a small dog's head. The great chief walked him a quarter of a mile to the scene of his battle against three hundred troopers under Captain Custer, whom his band had exterminated a few years before and in sign language explained details of the fight.

Lord Desborough and Gilbert Leigh, an English friend and a Member of Parliament, came out to stay. "A few days later a messenger rode in to say that Leigh was missing and asked us to send every available man to search. By the time we reached their camp his body had been found by Bob Stuart, the trapper. Apparently in the twilight he had mistaken the tree-tops of the pine trees sticking out of a deep canyon for some cypress brush, and had walked on and fallen a hundred feet sheer."

Leonard now ordered Moreton to return to civilization. On reaching New York he found that two former acquaintances from London, Oscar Wilde and Lily Langtry, were scheduled to arrive on the scene. Moreton had been among Mrs. Langtry's numerous early admirers. He had given her *Redskin,* the horse she rode timorously when accompanied by the Prince of Wales, but he ceased going to tea at her house because Prince Rudolph of Austria was an "inconveniently frequent visitor there in whose favour *les convenances* obliged me to give place." Mrs. Langtry had introduced him to Wilde and now the poet was beguiling New York. Moreton joined in the famous dinners where William Travers and Lawrence Jerome helped Wilde "like mid-wives to deliver his famous *bons mots.*"

In 1885 came the great cattle disaster which wrecked ten millions of British capital. Cleveland, the new American President, ordered the instant removal of half a million cattle from the Indian reservation of Oklahoma. Moreton's stockman advised quitting Wyoming before the southern herds arrived. Moreton cabled the directors of his company asking leave to drive his forty-five thousand head of cattle on the hoof to Canada, but they looked at the distance on the map and refused. A kindly duke became chairman of the company. "This lent confidence, though it did not improve the grazing." Two winters later the herds had been starved down to three thousand. Wyoming was eaten out!

Moreton dispatched his wife to England where a fourteenth-century manor house on the Frewen estates awaited her. On June 23, 1885, he made a final note in his ranch visitors' book: "Am leaving to-morrow via Superior for England, and this abode of pleasant memories and good sport is to be abandoned."

Moreton strove to move his dying herds northward. In a hardly known natural harbor at the end of Lake Superior, he bought and cleared a thousand acres of rough swamp and forest. Sheds for a thousand cattle were built, and he fed them with refuse from grain elevators. After a long unsuccessful battle to obtain permission to ship the remnant of his herds to Britain, Moreton sold for a song the thousand acres on which West

Superior City now stands and so missed his second fortune. He was always just too early or too late.*

Eventually he resigned, passing the company on to Horace Plunkett, who described the saga as "an example of Moreton's brilliant imagination and even prophetic vision aborted by a fatal inability to face inconvenient facts." Lord Rosslyn, a director, wrote: "Your only fault latterly has been you could not raise money fast enough."

This particular fault remained with him through life. Funds never caught pace with his schemes.

When asked if Frewen were rogue or fool, Lord Desborough, who had lost thousands because of him, answered: "Worse than either. He is a genius."

Ten millions of British capital had literally "gone West" and young Mr. Frewen, who had landed in America eight years before with sixteen thousand pounds, returned to his own country with an overdraft of thirty thousand. Unable to recognize defeat he wrote airily, "What had destroyed us was the magic growth of settlement and prosperity of the Great West—that and a bull-headed President."

No one could say Moreton was not a trier. No one could call him a satisfactory son-in-law, either.

But the story had only just begun. Moreton's mania for changing the world over to bimetallism had already caused the Washington Senate to dub him "Silver Tongue." He had yet to earn the nickname of the century: "Mortal Ruin"!

---

* Streets and schools are named after Frewen to this day, but the inhabitants of West Superior City do not know if he was a missionary or a lumberjack.

During the years of the great cattle catastrophe, Clara Frewen had settled into Brede Place, a beautiful, old, gray stone house lying derelict on the outskirts of the Frewen estates in Sussex. Built in 1350, it had not been inhabited except by ghosts and gamekeepers for over two hundred years. The old beamed ceilings and walls, the winding oak staircases and vast fireplaces delighted her. She created one of the most interesting homes in England. Roses and yew hedges and sweet-smelling shrubs encircled the dreaming gables, and (for she was not Mrs. Jerome's daughter for nothing) a procession of royalties and famous people came to plant trees for her.

There was no running water, but servants hauled it in pails from a nearby well, and the earth privies were emptied exactly as in Elizabethan times. Servants carried candles and arranged flowers and cooked huge meals in the brick-floored Tudor kitchen. Clara loved this place, the only real home that Moreton ever gave her.

The villagers felt it good to see a squire's lady in the big house. Here, amid the flowering Sussex slopes, she found peace, and three small children completed her happiness.

Occasionally Moreton came to stay, but not very often, for though ready to lecture the House of Commons and the Washington Senate on their currency needs, he proved singularly averse to paying his own servants' wages, preferring to keep them penniless "as part of the family." Strangely, they stayed on.

Leonard Jerome disapproved of these singular policies and refused to subsidize the Frewen home, but he gave Clara a London house in Aldford Street, and here she entertained Moreton's friends for him. Talk of high finance rang at her dinner table. Randolph's brother, the Duke of Marlborough, a convinced bimetallist, and the economists Lord Courtney and Lord Wenlock incessantly held forth in "the pretty mauve silk drawing room with the buffalo head on the wall." Clara did not understand one word of finance; she sometimes wondered if they did either.

Having lost every penny in Wyoming, Moreton now resolved to convert the entire world to a different currency standard. He describes his passion thus: "When I was a little lad I had visited nearly every nest of our British birds, but that of Richardson's skua I had never seen. I heard that afar off, on an islet near Skibbereen there might be seen the nest of this little gull. I pined for the sight of it. I was not allowed to go, and I have never since seen it at its home. The void seemed to sterilize my childhood. I recall it all these years after as one of life's disappointments. There it is! and similarly I came toward early middle life to the conviction that there was but one problem that really mattered—the great problem of Exchange." Money would ever prove elusive as the skua.

The self-appointed herald of bimetallism, tariffs, federalism and imperial preference, he darted around the world, entertained by princes, listened to by chancellors, and admired by sportsmen for his prowess with horse and gun. When creditors pressed for payment of his personal debts, he rewarded them by counter-offensives written on note paper headed "House of Lords," "The Bank of England" or "The White House." He wished it to be understood that "if I am at Washington I am there for no other purpose: if I turn up in Calcutta, in Hyderabad or Lahore, or Sydney or Ottawa or distant Auckland, it is to learn the currency needs of those far-flung communities and to see whether some welding heat can be generated here and there, such as may close that frightful fracture in the exchanges between eight hundred millions of silver-using peoples and the five hundred millions who finance themselves with gold."

Excellent, but the fissure in his own bank account might have been closed first. No hints from his father-in-law dampened Moreton, and he relates blithely an incident in the lobby of the House of Commons when Bright, the famous free-trader passed by.

"Lord Courtney clutched at Bright and said 'Do you know anything about this currency problem?'

" 'No,' said the other icily glaring at Moreton, 'but I am credibly informed there are people who do.'

"Had I tried to explain to him that there could be no Free Trade without fixed exchanges he would have said from sheer ignorance like Gladstone, that 'Bi-metallism is Protection in disguise.' "

It was experts' ignorance which galled Moreton. He could forgive the bewilderment of simple sporting friends such as a master of foxhounds who came up in Mount Street asking, "Frewen, what is all this about bimetallism? I read your speech in the *Times* to-day. Desborough tells me you can explain it in a few words." Moreton would good-naturedly take the arm of such a fellow and, leading him into one of the smart London clubs, deliver a harangue over lunch or dinner. "Thank you very much, Frewen, I feel I've learned something today," the ordinary Englishman would say, and go off more puzzled than ever. "Uncle Moreton had a first class mind untroubled by second thoughts. . . . He passed so quickly from the truths of political economy to the pitfalls of fortune hunting that it was difficult to know whether he was trying to enrich himself or the whole wide world."

A sporting trip to Egypt led to the discovery that the Nizam of Hyderabad was suffering a leakage of ten thousand pounds a year from his coffers. Moreton met the Nizam's exiled Prime Minister Sir Salar Jung in Cairo and speedily converted him to all his theories, political and financial. Sir Salar proposed a pleasure trip through the Balkans, and they moved off to Athens and Constantinople with a suite of turbaned retainers. The Dardanelles crisis was rising. Moreton "felt the pulse of the Turk" and decided that it was time the European powers took over Byzantium from the infidel "to become the winter resort for half the tired millionaires of the working world, with their steam yachts and private railway cars. Consider its amenities: the countless isles of Greece . . . the sweep of the blue Aegean . . . the great sporting solitudes of the Black Sea littoral," etc., etc.

The Sultan treated Salar Jung with consideration and sent his chief naval aide-de-camp to act as a guide to sight-seeing. "Sir Salar was more or less unmarried and proposed to me to discover for him a Turkish lady who would return to Hyderabad." Moreton spent hours in a harem trying to buy a wife, but the lady proved too expensive.

The party moved off to Vienna, Berlin, and Paris. Moreton's views on the means necessary to stabilize every country he passed through deeply impressed Sir Salar. Reaching England, they all proceeded to visit Clara, who had taken a house for Goodwood Races. Moreton cheered up her party with his Indians. "Amuse them," he ordered. So accordingly, Randolph's brother brought his coach, and Count Charles Kinsky (the handsome Austrian who rode his own horse Zoedone to victory in the Grand National of 1883 and who remained a lasting admirer of the Jerome sisters) brought an entire Hungarian band.

Sir Salar was enchanted. Then, forgetting that he had been exiled, he obeyed Moreton's orders to return to India. Moreton cajoled the party along, promising Salar that he would prevent executions on arrival. This he did by invoking the help of a racing friend, Lord William Beresford, who was secretary to the Viceroy.

Clara stayed alone in England while Moreton "straightened out the finances of Hyderabad." He lived in Sir Salar's untidy palace, in quarters of "rather tawdry Oriental splendour, but opening out upon a palmcourt with fountains." Sport was produced for Mr. Frewen, and he enjoyed the races which the great nobles attended in bejeweled Durbar costumes. The Nizam seemed to form a high opinion of him, and Moreton's busy mind started on various new plans. "When I left I was full of a great irrigation project which would have utilized some fifteen million acres of the wonderfully rich sugar-cane lands." He had also discovered an extraordinary series of frauds in the official yellow books and these he presented to a select committee of the House of Commons.

Clara's diamond necklace, the wedding present from her father, had been sold "because of pressing urgency" (when Leonard discovered this he angrily cut Moreton out of his will). Now the Nizam offered a tiara of brilliants for Mrs. Frewen, but for some reason Moreton refused it. Instead Clara was asked to present the ladies of Hyderabad at court. Queen Victoria, mistaking her for a Vice-Reine kissed her, and to her amazement received a kiss back! Poor Clara, blushing with confusion and trying to marshal her Indians who did not understand a word of English, saw the Prince of Wales shaking with laughter and realized she had made a unique breach of etiquette. Vice-Reines receive kisses. Only other queens kiss back!

After fixing Hyderabad, Moreton's next venture was a gold-crushing machine, designed to extract gold from all the mine heaps of the world. Currency investigations had shown there was not enough gold in the world. He proposed to increase it.

A model machine was set up on Clara's dining table. The Prince of Wales, Lord Randolph Churchill, and Mr. Leonard Jerome admired it dubiously while London society eagerly invested thousands of pounds. Moreton, deciding to "skip Africa and India for the first experiment," acquired a share of Broken Hill Mine and sent the invention to Australia. But the machine only worked in miniature. When put into actual practice the ore crushed the crusher! Had Moreton but kept his share of Broken Hill he would still have been a rich man, but he let it slip through his hands like Superior City and, selling all, hurried off after a new haul.

A series of schemes followed, and Frewen's long articles on how the Empire should be run appeared in the *Daily Telegraph*. When Moreton was in India, a shy youth had committed to his care the manuscript of *Plain Tales from the Hills,* which Moreton pressed on various publishers in vain. The *Daily Telegraph* returned the stories as "not up to the paper's standard." Kipling's fame broke soon after, and Moreton used the *Telegraph's* letter to tease them into publishing his own views.

After one plan to bring Siberian timber to England by a northwest passage (open three weeks in the year) came another to collect bats' guano from caves in Texas (this ended when samples killed his friend's gardenias). He obtained an option on trams in Denver but let it slip while on a hunting adventure. Leonard Jerome watched with misgivings which slowly turned into amazement and anger. He lost trust in his son-in-law long before London society did. Winning new capital with his smile, Moreton launched one splendid crash after another. Before the investors ever recovered from their surprise he was asking them for more money for a fresh venture. An American senator asked him to find an English house to handle Pacific Railway stock (in which real wealth lay) but he took it to Sir Ernest Cassel who "did not think much of American railways." Then came the first nonpoisonous disinfectant, made from specially treated sea water. Moreton poured it on fish at dinner parties "to stop putrefaction," which displeased hostesses. Rhodes entered into a long entertaining correspondence on the subject, but "owing to its smell" Moreton had to relinquish his hold on what later won fame under the brand name of "Milton."

During all these years Clara struggled to make a lovely setting for her family at Brede and to entertain with brilliance in London. Her father helped her, for she was a gentle flower ill-suited to such a husband. But a program of Frewen calamities lay ahead, which not even Leonard's imagination could have encompassed. The Ashcroft Sulphides, with nearly a million in capital, seemed about to reap a fortune when Moreton's option in America proved to be not "entirely correct in its legal form." The company was thrown overboard. Moreton immediately tried to float a new one with a fresh three quarters of a million "to enable Stead the economist to edit his own newspaper." But in Stead's words, "I defy the Archangel Gabriel himself to do a smart Dialogue upon Bi-metallism." Moreton never ceased to work behind the scenes for his silver plan both in England and America, and his persistent lobbying on both sides of the Atlantic did result in penny postage between the two countries. Leaving Clara with her faithful unpaid servants, he explored the resources of the whole world. Prince Rupert, a Pacific port, "the shortcut to China and Japan," nearly brought another fortune. So did the pine and cedar of Kenya. "Fifty years to exhaust forest," cabled Moreton, but his friends were exhausted too. "He believed that, with the best friends as with the best horses, he could get anywhere." But not if you ride them stone dead.

"Being thought rich is the next best thing to being rich," said Moreton. His father-in-law did not agree, but what could he do with this "thwarted Elizabethan," who "worked like a typist, lived like a dreamer, travelled like a King"?

"He left babies on other people's doorsteps," complained Dr. Jameson.

But in the welter of his gigantic, disastrous schemes it is hard to measure exactly the slightly larger-than-life figure of Mr. Moreton Frewen.

Ⅰ︎N October, 1884, Leonie married Lieutenant John Leslie of the Grenadier Guards in Grace Church. The event caused considerable excitement in the brittle little social world of New York City, for the youngest Miss Jerome had dallied with several Americans and Leonard fervently hoped that at least one of his daughters would settle in his own land.

For several years Freddie Gebhard, described as "an amusing fellow who could perfectly render imitations of a cock crowing" and as "the most fascinating of playboys," had tagged at her heels. Despite his riches, which impressed other mamas, Mrs. Jerome refused to admit he would make a desirable son-in-law, but Leonard liked him. They spent a few weeks together at Saratoga, enjoying the fabulous casino called Canfield's Clubhouse. Once Freddie Gebhard won ten thousand dollars there. He "joshed" Canfield late at night. "Don't worry Dick. I'll come over for breakfast in the morning and you can get even." Everyone liked Freddie, but Leonie announced, "If I hear Freddie crow like a rooster again, I shall go mad."

So that was that. Freddie bounced on the rebound to Lily Langtry, to whom Moreton introduced him "to stop any grizzling over Leonie."

His youngest daughter had maddened Mr. Jerome by leading on Charlie Fitzwilliam, one of the eight sons of Earl Fitzwilliam

261

of Wentworth in England. Several letters survive and tell a most uncomfortable story. "Darling Kismet," wrote Charlie on an October day in 1880 when Leonie was returning to America. "One line just as you start to wish you happiness and comfort, cheer yourself darling with this assurance. I am thinking of you with the tenderest truest and most devoted affections it is possible for any man to have for a woman. Darling Leonie," etc., etc., etc.

On the following New Year's Day when his father, rich, cross old Lord Fitzwilliam, master of four packs of hounds and acres of Yorkshire coal mines, had threatened to cut his allowance, Charlie wrote seven lugubrious pages:

> . . . Oh my darling will you let this new year bring us both true joy and happiness? Do but let me come to you (etc., etc., etc.). Let the very troubles we have endured only endear us so much the more one to another. You have wanted to please your Father, your Mother, yourself and me all at the same time. I do wish most sincerely I had come out, for you say that if we had married you would have been happier than you now are. I know you care for me darling. Why should we both be so miserable. You say you thought you could have married Freddie but now you find it impossible, that you would only spoil his bright young life. Oh my darling (etc., etc.). Be my Kismet again. I would do my best to endear myself to your people and I think I could make your Father feel he had not trusted his daughter's happiness to one who was altogether unworthy of her. We might travel about for a year or so. Go to China, Japan and India if you liked, till my father could get me some good appointment. In the meantime I might help Moreton with his affairs so as to be near you and your people. Of course we should never be very well off but we should have enough to get along with. My darling Kismet do tell me from your heart does your happiness depend upon me? Or is there anything about me you don't like. Are you afraid you might not be happy as my wife? I am only too anxious to please you if I knew how.

You say you cannot marry Freddy and unless you have some good reason against me what will you do Leonie? I always told you I did not in the least mind your temper etc. Anxious to satisfy your parents you have sacrificed your own interests to theirs, but you cannot make a marriage your heart revolts against. . . .

Ever yr kismet,

Charlie

Leonard had been exceedingly annoyed by Lord Fitzwilliam's attitude, and Moreton certainly did not need a helper of this caliber in Wyoming. A last sad letter ends the tale:

"I am writing with Randolph's consent. I had a talk with him this morning and he is so strongly of opinion that it would be detrimental to your interests that I should see you, that I fear I must, God knows; how unwillingly accede to his wishes. You won't judge me too harshly, but rather by what you know than by what others may say now that I am in my luck. I am to start for India on Thursday week, without a friend or acquaintance. . . ."

Exit Charlie Fitzwilliam, but Freddie Gebhard did not succeed in taking his place. The winner proved a good stayer. The only son of Sir John Leslie, of Glaslough, Monaghan, and Lady Constance Leslie, a frail Victorian beauty with a will of iron, Leonie's favorite beau had sneaked across the Atlantic to push his suit out of view of the family. But "Pink Jack" as they called him, had seen active service in Egypt and distinguished himself under fire, which was more than Freddie or Charlie had done. Leonie could not resist bravery.

Her wedding album contains comments from the papers of the day. "Social circles have been stirred to their utmost depths by the announcement of the engagement of Miss Leonie Jerome to Mr. John Leslie a lieutenant in the Grenadier Guards. Mr. Leslie is a handsome young Englishman, owning a fine estate, and although not yet bearing a title, yet belonging to one of the oldest families in the kingdom."

"His income amounts to about £30,000 a year, or $150,000, and with this he will be able to provide every luxury for his fair bride." (One might hope so.)

"Mr. Frank Griswold acted as best man. . . . The bride was more than beautiful, she was regal—and glittering (Jack had snatched what diamonds he dared from the family coffers before leaving Ireland). . . . Mr. Jerome escorted his daughter and gave her away, and you may be sure he did it with grace, mingled with regret, for Leonard Jerome is a man of dignity, heart and feeling, hard man of the world as he is supposed to be. It may please the *Post's* lady readers to know what the bride wore. She did not wear a wreath of roses, but she wore a bridal veil of point lace held with pearls, diamonds and orange-blossom. Her dress was of white brocade draped with lace. The corsage was cut low Pompadour style and decorated with a diamond star on either side. . . . The guests included the Astors, Lorillards, the Jays, Baron Frederick Blanc, William Travers, Ward McAllister, Mrs. August Belmont and Mr. James Gordon Bennett. So you see that the Commodore, in spite of his love for yachting, polo and other unholy things, has finally got into good society. Mr. Bennett spends a great deal of money in a lavish, showy, self-indulgent way, but he can't begin to use up his income!" The same columnist of the *Post* continued: "It will be remembered that the bride's sister married Lord Randolph Churchill, a brother of the Duke of Marlborough, but an abler and a better man than the Duke who is badness personified."

Well really!

The happy couple walked out of church to the strains of "The Grenadier Guards," and sailed away to England. No easy life awaited that unsuspecting "bride with large brown eyes and a lovely smile."

The Leslies were sore displeased. What was New York society? And why did Mr. Jerome "drive cart" on Fifth Avenue? These and such questions were relayed to Mrs. Jerome, who took them all as insults and rushed for her smelling salts. Leonard laughed at the reference to his four-in-hand, but he worried because there was no fortune left to settle on his youngest, and he was too tired to make one for her. His great health had begun to fail.

A description of him at this time comes from a New Yorker's pen:

"Every afternoon a tall, large, bony figure walks slowly into the Union Club; proceeds directly to the billiard room; is warmly welcomed by the two or three persons who are knocking the balls about while awaiting the newcomer, and begins at once a game of pool. The large, tall, bony figure is attired in a loose-fitting, old-fashioned black frock coat, a white waistcoat and grey trousers. The face is bronzed by exposure to the weather; the grey eyes are large but heavy-lidded; the hair is iron grey and closely cropped; a long drooping moustache conceals the mouth and adds to the semi-military appearance of Leonard Jerome . . . Once he dominated Wall Street as Jay Gould does now; but his was a merry despotism, and he was loved where Jay Gould would be hated."

Occasionally he stepped once more into the limelight, such as when he protested against fraudulent voters' going to the polls in Ohio and Indiana, or when he defended the betting system at Jerome Park, but in the main he lived quietly, immersed in sporting and musical interests.

With August Belmont he was regarded as a *doyen* of the Academy of Music where the best opera was heard until the opening of the Metropolitan in 1883. The old Academy had but eighteen boxes, and the new capitalists such as J. P. Morgan, the Vanderbilts, Rockefeller, Jay Gould, and William Whitney were kept out. "The social value of a box at the Academy was

265

inestimable; its economic value could only be gauged by the number of millionaires who, wishing to possess a box, were denied that privilege." When August Belmont, chairman of the Academy, heard that the Vanderbilts were heading a crusade to construct a vast new opera house where they could have all the boxes they wanted, he offered to add twenty-six to the Academy, but the war between old aristocracy and new millionaires was on. The Metropolitan Opera had a great opening. According to *The Dramatic Mirror*, "The tiers of boxes looked like cages in a menagerie of Monopolists." Two years later the old Academy closed down and Mr. Belmont and Mr. Jerome had to seek their musical entertainment among the "upstarts."

When Mrs. Jerome followed her three daughters to England Leonard shut up his house in Madison Square and moved to the Brunswick Hotel on Fifth Avenue, which was considered "headquarters of the aristocratic horsey set." The annual spring and autumn parades of the Coaching Club assembled here, and the elect would return afterwards to celebrate. Now that his family had left him entirely alone, it was something to have the company of fellow sportsmen.

Leonie's husband resumed his military career. In those days soldiering in the regiments of Her Majesty's Guards consisted chiefly of horse sports. Officers were supposed to hunt regularly with a view to training their eye when chasing enemy cross-country; they also rode steeplechases to show how they could lead a charge, and polo was becoming a fashionable expensive game. Occasionally Lieutenant Leslie went to camp or led his troop out on maneuvers. England in the eighties demanded little of an eldest son. Life had been made sweet for him with gun and rod. Horses and yachts were his due. Since Lord Grey's Reform Bill of 1832 had taken the power of government out of the hands of the agrarian aristocracy class, a curious atrophy had set in. Sense of responsibility seemed to be replaced by sense of snobbism.

Moreton Frewen's unbiased pen describes the "vast numbers of rich, well-dressed, idle people who constituted the society of the day."

John Leslie's father had been a member of Parliament until defeated by Parnell's secretary, Tim Healy. Then he withdrew from Irish politics forever, and did not expect his son to take up the cudgels. A charming fellow with blue eyes, pink cheeks, and fair hair, Leonie's husband belonged to a caste and had been brought up according to the caste system. Educated at Eton and entered into the Guards, he was not really expected to do very much except enjoy himself, marry a nice girl chosen by his parents, and eventually inherit large Irish estates.

In the eyes of New York society, Leonie had made a smart match with a nice-looking Grenadier, with a huge romantic place somewhere in the background. He was rich and the son of a baronet—whatever that might be. No guess could have been made at the responsibilities attendant on marrying an elder son of landed gentry in Ireland. The Jerome girls had been educated to be ambassadresses, princesses, or patrons of art. The management of thousands of acres of farmland, forest, and bog in a country where the peasantry were approaching revolution had been left out of the curriculum.

Sir John and Lady Constance retreated to Ireland and did not receive their daughter-in-law on her arrival in London. She was merely sent to tea to be feted by Miss Julia and Miss Emily Leslie, two maiden aunts who lived together in Bourdon House, off Berkeley Square (preferring luxurious spinsterhood if they could not, like their sister Christina Marchioness of Waterford, marry into the upper strata of derelict peers). Julia reported severely on her hairdo, complaining that she had no fringe. But this ominous verdict was counteracted by kindly, music-loving Emily, who discovered Leonie's knowledge of composition. The Leslies then unbent sufficiently to send a summons to the young couple to spend a Christmas at Glaslough. They traveled across the Irish Sea and arrived one rough winter's night in the big stone hall hung with antlers and armor. Little Olive Leslie, Jack's fifteen-year-old sister, ran down the stairs and stopped dead at the sight of the elegant lady in the hall. Leonie was standing there alone, looking very slim in a tight-fitting gray dress with a big bunch of violets pinned to the neck.

The week's visit passed quietly. Lady Constance could find nothing to criticize in her new daughter-in-law except that she "would overload the Christmas tree."

By January 1 Leonie was back in London picking up threads with which to weave a life of her own. She started a diary. Pink Jack was absent-minded. He missed parades, and having arranged to take his wife out to lunch, forgot and left her standing on the doorstep! Such incidents loomed large in her first months of marriage. However he took her to the theater with Jennie and the Duc de Morny. They saw Mrs. Langtry in *Princess George*: "such a fiasco, can't act and is badly made up, red hands. Freddie Gebhard with the mother. Looked ashamed of her, rather disgraceful." Visits to the Leslie aunts continued, "Emily off to a prayer meeting. Julia foul," interspersed with musical evenings with Mrs. Ronalds, Lady de Clifford, and Consuelo (Duchess of Manchester). On February 5 "Lady Blanche Hozier comes in with news of the fall of Khartoum consternation! Lady de C., Jennie and I drive to the Tower and lunch with Jack who is on guard and inspect the damages made by dynamite by an admirer of General Gordon." Then came a "vile letter from Jack's mother —makes me blue—feel so wretched."

Unfortunately, Leonard remained in New York. If only the fathers-in-law could have met, the strain would have ended for, horses and Italian opera were the great interests of both gentlemen and Leonard would have put an end to Lady Constance's nonsense.

In February the Leslies returned to town and on the fourteenth Jack was asked after coming off guard to bring his bride to Stratford House to be re-inspected in a London setting. "Dreadfully out of spirits" writes poor Leonie. "After lunch Lady C. receives us. Children all in the next room. Very formal and stiff. Then they come in, we sit in a row and discuss the war. I talk to the governess, etc. So dull and tiresome."

Lady Constance had "an awful temper." As a young bride she had always "jumped on to the window-sill in Berkeley Square and threatened she would dash herself down if not yielded to in every dispute."

Stratford House *, was a nobly proportioned Georgian edifice, with splendid drawing rooms and no sanitation. The Irish staff, including footmen and stableboys whom they brought over from County Monaghan, each spring invariably got sore throats and diphtheria, which they attributed to the treacherous London climate. No one dreamed of inspecting the undrained cesspool that terminated underneath the kitchen floor. From the upper stories of this white temple the senior Leslies enjoyed the grandiose side of each London season.

Whenever summoned there, Leonie arrived trembling with nervous indignation, but she determined to show no emotion and to put the Leslies in their place. Soon Sir John, who had known Chopin, Rossini, and Mendelssohn, appreciated her touch on his

---

* Later Derby House, now Hutchinson House.

piano—that Broadwood grand on which the great Anton Rubinstein also came to play. Lady Constance thawed slightly. It seemed exceeding strange that a "Colonial" with that questionable Second Empire and barbaric New York as a background, should play so much better than her own daughters who, despite much scale practice with their old governess, could hardly differentiate one tune from another. Eventually Jack and his wife were invited to stay at Stratford House (and here in a fine bedroom of supreme discomfort two of Leonie's sons were born).

A few months before Leonie's first child was born, Lady Constance presented her daughter-in-law to Queen Victoria. The "Drawing Room" which took place in the afternoon does not sound very stimulating. "Sit in carriage long time. Go in. Stand an hour. Queen still there. Kiss her hand. Princess shakes hands. Curtsey to the rest. Prince shakes my hand and congratulates."

During the remainder of the spring Leonie found herself sitting through the quiet afternoons with her hands folded, listening to the old man's reminiscences. One of his brothers, Charles, had accompanied Lord Hartington through the lines of both armies during the American Civil War. Another brother, Tom, occasionally called at Stratford House and himself related the episodes which led to the Charge of Balaclava. "Wait until you get to Glaslough," old Sir John would tell Leonie, "Then I must show you with all the letters and things that will be yours some day."

But Lady Constance was quicker at "letters and things" than her old husband. A true Victorian, she went through every box and diary, snipping out with scissors that which she considered "improper," leaving in many cases a mere filigree of paper to tease posterity. Happily she missed the eighteenth-century letters concerning the outcome of a game of hide and seek played on the top story in the 1730's. Sir John's great grandfather, aged sixteen, and the young daughter of an Irish Earl had hidden in the linen press and not been found for two hours. The resultant baby girl was brought up as a spoiled pet by her mother's family and eventually became the ancestress of a particularly brilliant line of statesmen.

The months Leonie spent in London were easier than those which had to be devoted to amusing her mother-in-law in an Irish country home. Lady Constance had, in 1876, made her husband dynamite the old square Castle Leslie and build in its stead an immense rambling Victorian edifice with superb views of the most beautiful lake in Ulster. By happy chance he had imbibed sufficient taste during Italian travels to design the interior proportions, and to vault ceilings and paint frescos pleasingly. An entire marble fountain was transported from Florence, Michael Angelo's cloister of Santa Maria degli Angeli in Rome was reproduced "to lead to the library and billiard room" and a Della Robbia fireplace as well as the contents of Venetian *palazzo*, arrived.

When Mrs. Jerome visited Glaslough, the mothers-in-law eyed each other like two formidable hens. The big walled demesne, with its gray lake and great dripping trees, struck Mrs. Jerome as "bleak and sad" and the Gothic lodge gates as "outlandish." As for the huge new house with its senseless wings of museum corridors, which old Sir John on a step ladder was covering with Italian-style frescos, it delighted her not at all. She merely wondered if his paint brush could compete with the decorations of green mold creeping over every unused room.

"It was different in the Tuileries," she remarked rather too often.

Lady Constance cut short her derision: "Louis Napoleon used to hang around London hoping to be invited for a meal anywhere. He often stayed at Came, our home in Dorset and we thought him *so* dull and *such* a poor sportsman, penniless too, but this did not prevent him trying to bribe me with barley sugar because he wanted to marry my eldest sister Lady Fortescue. Our father was on Cathcart's staff at Waterloo and he had a very poor opinion of *all* Bonapartes. He refused Louis Napoleon point blank!" Although herself scorning the Irish squirearchy, it was unbearable to see Mrs. Jerome intoxicated by the vulgar glories of the Second Empire and unimpressed by Leslies.

With the merits of their children, the Second Empire, and the Regency to disagree on, these long-drawn-out meals in the Glaslough dining room hung with family portraits must have become insufferable. Happily, dear old Sir John was growing deaf.

Lady Constance had devised an enormous centerpiece of flowers for her dinner table. This she spoke of as *"un cache mari."* "After thirty years of marriage," she said, "one simply cannot see the same face chewing every day."

Doubtless it was a relief when the time came to close down the Irish country home, and ship horses, carriages, and servants to London for the season. Leonie could then lead an independent existence, and she became one of the most sought-after young women in English society. Invitations to travel on royal yachts proved far more alluring than long unwanted "rests" in the depths of Ireland.

Among the stories she used to tell about herself was one concerning the summer after Clara's wedding.

Leonard had written her that a great friend was coming to London and that she must be particularly nice to him. At a large dinner of Jennie's she found herself sitting next to a charming gentleman whom she remembered in Papa's racing set. She held forth on what he ought to do and see in Europe with all the authority and assurance of her twenty-five years. "I explained the sports of England, the Tower of London, and Hampton Court and ended by telling him rather patronisingly all about the Derby. 'That will take place next week. You really ought to see it.' "

" 'Yes,' said Mr. Lorillard humbly. 'I hope to. I won it last year.' "

ㅤ

ㅤ

Lady Randolph Churchill in Connaught Place, Mrs. Moreton Frewen in Alyford Street, and Mrs. Jack Leslie in various small houses adjacent to Stratford Place—these were the three most brilliant and original young hostesses of London in the eighties. They entertained on a shoe-string, making their own charm and wit substitute for the grandeur and pomaded footmen they could not afford. Leonard found his daughters grown into ladies of high repute in intellectual and musical circles; during his brief visits he only wished they had more time to spare for "poor dear papa!" His grandsons delighted him, despite the strange English upbringing which made them seem reserved and different from the boys of his own recollection. How far off was that scene of western New York, the scene into which he had been born where every youth breathed the clear air of an untouched land, and planned to create a pattern of his own. English children found a world readymade; they were informed of their setting and expected to conform. They heard much of the importance of gentlemanly birth but not of Leonard Jerome's definition: "The character of a gentleman I consider within the capacity of all—at least it requires no extraordinary intellect. A due regard for the feelings of others is in my judgment its foundation."

The education of Jennie's eldest son during this period, when Grandfather Jerome can have been but a vague benevolent figure appearing annually from across the Atlantic, has been described in detail. Winston begins at the time when his father was in full ascendancy: "I was first threatened with school when I was seven years old. At the time I was what grown-up people in their off-hand way called 'a troublesome boy.' Although much that I had heard about school had made a disagreeable impression on my mind, an impression thoroughly borne out by actual experience, I thought it would be fun to go away and live with so many other boys, and that we should have great adventures. Also I was told that school days were the happiest in one's life. All the boys enjoyed it. Some of my cousins had been quite sorry—I was told—to come home for the holidays. Cross-examined, the cousins did not confirm this; they only grinned."

He described the dark November afternoon when Jennie took him to his preparatory school, and as the sounds of the beautiful Lady Randolph's carriage died away, a small sad boy was led to an empty classroom and handed a Latin grammar. "Behold me then on a gloomy evening, with an aching heart, seated in front of the declension of *mensa.*

"What on earth did it mean? It seemed absolute rigmarole to me. However, there was one thing I could always do; I could learn by heart.

"In due course the master returned.

" 'Have you learned it?' he said. 'I think I can *say* it sir,' I replied, and I gabbled it off.

"He seemed so satisfied with this that I was emboldened to ask a question.

" 'What does it mean, sir?'

" 'It means what it says. *Mensa,* a table.'

" 'Then why does *mensa* also mean O Table,' I inquired, 'and what does O Table mean?'

" '*Mensa,* O Table, is the vocative case,' he replied. 'You would use that in speaking to a table.'

" 'But I never do,' I blurted out in honest amazement.

"Such was my first introduction to the classics from which, I have been told, many of our cleverest men have derived so much solace and profit."

He entered Harrow after submitting a Latin paper adorned solely by a blot and several smudges. Evidently the headmaster reckoned he could entice more promising efforts later from the son of the brilliant Lord Randolph and did not wish to turn him down. Winston was placed in the lowest division of the bottom form, a situation which he later regarded as advantageous for, instead of struggling with Latin he was taught English. "We were considered such dunces that we could learn only English. As I remained in the Third Fourth three times as long as anyone else, I had three times as much of it. I learned it thoroughly. Thus I got into my bones the essential structure of the ordinary British sentence which is a noble thing."

The masters became maddened by the selectivity of this boy with his naughty blue eyes and rather pugnacious little face who remained impervious to chastisement and closed his mind against learning all that bored him. At intervals he showed a remarkable memory, reciting over a thousand lines of Macaulay's *Lays of Ancient Rome,* which happened to appeal to him; but generally he lowered a shutter around his brain as if to protect it against the accumulation of useless knowledge.

"In retrospect my school years form the only barren and un-happy period of my life. Actually, no doubt, they were buoyed up by the laughter and high spirits of youth. But I would far rather have been apprenticed as a bricklayer's mate, or run errands as a messenger boy. It would have been real; it would have been natural; it would have taught me more; and I should have done it much better."

This was the verdict of one who mingled ducal and pioneer blood in his veins, and who, from the beginning, felt the essential experiences and felt the futility of wasting time. Young Master Churchill could not and would not see the trees for the wood. He refused to pick up twigs he did not want. No punishment altered this resolve.

He also differed from others in his readiness to show emotion and in his moral bravery. A letter to his mother from Harrow reads: "I am getting on in drawing and like it very much. I am going to begin shading in sepia. Everest came down yesterday." Everest, his beloved old nurse, had arrived in a poke bonnet, and Winston walked her round the school and kissed her good-by at the station. No other boy would have dared to reveal this simple loyalty and affection for a nurse. The story went like wildfire around the school, arousing jeers among the more conventional and less courageous, but Churchill showed a curious toughness in withstanding the criticism of this kind.

The adored *"Tante* Leonie" often looked after Winston when his parents were abroad. In 1884 when Winston was thirteen years old, he begged a favor and Leonie, who always had time to do a good turn even when it was just for a small boy, wrote to the author Rider Haggard: "The little boy Winston came here yesterday morning beseeching me to take him to see you before he returns to school at the end of the month. I don't wish to bore so busy a man as yourself, but will you, when you have time, please tell me, shall I bring him on Wednesday next, when Mrs. Haggard said she would be at home? Or do you prefer settling to come here some afternoon when I could have the boy to meet you? He is really a very interesting being, though temporarily *uppish* from the restraining parental hand being in Russia."

Mr. Haggard was kind and gave Winston a copy of *Allen Quartermain*. Winston wrote to thank him. "I like *A.Q.* better than *King Solomon's Mines:* it is more amusing. I hope you will write a good many more books."

She found her lonely, snub-nosed, freckled little nephew full of fun and unself-conscious. "He doesn't mind everyone calling him 'copper-top'." She tried to give him a good time—too good a time according to his grandmother, the Duchess of Marlborough who, in a letter deeply bordered with black, and weighted with black coronets writes thus from Blenheim:

Dec. 27, 1887

"My dear Leonie,
I must say I am very much disappointed at Winston's not being allowed to come here for a few days. I had made every arrangement to take great care of him knowing he is susceptible to colds, and I do not think there could have been as much danger as there is in going to Pantomimes in London. Besides I feel it's all an excuse of that horrid old Everest to prevent my having him and his being happy with his cousins without her.

I feel that Randolph and Jennie would not have objected to my seeing a little of him as really I hardly ever see him, and must say I am very much vexed. He is not fit to go to Harrow if he is not fit for a visit here. The house is quite warm. But it cannot be helped. I have heard nothing from R. and Jennie, but the newspapers are full of them. I hope you are well and enjoying a happy Xmas. With much love.

Yours

F. Marlborough.

Jennie and Randolph had gone to Russia leaving their fourteen-year-old son and his old nurse in Leonie's charge. Winston has clearly described his feelings for his mother: "She shone for me like the Evening Star. I loved her dearly but at a distance. My

277

nurse was my confidante." * While Winston thoroughly enjoyed himself in the company of his favorites, his parents visited St. Petersburg and Moscow, sleighed, tobogganed, and skated, and were received in audience by the Tsar. Jennie found the Russian aristocracy lived in "overheated apartments far worse than American ones"; and, while the women struck her as beautifully educated, this seemed pointless as they took no part in guiding their men in politics or any other career. The memories she carried away were of snow-covered plains, a gracious Tsarina, wonderful jewels and Tzigane music. The memory she left (one which long survived the dispersal of the Russian court) was of "the most beautiful black-haired woman ever seen, who danced light as a moth on skates."

In England the newspapers boiled and bubbled, the *Times* in particular warning the Tsar that Lord Randolph, "the most versatile and volatile" of English politicians, should not be accepted as having official status. "Meanwhile the object of this merry chatter was enjoying himself. When the word has gone forth that a visitor is to be well received, he need not trouble about details. Everything moved *sur les roulettes:* railway officials and Custom House officers are transformed into attentive servants—often a considerable transformation."

Unaware, or uncaring, of editorial comment at home, Randolph drove "in bright sun and bitter cold to the Winter Palace, and after long delays, relieved by cups of tea, in interminable corridors adorned by wonderfully dressed servants with *panaches* of red and orange . . . he was conducted to the Emperor's apartment." Their talk, which lasted nearly an hour, concerned the possibility of maintaining peace between their respective countries.

On the following day Lord and Lady Randolph were com-

* Winston used to visit Everest in her old age and confessed that this friendship led him to realize the plight of many who were not, like her, pensioned in retirement and to press for old-age pensions.

manded to a party at Gatschina. "The marked consideration shown to the English visitor increased the gossip—good-humoured and spiteful alike at home." And in St. Petersburg the whole of society devoted itself to amusing the distinguished couple. Randolph wrote his mother: "I am sure in England it would bore me dreadfully to go to all these dinners and parties and things, but here it amuses me. I wonder why it is. . . . You must not believe a word the newspapers say. I was most careful and guarded in all my communications, and confined myself to general beaming upon everyone. Lord Salisbury may or may not be angry, but I am certain that my going to Russia has had a good effect and can, at any rate, do no harm."

On arriving back in England they found the *Times* devoting three columns to speculations on the possible import of Randolph's visit to Russia. It seemed as if this dynamic and controversial figure, whose every excursion conjured up excitement, could not fail to soon return to power, but Jennie wrote to her sister Leonie, and there is a sadness in her assessment of the facts:

2 CONNAUGHT PLACE
        W.

Dearest Snippy, I confess I have been a brute not to have written, but what with letters to R. and the Duchess, besides others and my painting and music I haven't a moment. I shall be *so* glad to see you dear—but I do not think that I shall be over until the 6th or 7th of March as I want to go to the Drawing Room here on the 3rd on account of the Queen (being offended at Randolph's resignation). The Duchess writes that you are considered the "belle of Dublin!" You must not be low dear. I shall soon be over and intend staying the whole month. I feel rather in the dumps myself to-day. I dined last night with the Salisburys where they had a dance afterwards. I had a long talk with Ld. S. after dinner but I did not get much out of him. He was very shy and nervous and I had the greatest difficulty to get him to speak of Randolph. It is too long to repeat but I rather had the impression that they could never come together again. Don't repeat this, of course it is impossible to say what may happen in the House. As Arthur Balfour said—their difficulties haven't commenced yet and when they do—they may have to go to Randolph. But Snippy I feel very sick at heart sometimes. It was such a splendid position to throw away. In the bottom of my heart I sometimes think that his head was quite turned at that moment and that he thought he could do *anything*. However "it is an ill wind that blows *no* good" and R. has been so much easier and nicer since that I ought not to regret the crisis. He writes most affectionately and very often and I hope all will be righted when he returns. . . .

Yr loving

Jennie

If, sensing the failing powers of Randolph, Jennie felt her heart ache, yet she continued to keep up a brave front. The most interesting people of the day—ambassadors, statesmen, writers and artists—flocked to her house. From Mrs. Ronalds she learned how to launch struggling musicians. One day a young pianist came to her from Poland. He carried a letter of introduction from a mutual friend, and after a cup of tea, during which she noticed he seemed very nervous, Jennie said, "Come on let's try a Beethoven duet together."

"You're too good," she laughed at the end. "You leave me breathless. I shan't play with you any more."

During the next days she gathered all the people she knew in London who were capable of judging an artist fairly. The young man received an appreciation which enabled him to approach his first concert in the St. James Hall with confidence. The place was only half full.

Jennie placed herself in a seat in front of the critics and listened to their comments: "There's not much in this fellow," said one. "He would be all right" said the other, "if he would leave Chopin alone, which he plays against all tradition."

Jennie could not resist speaking loudly to the friend beside her: "Stephen Heller, who was Chopin's pupil, taught *me* and *he* said that Chopin himself never played his works twice in the same way."

A year later the pianist returned to London. This time his audience stormed the stage to kiss his hand. When he came to tea with Jennie, he took both her hands in his. "Come on," Paderewski cajoled, "Let us try that duet again. I shall not feel so shy this time."

ETWEEN THE OLD DUKE OF Marlborough and Mr. Jerome there had never been many words, but Randolph's brother, the bimetallist eighth duke, joined the wide circle of admiring younger men who surrounded Leonard. He also became one of Moreton Frewen's cronies, and they scraped up several "marvellous ideas" together. Righting of the monetary systems of the world held more allure to both men than the improvement of conditions within their personal orbits.

Moreton's glib pen pronounced judgment on his associate thus: "I have known also one or two quite first-class minds whose achievements have been nil. Take George, eighth duke of Marlborough, an almost incomparable mind; indeed in receptivity, range and versatility hardly to be matched. . . . But to play the whole great game there must be the really master mind. . . ."

Despite a certain receptivity and range this unfortunate duke seems to have failed as patently as Mr. Frewen. After his wife, Lady Blandford, divorced him, Marlborough turned to chemistry on a grand scale and set up a laboratory on the top floor of Blenheim where he devoted himself to experiments in electricity and metallurgy. When the Frewen ore crusher failed to extract gold from boulders, he could more subtly try to convert it from other minerals. Under Leonard's supervision he also made tentative efforts to discover happiness with a new wife from the millionaire set of New York city. But even in this operation success remained elusive. For the eighth duke no alchemy was able to transform the dross of life.

The environments into which Leonard's daughters stepped after marriage produced a curious assortment of characters. Moreton Frewen's friends constituted half the British sporting aristocracy, and he brought them to Clara's house to mingle with European royalties and musicians whose company Moreton did not always relish. Sir Arthur Sullivan (of Gilbert and Sullivan) once scribbled her a note while arranging a dinner for H.R.H. the Duke of York. "I want another lady without a man badly. Will you come to my rescue and I will give Moreton any satisfaction he desires afterwards, either pistols, swords or Utah shares!"

Leonard regarded Moreton as less amusing every year.

Now that Leonie had won her battle with the Leslies, the most genial of the British in-laws proved to be old Sir John, whose fund of ancedotes covered all the years during which Jerome had known only the turbulence of early America. Sir John had been a member of the hallowed Marylebone Cricket Club since 1841 and had seen his first Derby in 1839. "In his youth prize fighting was the national sport and the 'champion of England' was, after the Arch-bishop of Canterbury, unofficially the second person in the realm."

To Mr. Jerome he could give an eyewitness's account of the famous fight between Sayers and Heenan, which had raised such feeling between England and America. "Sayers faced his rival like a polo-pony against a dray horse, and though his right arm was soon put out of action fought thirty rounds with his left until Heenan's face was a red mash." Sayers' backers broke the ring rather than lose their money, and the fight was declared a draw. This was the last time that deputations from the House of Lords and House of Commons attended a prize fight, and it was the gory, if glorious, end of the old English boxing without gloves.

A curious "at home" was given by Lord Caledon in the late eighties to which Jack Leslie took his bride and her father. The Caledon estate walls met those of Glaslough in Ireland, so the families were well acquainted and Leonie's four sons ran wild in the Ulster woods alongside the four sons of Lord Caledon.* Apart from being a good neighbor, the noble Earl was also a sportsman of repute; he had trailed alone across Wyoming, lived as a blood brother with Blackfoot Indians, shot bears with Moreton, and brought a buffalo back to his deer park.

After many years of travel it dawned on his lordship that the time had arrived when it became incumbent on him to make some effort to entertain in London society. His grand house in Carlton House Terrace overlooking the Horse Guards Parade was opened forthwith and stocked up with servants raw from the bogs, according to the wont of those who owned Irish estates.

Invitations went out for what Leonie and her husband assumed to be a soiree dedicated to some art. They arrived in a gilded drawing room to be received by the Countess of Caledon looking somewhat dazed beneath her tiara. "Sports have been arranged upstairs," she said. A bevy of gentlemen escorted ladies

---

* At present these sons are the Earl of Caledon, Field-Marshal Earl Alexander of Tunis, Honorable Herbrand Alexander, and Honorable Sigismund Alexander.

in jeweled evening dresses up the magnificent staircase to the ballroom where, beside a roped ring, Lord Caledon was greeting guests and supervising referees at the same time.

"I will never forget entering that room," Leonie used to say, "for the name of the boxer being called out was Billy Blood! A terrific fight then took place which made the chandeliers swing and I can remember the tremor which went through the men as someone shouted, 'He's drawn the claret!' and a scarlet stream shot from the nose of aptly-named Billy. The gentlemen may have enjoyed it but not the wives who stood with faces growing longer and more horrified at every round. 'Claret' proved the last straw and most ladies cleared off, clutching their silken trains. Refreshments were served in the next room to those who could bring themselves to swallow and our dear Irish neighbour all charm and affability (though rather a shy man) beamed on his friends saying, 'I thought it would be nice to have something a little different.' "

When Leonard returned to America after a month spent almost entirely in the proximity of Leonie and Jack, he wrote her a tactful letter. In the fashionable worlds of New York and Paris only the worldly endowments of Lieutenant Leslie were discussed: he was good-looking, he was rich, and some sort of title would come his way. Lucky young man! Probably conceited, thought the envious. Leonard's vision was more acute. The pink cheeks that reddened so easily, the blue boyish eyes, and old-fashioned courtesy of "Jacksy" hid a painful shyness, which was in no way being dispelled by his irrepressible, scintillating wife. Leonie was at that time impetuous and so full of vitality and *joie de vivre* that she had not time to notice the effect on a husband consistently forced to take second place. Society proved heartless. Leonie "made parties go." She was inundated with invitations which added, almost as an afterthought, "and bring Jack too." He felt himself tagging at her heels, merely tolerated while the exuberant young lady he had married became the star of every gathering.

Only Mr. Jerome noticed his discomfort. Because Jennie had married the most brilliant parliamentarian of the century, a like situation had not been able to arise, and Moreton, of course, was a steam roller in his own right. But Leonard realized that Jerome verve often needed curbing. How to accomplish this task?

The letter he wrote her was not very long, and she kept it all her life, taking it out to read over whenever she might have thoughtlessly dominated an evening. The last sentence read, "Do not forget that you have married a very amiable and gallant gentleman who will never *show* when his feelings are hurt but who will be unable to forget the slights of society when it is made apparent that you are more wanted than him. It will rankle in the future. A man may say nothing but he will never be able to forget."

These timely words helped an uneven match to culminate in long years of happiness. Many of Leonard's letters of 1888 survive. There is also a sarcastic note from Lady Constance to the Duchess of Marlborough (who had always assured her that since taking up politics Jennie had made a "very good wife") to say: "Old Mr. Jerome starts on Saturday for America to make a new fortune for Clara and Leonie." Obviously she rejoiced in the discovery that, despite Leonard's reputation, he could now offer but meager financial help to his daughters.

In actuality, he had abandoned efforts to earn big money on the market. Having settled all he possessed on his girls, he simply kept an eye on his race horses and lived contentedly in a room of the Brunswick Hotel where the Coaching Club met annually and he saw sporting friends. (Conveniently the hotel had been forced to reduce its rates after a Bowery gangster had wrecked its social standing by bringing an after-sleighing party for supper into the unsuspecting restaurant.)

During the spring and summer of 1888 Jerome was struggling to transfer his original American Jockey Club to a new race track financed by the rich John Morris; for since 1887 the City of New York had threatened to extend an aqueduct and reservoir over Jerome Park. "To give up Jerome Park, to see the American Jockey Club decay was a bitter blow to this man of energy and brains. It was like seeing a loved child shrivel and die. . . ." Mr. Jerome determined to build before he died a new home for the association founded in his prime. Months passed before he succeeded in raising a dollar. Carry him back twenty-five years and he could have millions for the asking; now he could interest no one in his plans. It was the joke of the day to ask him if he had yet found the four hundred dollars with which to build the new track. He bore the taunts with resignation and went about his business. On a certain day, when the question was put to him for the hundredth time, he responded with the light of vindication burning in his eyes, "No, I have not found the four hundred but I have found forty million."

He had met John A. Morris who was ready to use his fortune building a new course, "the million-dollar track." Once again Leonard burned with enthusiasm and the public's interest flared anew in racing.*

On April 4 he wrote Clara (who remained on patrol in London): "Coney Island Jockey Club: . . . We are getting on nicely. We have 292 acres, all the land we want except ten acres in one corner which we will have in a day or two. The work of surveying and laying out the track has commenced. Morris is in high spirits. . . .

"I dined last night with Kitty [his niece Mrs. Mott, daughter of Lawrence and Sister Carrie]. Awfully small dinner of 16! Lord Walter Campbell on her right and the celebrated orator—a

* New York *Tribune*.

lawyer Fergerson on her left *between Kitty and her mother.*
Judge what a charming time he must have had entertaining
Carrie! Kitty of course devoted herself wholly to the Lord. Kitty
was fairly dazzling with her diamonds. Her dress was *very* low
while her mother had a shawl pinned tightly round her neck. I
looked at Carrie many times while the lawyer was trying to entertain her. She never smiled once or even opened her lips as far
as I could see."

Red Indian blood can lend more dignity than charm to old age!
Mrs. Lawrence Jerome would have been extremely annoyed,
however, had anyone ever remarked on her resemblance to a
meditating Iroquois.

Another letter from Leonard to his wife reads:

WASHINGTON D.C.

. . . You must not worry about my health. I am at the
present writing in perfect condition and if I get ill I promise
to let you know at once. They tell you it's a shame that you
let me come off here alone, that you ought to come out
and take care of me. What nonsense! They simply don't
know what they are talking about. Alone! Why I am in the
midst of a host of friends and relatives who would fly to
me instantly if I were ill. As to your coming out you would
make a great expense, bore yourself and do me no good.
And I don't see why, if I am comfortable, you should take
a step that is sure to make me otherwise. When in town I
have a small room in the rear of the Brunswick sixth story
where I sleep and dress. It gives square to the sun and is
warm enough without a fire. I am as comfortable in it as if I
had the whole house. I spend my time mostly at the Jockey
Club and its office. At the office horse-talk and business, at
the Club meals, library, whist, billiards, talk with friends.
When it gets a little warmer I shall be off racing, yachting,
visiting and knocking about generally. If you had any go
in you like either of the girls and could mount your horse
and keep up, we might knock about together and enjoy

it. But you haven't a bit of taste that way and never had. And you couldn't stand that sort of life now even if you liked it once upon a time!

And you say you should be here in duty bound *to take care of me!* What stuff! I don't want to be taken care of and what's more I *won't* be, not by anybody. I gave Eugene [a Jerome nephew] to understand that. The first day his wife pounced on me as if I were a newly arrived poodle and fairly smothered me. She ordered a huge wardrobe into my little room. I ordered it out and told her I preferred to unpack myself as if I put away my things myself I knew where to find them. Of course in being together we could indulge in our habitual confidential talks and they are very pleasant and this is about all the good that would result from your coming out. I shall make up for that by writing you very fully. . . .

Randolph is doing magnificent work. Every move he makes strengthens his record. I hope we shall have good news of Moreton soon. Hope you are not pinching too closely. No necessity of it. Love to all.

Perhaps she felt a twinge at her husband's words. There had been a time when she longed for the capacity to show that mixture of helplessness and audacity which Leonard desired in women. But this fat lady encased in whalebone and stiff silk and rustling jet who had installed herself in London as a guardian of her daughters knew it was now too late for regret. "If you had any go in you like either of the girls and could mount your horse and keep up——" Once the words would have hurt. Now she could smile philosophically and admit the truth. She had never been able to keep up with Leonard. It was not in her to ride plunging horses, or hit high notes or knock about. Now it would be best to remember only that far romantic past in Rochester. With a wistful sigh, Mrs. Jerome took up her quill and agreed: she had never had "a bit of taste that way."

IN LATE JULY, LEONARD SAILED ON THE *Umbria* and by September 1 he was back in New York. The city and its modes of life altered with surprising swiftness, and many of his old friends were dying off. Rough old Commodore Vanderbilt had gone to his grave, leaving behind a dynasty of brash patrons of art to build themselves palaces in various European modes, to argue precedence in and out of dining rooms, and to marry a variety of titles. In 1887 William Travers, Leonard's great friend, had died in Bermuda after a last gay letter ending, "The waiters get the change and the hotel gets the rest."

Now Lawrence suddenly cracked. He and James Gordon Bennett had been known for their frolics together in America and France for many years. During the last decade their pranks on the Paris-Bordeaux Express had baffled countless travelers. Even in late middle age they feverishly "created jollity" by impersonating escaping madmen, hysterical jilted lovers, etc. Their jokes, which became steadily rowdier and more uncouth, appealed to their epoch. Bennett kept his own four-in-hand coach at Pau, and one day when Lawrence complained about wild driving he shoved his friend inside to be "quiet and safe." Bennett then galloped his horses off at speed. When they came to the formidable Morlaas hill the horses ran away. While Bennett tugged at the wheelers' reins, his secretary, clinging on for dear life, was ordered to take the leaders. At last the coach rattled to a standstill and Lawrence stepped out white in the face to remonstrate. Then he saw Bennett pouring with sweat and shaking. "Whose joke was it, anyway?" he asked. The secretary collapsed. "Not mine."

Bennett's final prank (presumably while on an excursion outside of that "good society" mentioned by the *Post*) was to take over a certain establishment in Paris, go to bed covered with bandages, and set all the girls nursing him. At three in the morning the same long-suffering secretary was sent by brougham to wake Lawrence saying Mr. Bennett had suffered a fearful accident. Lawrence arrived posthaste and knelt beside the swathed figure before he looked around at the twenty strange nurses. A burst of laughter and magnums of champagne followed. Happily Lawrence's wife, Aunt Carrie, did not hear of this episode. A strict teetotaler, she had already snubbed Leonard at a dinner party when he defended the drinking of wine. He quoted the Miracle of Cana at which she snorted, "In that case, our Lord showed poor judgment." After which there was nothing more to be said.

Lawrence's first stroke had laid him out after a fishing party in Maine. The Duke of Marlborough, a departing guest, received at the station an urgent telegram to return. "Another of Larry's jokes," he said and continued his journey.

A few months later Larry finally collapsed. New York headlines: "Lawrence Jerome dying: the Prince of Good Fellows Slowly gives up the Fight." "The merriest spirit in all the world goes when Lawrence Jerome crosses the dark river." Then he was gone.

At about this time Clara Jerome developed a most unlikely friendship with a Frenchman named Monsieur Eiffel who was busy on a "construction of amazement" for the forthcoming *Grande Exhibition*. He delighted her *salon* with little engineering sketches and took her to the top of his celebrated tower, signing a picture of it saying that she was the first woman in the world to have been so high. It was *the* adventure of her old age!

In 1888 Leonard planned to meet his wife and daughters in Paris for Christmas and offered to pay everyone's expenses.

"The scheme strikes me as very sensible, very possible and very jolly. Clara should take her children by all means. I have proposed to let Jerome Park for ten years—think I will get it. The three courses will then work in perfect harmony, Jerome P., Sheepshead and the New Course. We will make Jerome P. the *Auteuil* of New York not altogether steeplechasing but principally. It is admirably adapted to steeplechasing and too cramped for modern flat-racing. The New Course will open May 30. Jennie and Randolph have promised to come over for the occasion. You may be sure it will be a great event. Travers [Jerome] made a great hit in the Trial of Emerson . . . spoke for over an hour: compliments on all sides."

Travers Jerome carried exactly the same mixture of blood as Leonard's three daughters. He was half Hall, half Jerome. What would the uncompromising Puritan Catherine and roistering, light-hearted, uncontrollable Lawrence produce? Leonard watched this nephew with admiration and with astonishment. Travers was tough—that might have been expected in a Jerome, but he showed a streak of iron completely lacking in his father's make-up. Prank-playing Lawrence only wished to make the world laugh. His son wished to make it honest!

"And by heaven he nearly succeeded!" commented a fellow lawyer. Within a year of Lawrence's death Travers was well launched on his career as New York's famous attorney-reformer. He fought corruption, he fought graft, he fought Tammany Hall. Travers' upbringing had been Puritan, his zeal was that of the Inquisition. In the most spectacular of legal careers Travers organized many an auto-da-fé, and the press reveled in his exposures. He hounded the racketeers of New York City and flayed the owners of vice haunts not because they were naughty but because they bribed the police. Travers disliked hypocrisy. He wanted all the spades called spades and the bosses of Tammany Hall called them something else. "Everybody is talkin' these days about Tammany Hall growin' rich on graft," said State Senator Plunkitt, "but nobody thinks of drawin' the distinction between honest graft and dishonest graft." Certainly not Mr. Travers Jerome.

The slick guys must have hated him. Even Uncle Leonard was less uncompromising on one point. Among the extraordinary characters of New York was Richard Canfield, who ran the most exclusive gambling casino. Only millionaires were allowed into his palace on Forty-fourth Street. Stakes were higher than anywhere in the world and Canfield always kept five hundred thousand dollars in cash on hand to pay off house losses. Patrons were sometimes entertained in his office but never invited to the top floor where, in his private apartment, Canfield led a quiet gentlemanly life assembling rare books and interesting pictures.

He was a collector in the real sense. Unlike his friend J. P. Morgan who only bought up the museum-stamped masterpieces of Europe, Canfield studied the work of living artists and was almost unique among rich New Yorkers in showing discrimination. One cannot quite say that Canfield discovered Whistler, but—at a time when Leonie's friends, the "cultivated aristocracy" of London could only decipher Whistler's genius as "clever but a fraud"—Mr. Canfield was building up a collection of his best paintings. Canfield was proud to make a friend of James Mac-Neill Whistler, and the portrait of him ironically styled "His Reverence," now hangs in the Cincinatti Museum.

Leonard had just met Canfield at Saratoga where he operated the clubhouse. That was in the days when Freddie Gebhard was courting Leonie and at the same time trying to learn how to act as a man of the world from watching her papa. Leonard had never been a very big gambler but it amused him to guide rich youngsters. When Jerome first came to New York, a millionaire meant a man who owned a million dollars. Now the title was only bestowed on those who passed the ten-million mark. Fortunes were getting vaster and more complicated with great trusts consolidating them. Leonard had stepped right out of the category of wealth; horses were his only luxury, but his friends were the richest men of America. Jerome advised Freddie on how to play, and how to comport himself at the clubhouse. Soon he had found Canfield's views on art more stimulating than the endless gossip of the playboy world. "Such passion for the rare and beautiful gives one a feeling that the man is alive, much more so than most of his clients."

Now that his fortunes were gone, Leonard never stepped inside a New York casino but he visited that top story which the gambling Vanderbilts and Whitneys never saw. To the tall, curious Mr. Canfield, Leonard admitted that he "could not help liking Gebhard despite all the fuss." Freddie really had made himself into a national figure: he represented the adolescent male infatuated out of his wits, which is so dear an ideal to the average housewife.

"It is a pity," remarked Mr. Canfield, "when those who want to be gentlemen don't know how."

Canfield bluntly described his own conversion to bibliomania. At the age of thirty he had been imprisoned for six months and thus obtained time to read and study. "I don't care a rap about what other people think of me. I never did. So long as I know I am honest with myself, I am satisfied," he stated bluntly. Most New Yorkers agreed with this code of ethics. Only Travers Jerome continuously called the arty Prince of Gambling a "common felon."

Neither Leonard's wife nor daughters took much interest in cleaning up their cousins of New York. They were immersed in their own battles and triumphs.

In the autumn Leonard wrote: "I presume you are by this time installed in Paris. It seems to me a very sensible move. Paris is cold and wet in the winter but a thousand times better than London. I have written to your mother to go over, and Clara also. Why not? Don't try to live together. You have done it several times heretofore and successfully but it is not good policy. Something might occur in which you couldn't agree and then it would become disagreeable. Jennie and Randolph might come also? By the way, will you have my friend 'John Randolph of Roanoke' * and his tub with you? A very great additional inducement for me to come over if you do. I am myself entirely out of the way of gossip being immersed day and night in my racing schemes. Tell me how you propose to live, how to amuse yourselves in Paris. It is the place of all others for young people capable of enjoying the world's pleasures without running to excess. £100 bill enclosed."

The grandchildren splashing in their bathtubs grew ever more dear to him now that he felt the sands were slipping fast. These Christmas plans did not materialize, but Leonie produced a story which made him chuckle. Jack Leslie had made friends with a most charming Mrs. K——. When walking together at Sandown Races they met the Prince of Wales and "dear Jacksy introduced his fair companion. The Prince immediately asked her to accompany him, and his face lit up with such a smile that Jacksy knew he would not see her again for a long time!"

Mrs. K—— proved to be one of the most important influences in the Prince's life; in fact, her name is still well known on the continent where the Latins took an inordinate interest in royal romance. Leonie often visited her in Italy and once had the joy of standing beside her in the Piazza San Marco when an Italian guide passed by and called his party to a halt. "Do you

---

* Leonie's three-year-old son, now Sir Shane Leslie.

294

see the gentleman walking over there?" he asked breathlessly. His band of sightseers stared at the distant figure of Mrs. K——'s elderly husband walking across the square.

"That," hissed the guide, "is the lover of Queen Victoria!"

IF ONLY MORETON COULD HAVE let the silver question rest, he was promised material friendships, interests, and position. It definitely excluded him from the House of Commons. . . . While regarded abroad as a very prop of Empire, he was often without visible means of support. But there was an unconquerable element in him which kept him afloat.

Spectators of his struggles proved less buoyant. Mrs. Jerome, appalled and exhausted by her son-in-law's letters and schemes which Rudyard Kipling described as "apocalyptical," retreated to the seaside near Hastings where she hoped the air might revive her while she made personal economies "for honour's sake." "As long as a member of my family owes money anywhere I shall not have a fire in my room." And there she sat with hands folded staring into the unused grate of a cold boardinghouse. Leonard was appalled when he heard of this stoicism, but Moreton merely laughed. Corresponding with viceroys, presidents, ambassadors, ministers, and senators throughout the world he remained unimpressed by icy martyrdom. Clara groaned, "Mama won't have a fire while we owe *anything*," but Moreton had an easy way with creditors. "He carried them with his debts into his next scheme and repaid losses in the past by fairer hopes ahead."

Leonard had entertained hopes when his son-in-law led the Hyderabad delegation to the House of Commons but even here Moreton's position remained delicate "for while he was undermining the schemes of others he was advancing some of his own."

Meanwhile his gentle, blue-eyed wife continued to entertain in Alyford Street. Poets, cabinet ministers, and royalty hobnobbed in her mauve drawing room. Philippe d'Orléans and Count d'Esterhazy had been her admirers for a long time. Now Mr. Jerome heard extraordinary rumors. Clara, not content with the troubles of her husband, was taking on fresh ones which sounded uncomfortably like dynamite. The exiled King Milan of Serbia appeared on her doorstep each day laden with grievances and bunches of flowers. Moreton took him off (with a strapping Balkan foster brother) to shoot at a few country house parties and then himself departed on one of his celebrated tours. Milan continued to call daily at Alyford Street and the sight of a well-known Balkan king weighed down with gardenias caused comment in Mayfair.

Mrs. Jerome had always cherished a weakness for European royalties, but King Milan proved the exception. Like *Punch* of the time she could but hope that: "His Majesty did nothing consonant with the character of a plotter" and "conclude that the visit was in every way an innocent one, and that London is the better and not the worse for it."

Leonard's letters studiously avoid any reference to the subject which must have been uppermost in his wife's mind. Apart from news concerning his own horses and the successes of the three race courses he ran at Gravesend, Westchester, and Sheepshead, he mentions only a pleasant week on the Vanderbilt farm, and in September writes from the Union Club: ". . . I took a little trip last week, Saratoga three days, and Williamstown two days, where I stayed with Eugene. Fine weather, quite refreshing, good appetite, leg about the same.

"Eugene drove me over to see your father's house. It is a fine old English country house. Do you remember the house where we stopped when we drove down to Rockaway in a buggy some *several* years ago? Just such another house, wide hall running through the centre with a number of rooms on both sides. . . ."

Clara Jerome often thought of the early days of their married life. How simple everything then seemed! What a clutter of complications and distresses her daughters had collected with their English commitments—yet she herself had willed it. Determined to expiate for all the family follies and extravagances, she let another draft blow in. But despite Mrs. Jerome's refrigeration the facts remained rather warm.

Some of Clara Frewen's journals of the eighties still exist; page after page mentions the weather, the dresses she wore, and who she found "civil." "Dined at Ldy Blanche Hozier, Consuelo [Manchester], Ldy Lonsdale, Lord Hood very cherry. Leonie came in late, wore my blue—Leo and I walked down Piccadilly to buy a boutonniere. Ld. Dunraven to lunch. Mrs. Ronalds came in after. Moreton dined on guard. Leo and I dined alone and she practised while I read. . . . Blanche Hozier, Fanny Roche, and Wharncliffe and Leo dined with us. Sat about talking while Leo played. The Hozier nurse dear Bessie is leaving baby Clementine to look after Leo's boy. How lucky. Moreton so cross about my remark on the mistletoe. . . . Drove about all day shopping. Duke of Manchester to dine, Moreton very tired after Board Meeting. . . . Saw baby washed. Kings X Station at 1. No Moreton. Had to go all alone to Bretton. Big party. Dressed for the ball. White tulle and satin. Drove 7 miles."

She travels through the country homes of England; occasionally there is mention of the "famous pictures" and the "beautiful beds," but no descriptions emerge. She is usually without her spouse. It sounds a deadly round, creeping from swan feeding to reading of newspapers to gold tea gown for tea and other dresses for dinner. But whenever there is a ball she writes "danced like mad all evening" and lists the more pleasing partners. Moreton only appears as not turning up when expected, failing to write a promised letter, or as "very cross." In London she practices the piano for three hours and sees baby washed daily, politicians and lords and ladies come to dine, and things go wrong with the brougham. She dines at Randolph's house: "Sir H. Wolff, Arthur Balfour, (Lord Falmouth). Very dull considering so many clever men together." A daily walk with Leonie in the park often ends with lunch at Jennie's, where Winston flits in the background like a little ghost. "Randolph not much interested in children but thought Baby sweet. Winston came in to say goodbye as the poor little fellow had to go back to school." Arthur Balfour takes her to the opera "which finishes just as we get there." Lady Blanche Hozier (whose baby daughter Clementine would someday marry "poor little Winston") appears on almost every page; so does Lord Grey (Moreton's truest political friend) and Mrs. Ronalds, with her new harpists and cellists. Sundays always mean "the Park after Church." "Saw lots of pals under the trees but I wanted a man for luncheon so went to the Row." That was apparently the place to find one. Lists of grand names at parties end with "horrid sweet champagne, thought 11 o'clock would never come." The entries become fewer during Moreton's travels: "No news from Moreton today but a telegram he hopes for results . . . M. writes from Montreal . . . Good news from India . . . feel very blue." Then the pages are blank. Only a box of carefully tied letters show that she thought sufficiently of King Milan to keep his compliments.

Servia suffered from two rival royal families, the Obrenovics and Karageorgevics, who at intervals and by means of intrigue or assassination replaced each other on the throne. King Milan (Obrenovic) was at this time "ex" in name rather than function, for, although he had rid himself of certain troubles by abdicating in favor of his son Alexander, he continued to exercise considerable influence in his native country. Basing himself chiefly in Paris and Vienna he pulled strings at a safe distance while his wife Queen Natalie from whom he was separated chased him with her "tiresome Memoranda." She influenced her son King Alexander, turning him against his father, which Milan bitterly resented; and when he met Clara Frewen in London and fell in love with her, he made no secret of his wild hope that it might be possible to become free to marry again. What his proposals were concerning Moreton we do not know.

Clara fluttered and sat safe on her mauve brocade sofa, keeping the tea table between herself and over-dangerous plots. King Milan was an enormous man with bulgy, black eyes and what she described as "over-powering ways." The only one of his gifts that has survived is an exquisite little tortoise-shell music box with a tiny golden bird that pops out of the lid and delicately trills. King Milan's surname meant "bird" and no more fascinating reminder could have been made by all the jewelers of Russia who specialized in such trinkets.

The twenty-odd envelopes addressed to Mrs. Frewen, 18 Alyford Street, are all embossed with different regal designs of brilliant color. Large gold crowns supported by Serbian eagles and the name *Milan* in red and blue stand entwined with the Obrenovic motto *Tempus et meum jus.* For an exile he kept a splendid assortment of note paper.

The correspondence begins with a menu card signed by Paul Metternich, and then Milan who in his favorite joking way inscribed his name "1,000y" (*mille-an*), after which he writes *"non pas adieu mais au revoir."* Then come an assortment of crowned calling cards in different colors: *"Chère Mme Frewen. Je me permets de mettre à vos pieds ces quelques gardenias sachant que*

c'est vôtre fleur favourite. Vôtre bien reconnaissant Milan."
Others ask affectionately after her daughter, *la petite Clare,* ending: *"Je vous baise les mains et suis vôtre devoué Milan."*

A series of undated notes on different-colored note papers asking when he can come and see her to discuss ominous news from Paris makes us long to know what was really going on. Clara must have acted on his behalf in London, for Milan ceases to be "devoted" and becomes instead "greatful." All the letters are in French and full of puns:

*"Chère Mme Frewen. Dans le jardin de la vie pour parler le langage image d'un Oriental—ces quelques lilas et muguets peuvent être douces et avoir un parfum, tout comme vous, Madame, êtes bonne et aimable. Ils sont blancs et innocents tout comme mon langage est plus qu'innocent—même muet—*in the language of green flowering Albion, they seem like you, Madame, to appear innocent of a slow plot to obtain a professor for an ignorant savage.

"Look at his face. See how he blushes because he is ignorant. Throw one pitying look on this little bunch of mysterious violets. See how shy they are. Just so the savage will soon have to hide his face if he cannot say more than 'to learn or not to learn that is the question.' *Dois-je mettre au bas de cette page mon nom d'oiseau ou dire que je suis un Ass."*

This balderdash followed a suggestion that Milan should take English lessons. Most of his letters liken himself to a "bird of passage" and mention an accompanying gift—special bonbons from Paris, foreign cigarettes, a box at Drury Lane, the book they had discussed the day before, and torrents of various flowers all "deposed at her feet." With fine words. Several notes beg Clara to see him to talk over "the matter of great importance" and ask rather pathetically if "Lady Churchill" could help. Every morning regularly a box of her favorite gardenias arrived on the doorstep of Number 18.

300

Invited to lunch to meet a famous beauty he writes coyly to say that like the swallows he only admires the "beauty of nature and smile of spring," a lesson which apparently Clara has taught him. "Belonging to the race of birds, how could you wish me to be otherwise?" In November, 1890, he is writing *"Chère et charmante amie"* and begging for her advice. He is profoundly unhappy and grateful for her friendship: "An exile feels kindness more profoundly than others and all the more so as in this country I am not only unknown, but have all against me."

Moreton reappeared and, after expressing annoyance at the boxes of gardenias, proceeded to ask Milan to his club (where the poor King could not find the way in), and then to induce the *Pall Mall Gazette* to publish a political letter for His Majesty. Not knowing the customary formalities in England, Milan asked Clara for advice concerning an audience with Queen Victoria "at the risk of displeasing." The card with next day's gardenias reads: *"Chère et charmante amie.* I understand. Of course you are right. . . . Milan."

When the King departed for Belgrade he wrote pages of thanks for Clara's advice and help. He expected to return to Paris for the spring: "I don't expect to stay with my son more than two or three weeks and then to come back to Paris for *la belle saison* . . . I would like to follow Lord Randolph to Africa but because of my son I will have to stay in Europe, without being able to make any definite plans. *Dans le* 'struggle for life' *ma part est dure.* How I envy those who are free. My aim in this journey is to regain my liberty. Will I succeed? I don't know. But as it is my existence is odious. What shall I say to you concerning Paris. Nothing to interest you because I lead the life of a savage, seeing no one. Public life is absorbed by two things, the Empress Frédérick whose visit to Versailles and especially to Saint Cloud which is still in ruins, has produced an acute emotion and the sitting of the Chamber yesterday. They voted for the complete suppression of Pari-Mutuel, betting, book makers, etc. Many people think that it bodes the end of racing in France." A later letter from Vienna reads:

Chère amie,
Returning to Vienna from Moravia I went to the country for a week to friends and found your little letter from Paris —which I have definitely left—to carry my penants to Vienna and follow more closely for Serbia's sake, the intrigues political and private of my horrible spouse. It is a constant battle. Paris suited me personally, I departed leaving many friends but the government looked at me sideways and openly protected through the French Minister in Belgrade the intrigues of Queen Nathalie, who having played such a fatal role during my reign is now concentrated on the ruination of her son, who lets himself be led and cannot see that her acts and gestures have but one end, which is her own immeasurable ambition.*

One more letter remains. Sent by hand to Clara at the Hotel Vendome in Paris, it carries a gold embossed *M* over an inch long surmounted by the royal crown. *"Ma chère amie,"* he begins, but Clara considering discretion the better part of sentimentality has unfortunately cut out the comments we would most like to read.

Leonard thought that Moreton created sufficient havoc without taking on Balkan stew pots as well. When he came to Lon-

---

* Queen Natalie's intrigues ended in blood-stained tragedy. Milan's last public act was to write a letter to his son King Alexander forbidding him to marry Draga, one of Queen Natalie's ladies-in-waiting. His son disobeyed and later evoked great unpopularity by refusing to go to his father's funeral when Milan died in Vienna. In 1904 King Alexander and Queen Draga were murdered in horrible circumstances, and Peter Karageorgevic took the throne, riding from his coronation on his predecessor's white horse and using the Sixth Regiment, which had torn Queen Draga to pieces, to supply sentries at his palace. The *Daily Mail* remarked ominously that he began to resemble Alexander I, who walked "preceded by assassins of his grandfather, surrounded by those of his father, and followed by his own."

don and found his daughter "very blue" because Queen Victoria insisted on treating Balkan monarchs as if they were walking bombshells, "unwise to receive in audience" Leonard finally expostulated: "Why couldn't she have married a normal American and lived in my country!"

L EONARD JEROME HAD ACCEPTED stoutly the role of Phoenix. His daughters never realized they were devouring him. Letters to his wife throughout the summer of 1889 are obviously intended to restore her spirits: "April 6th. It has come off warm at last and there is comfort in visiting my ranches. I go out to the New Course on Sheepshead Bay and to Jerome Park about every other day. I mean to make young Morris give me a horse to drive. He might give me half a dozen and never miss them. I don't suppose they know into twenty or thirty horses how many they have. The enclosed cheque of course for Leonie. . . . *April 26th*. I dined with Morris yesterday and then drove over the Course. He is pleased with the whole thing and showed no signs of weakening though he had already paid $700,000. I shall send you the girls' money next week and £8 for the Epsom trainer."

Mrs. Jerome worried because Winston had not inherited his mother's sublime beauty. He rather resembled a naughty, sandy-haired little bulldog and seemed "backward except for complicated games with toy soldiers." It appeared "very difficult to tell what goes on in his mind." School reports were not complimentary; Jennie thought that the Army might offer a solution some day.

"Let him be," advised Leonard. "Boys get good at what they find they shine at."

But there was precious little shining at this stage. The spurt took place quite suddenly some eight years later. Then Steevens, most brilliant of war correspondents, would be writing of a junior subaltern: "He is what he is by breeding. He is the eldest son of Lord Randolph Churchill, and his mother is American. Lord Randolph was not so precocious as he was popularly supposed to be, but they begin early in America. From his father Winston derives the hereditary aptitude for affairs, the grand style of entering upon them, which are not the less hereditary in British noble families because they skip nine generations out of ten."

From his mother's side, thought Steevens, came the shrewdness, keenness, personal ambition, and sense of humor.

Leonard, interested as he had always been in breeding, refused to worry over his snub-nosed grandson. With that father and that mother—well, in a horse he would have seemed a likely winner. And what could you do with a stubborn colt but keep the reins light?

In July, 1889, the new track, Morris Park, was opened. It was Leonard's last venture. Foreseeing the doom of Jerome Park, he had perhaps been wise to make one huge effort to hold public interest. "A gorgeous Marquee was erected on the lawn but this did not replace the shaded slope at Jerome Park. The Gala Opening day brought out only six coaches whereas any day on the old course there were never fewer than twelve."

The Tribune wrote, "The outstanding feature of the Morris Park course is its immensity. The enclosure seems to have no bounds, the stables may be measured by miles. The betting ring would hold all the book makers in the U.S. and the Grand Stand looks big enough to seat all the race-going communities combined."

Toward the end of the year the press lamented the possibility of the American Jockey Club's disappearing if it proved unable to sustain itself in the vastness of Morris Park. "How strange the whole thing seems. The man who gave Jerome Park to the public is the man who has done most to take it away. Is this honourable and honoured institution to die?"

Leonard fought on, determined that his jockey club should remain in the hands of honorable sporting gentlemen and not be run by "tykes." He expressed himself strongly to a friend: "I tell you Sir, these men stop at nothing. They are capable of all kinds of peculiar work. They play to win. The public must pay and they see that it does. Really it seems a great pity that racing associations should do business to enrich these fellows." The just and the unjust combined to defeat his high aims. It was as though his Puritan ancestors had risen from the grave in judgment. Sister Catherine made one of her horrid remarks: "The Jeromes seem to have so much sense of honour and hardly any sense of sin."

Now he knew well there could not be much time left to tie up the loose ends of material arrangements, but he never let anyone know he was dying. After returning from England in May, 1890, Leonard Jerome wrote his wife: "I have your letter and am amused at the number of your hopes. Fortunately I can satisfy you at once on most of them. I am not 'safe and comfortable at the Brunswick Hotel' but I am all that at the Lenox. Sitting room, bedroom and bathroom—3 windows facing south. So much for hope No. 1. No. 2 you hope I am 'feeling better.' All right, I am. You hope my 'affairs don't bother me.' *They don't.*

"I have paid an ugly bill of taxes this morning of $4,586 and have plenty of money in the bank. I am delighted to hear Randolph won such a lot of money, also that Moreton's prospects are so encouraging and at last, though not least, that you are recovering from your illness.

"*The Sun* made a statement two days before I arrived that I was dangerously ill in London and would never see New York again! It has been contradicted since."

On May 15 he wrote: "My knee is better. I walk without pain only soon get tired. Kate has gone to the country. Travers has just made a great hit by the conduct of a case and an hour's speech in Court as Assistant District Attorney. He fought a great Tammany leader on a brutal assault and got him convicted and sentenced to one year's imprisonment and $500 fine.

"I have no use whatever for a servant. He would only be a nuisance. When one has been in the habit of putting on one's own shoes and stockings for 60 or 70 years it would become rather awkward to have another do it. Randolph has come out of the Temperance affair very nicely. I hope to live to see the day when he will be the great leader in that richest of all rich fields *Free Trade*."

All through the summer Leonard attended to his racing fixtures. A red leather program for the thirteen-day September meeting of the Coney Island Jockey Club at Sheepshead Bay still survives. The production is lavish. Every owner and trainer had one of these leather-bound programs with his own name engraved in gold letters on the cover. Unlike a modern race card, this booklet was not meant to be thrown away, but to grace a gentleman's reference library when the events it enumerates were over. Out of the hundred issued in the sunshine of that 1890 meeting, probably only this one remains, and that because Leonie's handwriting has penciled in "Dear Papa's last racing book."

The conditions of entry vary, the races are large and go up to seven a day, and the stakes compare very favorably with those in England at the same period.

Leonard Jerome's name appears as President of the Jockey Club (C. Fellowes and William K. Vanderbilt were Vice-Presidents) and also as the owner of three horses. He could no longer afford "fashionably bred stuff." But his name remained at the top of the racing world, and among friends his charm, his kindness, and his fire would never be forgotten. They said a man with such drive could never grow old.

In December, having played every card in efforts to perpetuate the strength and honesty of American racing associations, he left New York for the last time. There was little enough to close down; he merely paid a hotel bill and embarked with a couple of trunks, still hotly refusing to be bothered with a valet. Only four horses in training remained as commitments in the American continent. On arriving in England he scolded his wife severely for her icy moral vigil. He remarked impatiently: "That isn't the way to make other people do things" and taking a house in London, he ordered fires to be lit in *all* the grates.

His daughters were horrified to see dear Papa grown tired and worn. His banter could not reassure them, and for the first time they realized how incessantly they relied on him, writing continuously to ask him to do something, burdening him with their troubles because his shoulders had always seemed so broad. Now they were overcome with remorse at not having gone to America more often.

Leonard's nephew Eugene Jerome wrote apologetically to Clara Frewen: "I can understand how much you regret that one of you did not come over to him. But he would *not* consent to change his surroundings . . . it was his wish to remain at the Hotel Brunswick and we *had* to submit. . . . Had Uncle Leonard permitted me to do so I certainly shd have cabled you to come. When he sailed Henry Jerome went on board with him, and did all to make him comfortable. He would not listen to my getting a servant for him during the trip and had I been in a position I should have accompanied him. . . . None of his family here were inattentive to his true condition. On the contrary he was a constant source of anxiety. . . . During the past ten years he has taken the place of a father gaining my affection as a man and dear friend. He wanted to save you anxiety and I could not—against his wishes send you word. . . . Uncle Isaac died on Monday . . . Uncle Tom and your father are all that are now left of the nine brothers."

Once or twice Leonard dined out, in Jennie's house where Randolph still collected the most brilliant political brains in London, at Alyford Street where King Milan "did not greatly impress although obviously a kind man" and in Leonie's new house where she was arranging lectures to familiarize society with the *Ring das Niebelungs,* which had been produced some years previously in New York but was still considered too "queer and discordant" for a London audience. A well-known German exponent of Wagner lectured and his lady attendant sang the motifs. Leonard delighted in the Professor's efforts to keep the story of Siegfried *comme-il-faut* for the young ladies present. "Dee ladees mus not mind dis bad business of Sigmund und Siedlinde; it is *Schrecklich,* but it is only zee lofs of zee gods, vich do not count . . . Und here we have zee lofe motif illustrated by 'triolets' or 'triplets' as you say in English. . . ."

But Leonard's outings were limited. The bleak London fogs descended and his lungs ached. His daughters hardly left him, seeking to atone, rather late, for having taken so much. "If you make yourself into a rock," said Leonie later, "people *will* climb up and hang there." Of the three girls Leonie seemed to have solved her problems most happily. After the birth of her second son, Norman, at Stratford House, old Sir John had written her:

Well done My dear Leonie. Well done! Another son and punctual to the moment. These dear boys with God's blessing will be delightful companions and fight the battle of Life side by side. I was but 14 months younger than my elder brother who from the first confided in me so that I knew everything he thought of and was in all his pursuits a companion at school, at College and afterwards in the

World and no one knows the grief it was to me to lose him and have to take his place. Therefore these two remind me of former days and their destiny appears very similar. Little Jack (Shane, aged fourteen months) has made great progress and when he trots on his little feet with his little red shoes I see you in all his motions—and I may say that I never knew anybody bear their burden so gaily and trip about so actively as you did without all those necessities to Fine Ladies in interesting situations which one is accustomed to observe. But you are entitled to a rest from your labours. I should recommend a pause, and if these dear children had been girls not boys I should have given the admonition to Jack but according to my theory it is under the circumstances to you that I think this sage Counsel ought to be addressed.

Much luck to you,

Yr. affectionate father-in-law,

John Leslie

Jacksy had always teased his wife because she "trotted about indoors," and to his surprise Leonie answered, "That's my Indian blood—only don't let Mama know I told you, nor your mother either!" Her father-in-law had been completely won over, and Lady Constance was gradually relenting. After many years of careful observance and a good many stringent remarks she turned into a delightful old grandmother. Alas, she would live to see that second grandson Norman killed in the first month of the 1914 war; but the elder, grown from his little red shoes showed her volumes of verse before she died. At ninety Lady Constance's wit remained acute. Her last words, having been asked "How do you feel to-day?" were, "Pretty poorly I'm afraid . . ." and then with a faint smile, "and not very pretty."

To Jennie, who had tea with him almost every day, Leonard spoke encouragingly of Randolph's future, of that come back he must surely make. She did not argue, but the sadness never left

309

her eyes. Her husband was as ill as her father. Within five years he would be dead.

Of Clara, blue-eyed, affectionate, and still surprised by life's vagaries, he spoke most lovingly to the other sisters. She needed protection and soon he would not be there to give it. King Milan proceeded with admirable tact to send her rare old brandy for Leonard instead of gardenias. *"Quelques bouteilles de vieux cognac que j'ai procurer de Paris pour vôtre chèr malade,"* read his cards throughout January.

Moreton, blustering around the clubs, could hardly object to kindnesses for which he himself had no time.

And then in late February Leonard's cough grew worse. Clara insisted he must be moved from fog to the sea air of Brighton. He wondered briefly if it would not have been better to die in America, independently as he had lived, but it meant so much to see those he loved—even if they did fuss and hand him Bibles. The March winds blew hard and sea spray lashed the boarding-house windows. It was a drab place in which to say farewell, but Leonard had always been at heart a traveler untrammeled by possessions. He felt that America belonged to him and he to her. Such as he was she had made him, giving her vitality to his blood, her wide horizons to his mind. They would take him back to New York for burial. The "odds and ends" he left were in order.

Now the cough racked him and his heart beat an uneven measure. Clara's eyes widened with anxiety and his three daughters hovered like frantic angels around the big brass bed. Their faces grew carved into lines of despair as they realized the impossibility of preventing that fiery spirit from quitting them. "Don't go yet," whispered Leonie. But he was slipping into the shadows. Again his eyes turned toward the screen which occasionally hid a grandchild, and his hand found strength to wave at a small peeking face. He was finished. The future lay with them.

Little Clara, his six-year-old granddaughter, came, and Mrs. Jerome's hands could be seen tying her blue shoulder ribbons. Her adventures in life as sculptor and explorer could by no stretch of the imagination have been compassed by any man in the nineties, but the poems of Leonie's first son would some day echo the quality of a life that Leonard understood. The tempo of his own pulse throbbed in "Fleet Street."

> I never see the newsboys run
>   Amid the whirling street,
>   With swift untiring feet,
> To cry the latest venture done,
> But I expect one day to hear
>   Them cry the crack of doom
>   And risings from the tomb.
> With great Archangel Michael near;
> And see them running from the Fleet
>   As messengers of God,
>   With Heaven's tidings shod
> About their brave unwearied feet."

Jennie's eldest was at Harrow. Red-headed, blue-eyed, freckled, and "difficult," he still showed no outstanding characteristic save a determination which grownups seldom appreciate in the young. Winston Leonard Spencer Churchill. What would he come to? Where would his road lead?

The firelight glowed suddenly strong and flickered into unreal shapes, momentary as breaking waves. As Leonard's thoughts traveled through time, the Atlantic swung into his mind, the ocean he had crossed under storm canvas, the ocean which had divided him from his young. Now he must lay down his torch in this fog-wrapped island. Who of the grandchildren might lift it again? His own impetus in living gave him presentiment but the form of the future's violence remained beyond vision's range. A battleship of strange pattern steaming through the ocean to bring an English war leader to confer with America's President— around them long-snouted guns and planes and deep-dived death. . . . Too strange a jigsaw. . . . He could not grasp the pieces.

Leonard died quietly just before a wintry dawn lit the sky.